D0945521

HTML 3.2
Starter Kit

Jerry Honeycutt
and
Mark R. Brown

with

Jim O'Donnell   *David Wall*
Eric Ladd   *Bill Bruns*
Robert Meegan   *Rob Falla*
Robert Niles   *Todd Stauffer*

Matthew Brown

HTML 3.2 Starter Kit

Library of Congress Catalog No.: 97-65538

ISBN: 0-7897-1249-0

99 98 97   6 5 4 3 2 1

Interpretation of the printing code: the rightmost double-digit number is the year of the book's printing; the rightmost single-digit number, the number of the book's printing. For example, a printing code of 97-1 shows that the first printing of the book occurred in 1997.

Screen reproductions in this book were created with Collage Plus from Inner Media, Inc., Hollis, NH.

Composed in *ITC Century, ITC Highlander,* and *MCPdigital* by Que Corporation.

HTML 3.2
Starter Kit

CompUSA
310 764 6224
www.photody.com
3.2

SAMS
431 0524
669 4727
www.compusa.com

Credits

In memory of William C. Niles—Jerry Honeycutt

To my wife, Carol, and my daughter, Jenny, who are and have always been my inspiration, my foundation, and my best friends—Mark R. Brown

About the Authors

Jerry Honeycutt provides business-oriented technical leadership to the Internet community and software development industry. He has served companies such as The Travelers, IBM, Nielsen North America, IRM, Howard Systems International, and NCR. Jerry has participated in the industry since before the days of Microsoft Windows 1.0, and is completely hooked on Windows and the Internet.

Jerry is a leading author in the Internet field. He is the author of *Using Microsoft Plus!*, *Using the Internet with Windows 95*, *Windows 95 Registry & Customization Handbook*, *Special Edition Using the Windows 95 Registry*, *VBScript by Example*, *Special Edition Using the Internet*, Third Edition, *Using the Internet*, Second Edition, and *Windows NT and Windows 95 Registry Customization Handbook*, all of which are published by Que. Many of his books are sold internationally and have been translated into a variety of languages, including French, Italian, Korean, Japanese, Portuguese, Russian, Spanish, and Turkish.

Jerry is also a contributing author on *Special Edition Using Windows 95*, *Special Edition Using Netscape 2*, *Platinum Edition Using Windows 95*, *Visual Basic for Applications Database Solutions*, *Special Edition Using Netscape 3*, *Windows 95 Exam Guide*, *Netscape Navigator 3 Starter Kit*, *Using Java Workshop*, *Using JScript*, *Internet Explorer ActiveX and Plugins Companion*, and *Windows NT Server 4.0 Advanced Technical Reference*, all of which are published by Que. His work has appeared in *Computer Language* magazine and he is a regular speaker at Windows World, Comdex, and other industry trade shows on topics related to software development, Windows, and the Internet.

Jerry graduated from the University of Texas at Dallas in 1992 with a B.S. degree in computer science. He currently lives in the Dallas suburb of Frisco, Texas with two Westies, Corky and Turbo, and a bird called Opie. Jerry is an avid golfer; and has a passion for fine photography and international travel. Feel free to contact Jerry on the Internet at **jerry@honeycutt.com**.

Mark R. Brown has been writing computer books, magazine articles, and software manuals for over fourteen years. He was managing editor of *.info magazine*, when it was named one of the best computer magazines of the year by the Computer Press Association in 1991, and was nominated by the Software Publisher's Association for the Software Reviewer of the Year award in 1988. He's now a full-time freelance writer, who has contributed to over a half-dozen Que books, and is the author of Que's *Special Edition Using Netscape* series and the *WWW Plug-Ins Companion*. He is Webmaster of a site devoted to the topic of airships at **http://www2.giant.net/people/mbrown**, and can be reached via e-mail at **mbrown@avalon.net**.

Jim O'Donnell was born Oct. 17, 1963, in Pittsburgh, Pennsylvania (you may forward birthday greetings to **odonnj@rpi.edu**). After a number of unproductive years, he began his studies in electrical engineering at Rensselaer Polytechnic Institute. Jim liked that so much he spent 11 years at the school getting three degrees, graduating for the third (and final) time in the summer of 1992. When he isn't writing or researching for Que, he likes to run, row, play hockey, collect comic books and PEZ dispensers, and play the Best Board Game Ever, "Cosmic Encounter." You can find Jim on the Web at **http://www.rpi.edu/~odonnj/**.

Eric Ladd (**erll@access.digex.net**) is a task leader for Advanced Technology Systems in McLean, Virginia, where he leads a group of Internet developers that support the FDIC. By night, he toils endlessly for Macmillan Computer Publishing, coauthoring *Platinum Edition Using HTML 3.2, Java 1.1 and CGI*, and *Special Edition Using Microsoft Internet Explorer 3*, and contributing to several other titles. Eric lives in Washington, D.C., with his Boxer puppy, Zack.

Robert Meegan designs large software systems for manufacturing and research facilities. He has been working with computers for longer than he cares to recall. He can be reached at **rmeegan@ia.net**.

Robert Niles is a systems administrator and Web programmer for InCommand Inc., a company located in Yakima, Washington, that specializes in Internet and intranet applications.

Robert loves all things Internet, especially the Web and CGI in particular. He has been online since 1983, exploring the very nature of the online world. In 1984, he entered the military service as a communications specialist, taking a yearlong intensive course at the Presidio of Monterey as a Czech linguist. After completing military service, he returned to his home in the Yakima Valley.

Currently, Robert can usually be found with his head almost stuck to a monitor—no matter where he is. He specializes in the UNIX environment, Perl, and SQL.

Robert lives in Selah, Washington (Apple Country) with his wife, Kimberly, his son, Michael, and his daughter, Shaela. You can find him on the Web at **http://www.selah.net/** or via e-mail at **rniles@selah.net**.

David Wall lives in Utah, where he distinguishes himself by belonging to neither an organized religious group nor a militia. Mainly, he skis, perfecting the fine points of the high-speed inverted face-plant.

Bill Bruns is the network analyst at the Illini Student Union at the University of Illinois at Urbana-Champaign. He really wanted to work in television production, but got interested in computers while working on an undergraduate internship at *Square One TV*, a children's mathematics show produced by the Children's Television Workshop. Bill has been a technical editor for Que and has worked on such titles as *Platinum HTML 3.2*, *Java 1.1 and CGI*, *Running a Perfect Netscape Site*, and *10 Minute Guide to HTML Style Sheets*. Previously, he ran administrative computing at New York University's Tisch School of the Arts. Bill holds bachelor degrees in telecommunications and English literature from Indiana University, a Masters of Public Administration from New York University, and is a Certified Netware Engineer. You can reach him at **bruns1@prairienet.org**. He's also the Illini Union's Webmaster. Check out their pages at **www.union.uiuc.edu**.

Rob Falla (**rfalla@netroute.net**) is a professional HTML developer and part-time writer. He authored *HTML Style Sheets Quick Reference*. When not writing, Rob is usually on the Internet, learning about the next big trends.

Todd Stauffer is a magazine writer, host of the Peak Computing Radio Hour in Denver, CO. and cohost of the television show "Disk Doctors" airing nationally on JEC Knowledge TV. He's the author of *HTML By Example, Using HTML 3.2, Second Edition, Using the Internet with the Mac,* and four other titles. In addition, he's coauthured five titles, all of which have been published by Que Corporation.

Todd's articles have appeared in local and national magazines including *The Inside Line, Websight Magazine,* and *Windows Magazine.* He writes a regular column for *Peak Computing Magazine* called "On the Internet," available weekly on the Web at **http://peak-computing.com**. He also serves as an expert television guest on "Jones Technology Update" and the "Computer Zone" and gives occasional seminars along Colorado's Front Range. His story "Mac vs. PC: Sometimes it's War" won Peak Computing Online a "Hot Site" award from *USA Today.*

Todd has also worked as a freelance advertising writer, technical writer, and magazine editor, all in consumer-oriented computing. Outside of computing, he freelances as a car reviewer for the *Colorado Springs Gazette Telegraph* and as a travel writer/photographer for **http://members.aol.com/tstauffer/**.

Matthew Brown lives in the small town of Addison, TX, with his fiancée, Caroline, and their children Ramses, Cleo, and Bastian. Matthew currently works at National Knowledge Networks, Inc., as the Webmaster and local Windows NT expert. In his free time, Matthew enjoys listening to music, go-kart racing, and watching mindless television for hours.

Acknowledgments

Wow. This book took a lot of work by many people. The authors, of course, contributed many hours of bone-racking work to this book. The editors made sure that this book's content was on the up and up. There are a couple of very special folks that I want you to be aware of, though:

- Philip Wescott put together a fine group of contributing authors in order to get this book done.

- Mark Cierzniak and Steve Schafer are the development editors for this book. They kept their heads cool and allowed the authors to put together the best book possible. Thanks.

- Jim Bowie, the production editor for this book, is a joy. He works with almost unbearable details and schedules, but manages to keep his head screwed on tight.

- The technical editor—Jim O'Donnell—did a fabulous job of making sure the technical details were correct. They scoured over every line of HTML in this book, as well as the text content. They didn't just verify the facts, either; they often came up with great ideas for new content.

- The copy editors—Patricia R. Kinyon, Kelli M. Brooks, and Kate O. Givens—made sure the gibberish the authors banged out on the keyboard was readable and conformed to some sense of English structure.

- The contributing authors—O'Donnell, Eric Ladd, Matthew Brown, Bill Bruns, Robert Meegan, David Wall, Rob Falla, Todd Stauffer, and Robert Niles—were shooting at fast-moving targets. They did good.

- The Internet community contributed ideas for content and often provided solutions to problems for which we were stumped.

Last, but not least, I'd like to thank my coauthor, Mark R. Brown. His contribution to this book was significant. It was more fun with him than it would have been without him.

Jerry Honeycutt

Thanks, first of all, to the small group of knowledgeable writers who did the research and wrote down the words that comprise this book. Professionals all, I think that they have done a marvelous job of documenting a potentially formidable subject in an entertaining and enlightening manner.

I also extend my deepest thanks to the entire crew at Que. Please read their names on the masthead and try to imagine how hard these people had to work to make a huge and detailed book like this happen in such a short period of time. From this talented group, I'd like to single out Philip Wescott, Mark Cierzniak, and Jim Bowie for special thanks—Philip for his dogged discipline and diehard diligence in bringing together all the disparate elements of this tome; Mark for his sharp eye and controlled demeanor under incredible pressure, as always (it must be the cigars); and Jim for tying up all the loose ends. If you find yourself thinking that this book is pretty good, it's most likely due to something that these three did.

Closer to home, I'd like to thank Oran Sands for bringing me in the door at Que in the first place; Jim Oldfield for giving me my first chance (many, many years ago) to write professionally; and Benn Dunnington for an intense eight-year apprenticeship, which taught me to write improbably well under impossible deadlines. I'd also like to add to that list Mr. Frank Buxton, my seventh grade English teacher, and Dr. Isacc Asimov, famed author of science books (both fact and fiction), for helping me to discover the seemingly disparate but surprisingly well-intertwined career paths of journalism and science.

Finally, I would like to thank my wife, Carol, for her continuing encouragement and support. We writers tend to make a big deal about how tough the writing life is, though it's often writers' spouses who suffer the most. She's suffered her share, and more.

Mark R. Brown

We'd Like to Hear from You!

As part of our continuing effort to produce books of the highest possible quality, Que would like to hear your comments. To stay competitive, we *really* want you, as a computer book reader and user, to let us know what you like or dislike most about this book or other Que products.

You can mail comments, ideas, or suggestions for improving future editions to the address below, or send us a fax at (317) 581-4663. Our staff and authors are available for questions and comments through our Internet site, at **http://www.quecorp.com**, and Macmillan Computer Publishing also has a forum on CompuServe (type **GO QUEBOOKS** at any prompt).

In addition to exploring our forum, please feel free to contact me personally to discuss your opinions of this book: I'm **mcierzniak@que.mcp.com** on the Internet.

Thanks in advance—your comments will help us to continue publishing the best books available on new computer technologies in today's market.

Mark Cierzniak
Product Development Specialist
Que Corporation
201 W. 103rd Street
Indianapolis, Indiana 46290
USA

Contents at a Glance

Contents

Part II: Basic HTML

Part III: Advanced HTML

10 Frames   193

Part IV: Web Site Management and Tools

Part V: Appendixes

Introduction

You can't build a monument without bricks, and you can't make bricks without straw—everyone who has seen the film *The Ten Commandments* knows that. Likewise, if you plan to establish your own monumental presence on the World Wide Web, you have to start with the straw, and that's HTML.

The World Wide Web is built out of Web pages, and those pages are themselves created with the Hypertext Markup Language, or *HTML*. Though many folks talk about "HTML Programming" with a capital "*P*" (particularly recruiters), HTML is really not a programming language at all. HTML is exactly what it claims to be: a *markup language*. You use HTML to mark up a text document, just as you would if you were an editor using a red pencil. The marks you use indicate which format (or style) should be used when displaying the marked text.

What is HTML?

If you have ever used an old word processing program (remember WordStar?), you already know how a markup language works. In these old programs, if you wanted text to appear in italics, you surrounded it with control characters. For example, you might surround a phrase with control characters that make it appear as bold text, like this:

```
/Bthis text appears bold/b
```

When you printed the document, the first /B caused the word processor to start using bold characters. It printed all the characters in bold, until it reached the second /b. The word processor didn't actually print the /B and /b. These just "marked up" the text sandwiched between them.

HTML works the same way. If you want text to appear on the Web page in bold characters, you mark it up like this:

```
<b>this text appears bold</b>
```

The <b> turns on bold characters. The </b> turns off bold characters. These tags don't actually appear on the screen; they just cause the text sandwiched between them to display in bold characters.

Why you need this book

Everything you create in HTML relies on tags like these. To be a whiz-bang HTML programmer, you need to learn which tags do what. Fortunately, that's what this entire book is about.

A few other topics are covered in this book: page-design techniques, the HTML extensions you find in Internet Explorer and Netscape Navigator, graphics creation, and much more. You'll look at HTML and graphics-editing tools, and how to promote your site on the Web.

But, you explore these topics only as they relate to the main theme: creating your own Web pages by using HTML. The major goal of this book is to help you learn as much as possible about HTML itself.

How this book is organized

HTML 3.2 Starter Kit provides comprehensive information about HTML that you can use to build great Web pages. This edition has four parts, each dedicated to a particular concept, such as Web programming or objects. What follows is an overview of topics you'll find in each part of this book:

- Part I, "Overview of WWW Publishing," gives you a brief history of the Internet, World Wide Web, and HTML. In this part, you'll also learn about an approach to designing and implementing Web pages.

- Part II, "Basic HTML," introduces you to HTML. You learn how HTML documents are organized and formatted. You'll learn how to put text on a Web page. You'll also learn how to put graphics, lists, and tables on a Web page.

- Part III, "Advanced HTML," contains the meaty stuff. You learn how to use frames, forms, and image maps.

- Part IV, "Web Site Management and Tools," shows you how to manage your entire Web site. You learn how to get your pages onto the Internet and get your Web site noticed.

- Part V, "Appendixes," describes the editors, located on the CD, that you can use to create great Web pages. Also, you can find out here what's on the CD.

Conventions used in this book

This book uses various stylistic and typographic conventions to make it easier to use.

Shortcut key combinations are joined by + (plus) signs; for example, Ctrl+X means to hold down the Ctrl key, press the X key, and then release both.

Menu items and dialog box selections often have a mnemonic key associated with them. This key is indicated by an underline on the item on-screen. To use these mnemonic keys, you press the Alt key and then the shortcut key. In this book, mnemonic keys are underlined like this: <u>F</u>ile.

This book uses the following typeface conventions:

Typeface	Meaning
Italic	Italics indicate new terms. They also indicate variables in commands and addresses.
Bold	Bold indicates text you type. It also indicates Internet addresses.
Computer type	Commands.

 NOTE **Notes provide additional information related to the topic at hand.**

 TIP **Tips provide quick and helpful information to assist you along** the way.

Cautions alert you to potential pitfalls or dangers in the operations discussed.

 ### *What are Q&A notes?*

Q&A notes address problems that you might encounter while following the procedures in this book.

Part I: Overview of WWW Publishing

1

The Wide World of HTML Publishing

● In this chapter:

● **HTML was originally used for the creation of pages on the World Wide Web**

● **Both Microsoft and Netscape are advocating HTML as the GUI-creation framework for application development**

● **Even news and e-mail are strongly integrating HTML content**

Though the experts aren't in total agreement, it is generally acknowledged that the jackknife was originally invented for whittling. But once someone had that first jackknife in hand, they found that it was also pretty good for cutting string, driving screws, and picking teeth. It wasn't long before some enterprising jackknife manufacturer added blades specifically designed for those (and other) tasks, and the humble jackknife quickly evolved into the somewhat bulkier, but nonetheless more ubiquitously useful, Swiss Army Knife™.

The evolution of HTML has followed a similar path.

Originally developed for the creation of World Wide Web pages, HTML proved itself useful for many other, originally unforeseen tasks, and has therefore evolved over time into a bulkier, but much more useful markup language. Though the Web is arguably still the place where it sees the most use, HTML is now also called into service for the creation of corporate intranets, for spicing up e-mail and news messages, and even for developing GUIs (Graphics User Interfaces) for stand-alone and net-centric applications. Along the way, new functions and features have been added to HTML, so that the current standard (3.2, as this is written) bears little resemblance to its much simpler and less ambitious precursors.

This chapter looks at how, in just a few short years, HTML has become such a widely used and useful development tool.

The birth of the World Wide Web

Contrary to what the media would have you believe, the World Wide Web did not spring into being overnight. Though relatively new in human terms, the Web has a venerable genealogy for a computing technology. It can trace its roots back over 25 years, which is more than half the distance back to the primordial dawn of the electronic computing age.

The World Wide Web is actually just one of many applications that run on the Internet, a worldwide network of computer networks (or *internetwork*) which has been around in one form or another since 1961.

TIP **If you're curious about the origins of the Internet, read Bruce** Sterling's excellent article on the subject at **gopher://oak.zilker.net:70/ 00/bruces/F_SF_Science_Column/F_SF_Five_**.

By the mid-1970s, many government agencies, research facilities, and universities were on this internetwork (which was then called ARPAnet), but each was running on its own internal network developed by the lowest bidder for their specific project. For example, the Army's system was built by DEC, the Air Force's by IBM, and the Navy's by Unisys. All were capable networks, but all spoke different languages. What was clearly needed to make things work smoothly was a set of networking *protocols* that would tie together disparate networks and enable them to communicate with each other.

In 1974, Vint Cerf and Bob Kahn published a paper titled "A Protocol for Packet Network Internetworking" that detailed a design that would solve the problem. In 1982, this solution was implemented as *TCP/IP*. TCP stands for *Transmission Control Protocol*; IP is the abbreviation for *Internet Protocol*. With the advent of TCP/IP, the word *Internet*—which is a portmanteau word for *interconnected networks*—entered the language.

The Department of Defense quickly declared the TCP/IP suite as the standard protocol for internetworking military computers. TCP/IP has been ported to most computer systems, including personal computers, and has become the new standard in internetworking. It is the TCP/IP protocol set that provides the infrastructure for the Internet today.

TCP/IP comprises over 100 different protocols. It includes services for remote logon, file transfers, and data indexing and retrieval, among others.

TIP **An excellent source of additional information on TCP/IP is the** introduction to the TCP/IP Gopher site at the University of California at Davis. Check it out at **gopher://gopher-chem.ucdavis.edu/11/Index/ Internet_aw/Intro_the_Internet/intro.to.ip/**.

One of the best online guides to the Internet as a whole is the Electronic Freedom Foundation's Extended Guide to the Internet at **http:// www.eff.org/papers/bdgtti/eegtti.html**.

The Web explosion

There were a plethora of different data-indexing and retrieval experiments in the early days of the Net, but none was all-pervasive until, in 1991, Paul Lindner and Mark P. McCahill at the University of Minnesota created *Gopher*. Though it suffered from an overly cute (but highly descriptive) name, its technique for organizing files under an intuitive menuing system won it instant acceptance on the Net. The direct precursor in both concept and function to the World Wide Web, Gopher lacked hypertext links or graphic elements (see Figure 1.1). Although Gopher servers sprung up quickly all over the Internet, it was almost immediately apparent that something more was needed.

FIG. 1.1

Most Web browsers, like Netscape Navigator, can also display information on Gopher sites like this.

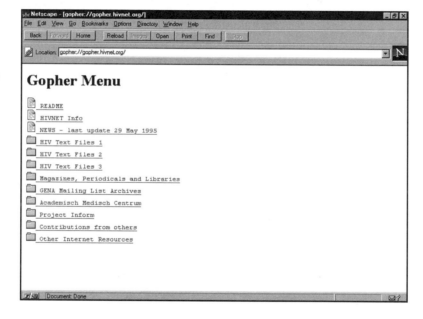

By the time "Gopherspace" began to establish itself on the Net, the European High-Energy Particle Physics Lab (CERN) had become the largest Internet site in Europe and was the driving force in getting the rest of Europe connected to the Net. To help promote and facilitate the concept of distributed computing via the Internet, Tim Berners-Lee created the World Wide Web in 1992.

The Web was an extension of the Gopher idea, but with many, many improvements. Inspired by Ted Nelson's work on Xanadu and the hypertext concept, the World Wide Web incorporated graphics, typographic text styles, and—most importantly—hypertext links.

The hypertext concept predates personal computers. It was first proposed by computer visionary Ted Nelson in his ground-breaking, self-published book *Computer Lib/Dream Machines* in 1974.

In a nutshell, electronic hypertext involves adding links to words or phrases. When selected, these links jump you to associated text in the same document or in another document altogether. For example, you could click an unfamiliar term and jump to a definition, or add your own notes that would be optionally displayed when you or someone else selected the note's hyperlink.

The hypertext concept has since been expanded to incorporate the idea of *hypermedia,* in which links can also be added to and from graphics, video, and audio clips.

The World Wide Web used three new technologies:

- HTML (Hypertext Markup Language) used to write Web pages.

- HTTP (Hypertext Transport Protocol) to transmit those pages.

- A Web browser client program to receive the data, interpret it, and display the results.

Using HTML, almost anyone with a text editor and access to an Internet site can build visually interesting pages that organize and present information in a way seldom seen in other online venues. In fact, Web sites are said to be composed of *pages* because the information on them looks more like magazine pages than traditional computer screens.

HTML is, itself, an outgrowth of the much more complex SGML, or Standard Generalized Markup Language. SGML is (rarely) also used for creating pages on the Web, though it takes a different browser to be able to view SGML pages. You can find out all about SGML at **http://www.w3.org/pub/WWW/MarkUp/SGML/**.

HTML is a markup language, which means that Web pages can only be viewed by using a specialized Internet terminal program called a *Web browser*. In the beginning, the potential was there for the typical computing "chicken and the egg problem": No one would create Web pages because no one owned a browser program to view them with, and no one would get a browser program because there were no Web pages to view.

Fortunately, this did not happen, because shortly after the Web was invented, a killer browser program was released to the Internet community—free of charge!

In 1993, the National Center for Supercomputing Applications (NCSA) at the University of Illinois at Champaign-Urbana released Mosaic, a Web browser designed by Marc Andreessen and developed by a team of students and staff at the University of Illinois (see Figure 1.2). It spread like wildfire though the Internet community; within a year, an estimated two million users were on the Web with Mosaic. Suddenly, everyone was browsing the Web, and everyone else was creating Web pages. Nothing in the history of computing had grown so fast.

FIG. 1.2
NSCA Mosaic, the browser that drove the phenomenal growth of the World Wide Web, is still available free of charge for Windows, Windows NT, Windows 95, UNIX, and Macintosh.

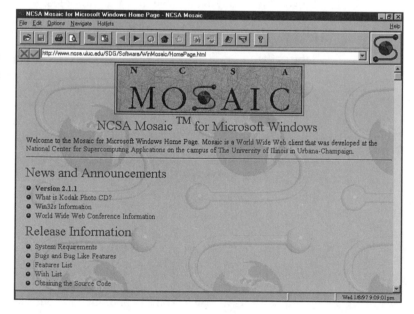

TIP For more information on NCSA Mosaic, check out the NCSA Web site at **http://www.ncsa.uiuc.edu/SDG/Software/Mosaic/**.

By mid-1993, there were 130 sites on the World Wide Web. Six months later, there were over 600. Today, there are over a quarter of a million Web sites in the world (more or less, depending on whose figures you believe).

Mosaic's success—and the fact that its source code was distributed for free—spawned a wave of new browser introductions. Each topped the previous by adding new HTML commands and features. Marc Andreessen moved on from NCSA and joined with Jim Clark of Silicon Graphics to found Netscape Communications Corporation. They took along most of the NCSA Mosaic development team, which quickly turned out the first version of Netscape Navigator for Windows, Macintosh, and UNIX platforms. Because of its many new features and free trial preview offer, Netscape Navigator quickly became the most popular browser on the Web. The Web's incredible growth even attracted Microsoft's attention, and in 1995, they introduced their Internet Explorer Web browser to coincide with the launch of their new WWW service, the Microsoft Network (MSN).

Established online services like CompuServe, America Online, and Prodigy scrambled to meet their users' demands to add Web access to their systems. Most of them quickly developed their own versions of Mosaic, customized to work in conjunction with their proprietary online services. This enabled millions of established commercial service subscribers to spill over onto the Web virtually overnight; "old-timers" who had been on the Web since its beginning (only a year and a half or so before) suddenly found themselves overtaken by a tidal wave of Web-surfing *newbies*. Even television discovered the Web, and it seemed that every other news report featured a story about surfing the Net.

The World Wide Web didn't get its name by accident. It truly is a web that encompasses just about every topic in the world. A quick look at the premier index to the Web, Yahoo! (**http://www.yahoo.com**), lists topics as diverse as art, world news, sports, business, libraries, classified advertising, education, TV, science, fitness, and politics (see Figure 1.3). You can't get much more diverse than that! There are literally thousands of sites listed on Yahoo! and other online indexes.

FIG. 1.3

If you really want to know what's on the Web, you need look no further than Yahoo!, which serves as a good example of an excellent Web site itself.

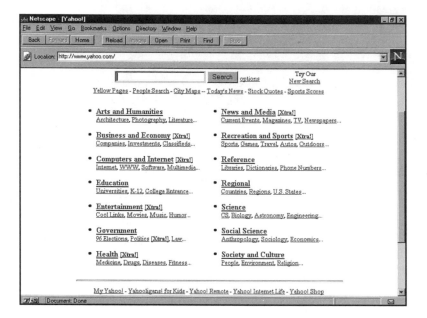

TIP For more information about the World Wide Web, consult the WWW FAQ at **http://www.boutell.com/boutell/**.

HTML in e-mail and news

HTML is also showing up in many other places you might not expect—electronic mail, for example.

E-mail was one of the first Internet applications. It changed the way scientists collaborated in the mid-60s, and continues to be one of the major applications of Internet technology. Millions more people use the Internet for e-mail than use it for Web surfing.

Perhaps, then, it should come as no surprise that HTML has made its way into e-mail messages. HTML affords the same benefits to e-mail as it does to Web pages or intranets: an easy and fun-to-use interface; integration of text and graphics; hyperlinks; and the ability to integrate video, sound, and applications inline, to name just a few.

Where e-mail is just a way to exchange text, HTML-enhanced e-mail can enhance and reinforce text messages with graphics or other "rich" information. After all, sometimes a picture—or sound bite, or video clip—is worth a thousand words, or more.

Hyperlinks mean the ability to link an e-mail message to Web sites or intranet information. Integrated applications mean the ability to include even "live" spreadsheets or other data into e-mail messages.

Extend this concept to newsgroups (see Figure 1.4), and you have the ability to turn static, all-text news postings into truly collaborative works. One worker can post an HTML message which contains an AutoCAD drawing, for example, and all the other members of the group can comment on it, adding notes or even making changes to the drawing itself.

FIG. 1.4

E-mail messages and newsgroup postings created with HTML can have all the look, feel, and functionality of Web pages.

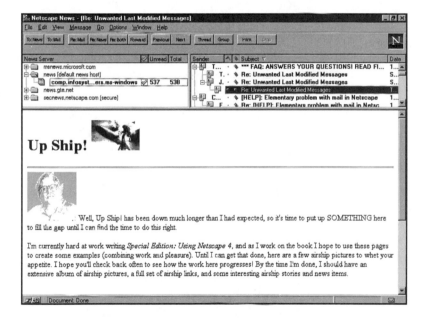

Clearly, HTML in messages—both e-mail and newsgroups—may have as much of an impact on the way people communicate and collaborate online as the Web or intranets have already had.

HTML for GUIs

But that's not the end of HTML's potential. Both Microsoft and Netscape are advocating that HTML be used as the basis for creating stand-alone applications, too.

That HTML's user interface is friendly and easy-to-use has certainly been well-established on the Web and corporate intranets. But, because HTML documents can also incorporate *active* objects like ActiveX controls and Java applets, HTML pages can act as containers for applications. HTML tags can be used to format text, graphics, interactive buttons, forms, and other objects on-screen which interact with the user just like any other GUI (Graphical User Interface). Incorporated into the HTML page are objects such as an ActiveX control or a Java applet (see Figure 1.5).

FIG. 1.5

This JavaScript-based online calculator is just a simple example of using HTML to create the user interface for an application program.

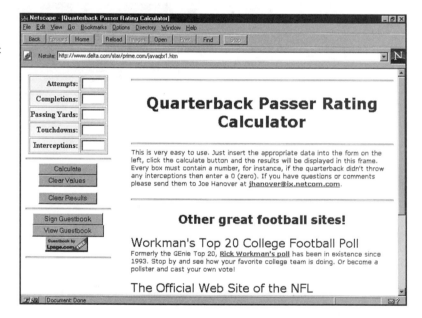

By using HTML as the GUI-development language, the developer gains a whole list of advantages:

- GUI development is sped up considerably. Rather than using a high-level language like C or C++, the GUI is created quickly with simple HTML.

- GUIs can be created by end users, or at least by relatively inexperienced personnel, which is cheaper and faster than tying up programmers.

- GUIs can be easily debugged and modified, further freeing up development resources.

- GUI development is not tied to application development. Applications can be of any type, from ActiveX controls to Java applets to JavaScript or VBScript applications.

- It's easy to develop applications that can access data locally, over a corporate intranet, and over the Internet without having to change the code.

- User interfaces are naturally easy to use and easy to learn, because they use the familiar Web metaphor.

Netscape is actively pushing Sun's Java as its development language of choice, while Microsoft would like to see developers using their ActiveX controls. But each supports the other and—most importantly—both advocate HTML as the GUI-development language.

As this concept catches on, you'll see more applications developed with HTML interfaces, and HTML will become important in its own right as a language for "gluing together" mini-application modules (or *applets*), no matter what language those applets have been written in. In time, it may be the majority of special-purpose software and shareware is written in this way, and even a percentage of commercial applications may be developed in this manner.

HTML Page Design and Implementation

● **In this chapter:**

- **HTML is not a programming language; it's a markup language**

- **Form follows function in designing pages**

- **HTML documents should be focused to draw the interest of your audience**

- **Real-world issues like copyrights, plagiarism, legality, and morality assert themselves in HTML page design**

J ournalist and critic A.J. Liebling wrote, "Freedom of the press belongs to those who own one." But with the advent of the World Wide Web, almost anyone can own a "press," which can potentially reach a much larger audience (the world) at a much lower cost (practically free) than any other form of information distribution that has preceded it.

But, what do you print with this press? There are really two issues involved: content and presentation. Because HTML documents are such a visual medium (or *multimedium*, to coin a new term), the way in which information is presented can sometimes seem to almost bury the information itself.

Marshall McLuhan was the first to recognize this principle. In his landmark analysis of television's effect on society, he declared that "the medium is the message," and that's as true a statement when applied to HTML documents— especially the World Wide Web—as it was when he philosophized about TV. Because they represent a whole new way to present and interact with information, HTML documents can have a tremendous impact on the viewer's perception of the information contained in them.

For example, a simple printed table of sales figures on paper can't convey the same levels and sub-levels of information that those statistics communicate when placed in an HTML table which includes links to the sales figures for the same periods in other years, a full set of charts and graphs which interpret those sales figures in multiple ways, and even photos and biographies of the company's top salespeople! It's clear that creating HTML documents demands a whole new way of thinking about information, and the ways in which that information is presented.

Before this chapter goes into the mechanics of creating pages with HTML, there are a few pages to get you thinking about what kinds of content you want in your HTML documents and how you might want to present that content.

What HTML is

It isn't a programming language. HTML is exactly what it claims to be: a "markup language." You use HTML to mark up a text document, just as you would if you were an editor with a red pencil. The marks you use indicate which format (or presentation style) should be used when displaying the marked text.

If you have ever used an old word-processor program, you already know how a markup language works. In older word-processing programs, if you wanted text to appear in italics, you might surround it with control characters like this:

```
/Ithis is in italics/i
```

When the document was printed, the /I would kick your line printer into italics mode, and the following text would be printed in italics. The /i would then turn italics off. The printer didn't actually print the /I or /i. They were just codes to tell it what to do. But the "marked up" text in between appeared in italics.

This is exactly how HTML works. If you want text to appear on a Web page in italics, you mark it like this:

```
<I>this is in italics</I>
```

The <I> turns italics on; the </I> turns them off. The <I> and </I> tags don't appear on-screen, but the text in between is displayed in italics.

Everything you create in HTML relies on marks, or *tags*, like these. To be a whiz-bang HTML "programmer," all you need to learn is which tags do what.

Of course, nothing in the real world is ever quite that simple. In truth, simple HTML gets a big boost in real-world page design from add-ons like Java and JavaScript, VBScript, CGI programming, style sheets, ActiveX controls, and other page-design extenders and expanders. Fortunately, this book covers those topics, as well. But, you can still get started in HTML page design by using nothing but a handful of basic HTML tags and a good text editor.

The only tool you really need

Because HTML is a tag-oriented text markup language that works with standard ASCII text, all you really need to begin creating HTML pages is a good text editor. If you're using a version of Windows, for example, good ol' Notepad will do just fine.

Listing 2.1 is a simple HTML document that you can recreate by using Notepad.

Listing 2.1

A sample HTML document

```
<HTML>
<HEAD>
<TITLE>A Simple Sample HTML Document</TITLE>
</HEAD>
<BODY>
<H1>Welcome to the World of HTML</H1>
<HR>
HTML documents can be as simple as this Web page, which
consists of just a single page of <B>text</B> and <I>links</I>,
or as complex as a 10,000 page corporate intranet site replete
with Java applets and CGI database access. <P>
In this book, we'll explore the possibilities of HTML, but
we'll also check out what can be done by adding other elements
to your documents.<P>
Click <A HREF="sample.htm">HERE</A> to reload this page!<P>
</BODY>
</HTML>
```

Don't worry that you don't know what these markup tags mean for right now—they'll all be explained in the next few chapters. Just type this sample document into your text editor of choice, and save it by using the file name "sample.htm." (Make sure your editor is set to save in simple ASCII text mode.) Then fire up your Web browser and load this file from disk. You should see a display similar to that in Figure 2.1.

 TIP **In Netscape Navigator, you can load a file from disk by selecting** File, Open File from the menu. In Microsoft Internet Explorer, choose File, Open, then use the Browse button to locate the file you want. Other browser programs work similarly.

FIG. 2.1
Netscape Navigator displays the simple sample HTML file from Listing 2.1.

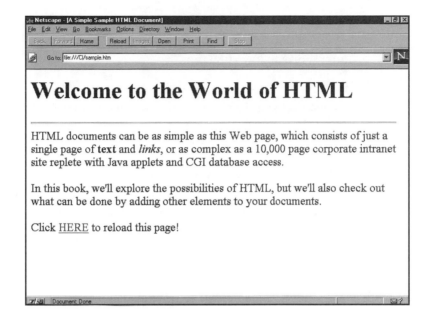

Of course, just as most carpentry projects are easier when you have a selection of power tools rather than just a couple of hand tools, the job of creating HTML documents is made easier if you have a selection of software tools to help you along. Appendix A, "HTML Editors: HomeSite, HotDog Professional, Web Media Publisher Pro, and BBEditLite," discusses a variety of HTML editors that speed and simplify the task of editing HTML, and many of the other chapters in this book describe graphics editors and other software tools to ease the creation of the other elements you'll want to incorporate into your HTML documents.

Image is not everything

Billy Crystal's Fernando character on Saturday Night Live used to say, "As we all know, it is better to look good than to feel good…and you look mahvelous!" Unfortunately, it seems that many HTML developers have a similar attitude: They believe it is more important for their pages to look good than to actually be good. For example, you can find plenty of Web sites that are loaded with colorful graphics and have a multitude of links to click; but, they often lack good, solid content.

It might be better to follow the advice of the 20th Century's most famous architect, Frank Lloyd Wright, who coined the mantra of modern architecture: "Form follows function."

Because HTML documents can contain so many flashy elements—graphics, animations, video clips, and even interactive games—it's easy for the message to be overwhelmed. When designing HTML pages, you need to continually ask yourself: "Is this really necessary?"

Before adding a page-design element, it should be determined that the element will actually enhance and emphasize the message your document is trying to communicate. What are you trying to say? Does that graphic, or sound bite, or table help you communicate your message? If the answer is "no," then you should rethink your page design.

The flip side of this is, of course, that if your HTML pages have excellent content but aren't visually appealing, people aren't likely to stay around long enough to find out just how good they are. People have a tendency to judge a book by its cover, and with so many well-done, visually attractive HTML documents out there, you're up against some stiff competition.

A case in point, chosen at random, is the Rutgers University Libraries Web site listing resources on American and British history at **http://info. rutgers.edu/rulib/artshum/amhist.html** (see Figure 2.2). Everything is here from the autobiography of St. Patrick to the North American Free Trade Agreement (NAFTA). Unfortunately, this unadorned list of links is unlikely to be discovered by anyone except academics doing scholarly research. There's a lot of excellent information here, but it's hidden by unspectacular presentation. It's not even that the index is badly done; in fact, the information is very well organized. It's just not presented in an appealing manner. (Note that this site has been awarded a "Top 5 Percent Web Site" recognition by Point Technologies, an award which was obviously based on its excellent content, not its presentation.)

If you're going to draw people in, you have to present your pages the way a politician campaigns: You've only got the public's attention for a quick "sound bite," so you must make your impression up front.

FIG. 2.2
This list of American and British history resources at Rutgers contains good information and is well organized, but the site suffers from bland presentation.

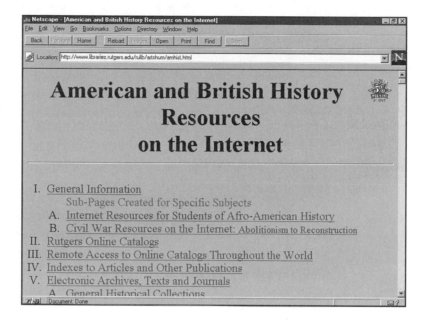

NOTE **Though you want to strive for good design, don't just shove a** whole bunch of extra elements down your viewers' throats—give them a choice! If you want to add Java applications, animations, sound files, video clips, and even background graphics to your pages, make them optional. Don't make your visitors automatically load a home page that is overloaded with lots of noncritical elements. Viewers with slow modem connections will especially appreciate the opportunity to *not* view everything on your pages.

The right stuff

We've established that looks aren't everything, but that without looks you'll never get your message across. Now, it's time to think about what that message will be.

Keep focused

Here's your new motto: "Keep in focus!"

Your HTML documents should focus on a single topic or, at most, a cluster of closely associated topics. If you're developing a Web site, for example, there are millions of different Web surfers out there, and most of them won't even slow down for a generic, generalized site. They want to find information and entertainment that suits their personal needs, wants, and tastes. The odds are that you'll never find even a handful of individuals who share your dual interests in, say, windsurfing and Baroque music. It would be suicide to mix the two on a Web page—those who are interested in one topic will be turned off by the other, and move on. But if you put up a site devoted to one or the other, you'll pull thousands of like-minded individuals in. (And remember, there's nothing to keep you from putting two separate sites on the Web!)

Above all, your pages should be interesting. Whether you're developing a Web site or even if you're just enhancing an e-mail or news message, your HTML documents should appeal to the audience you have identified for them, and should communicate your message clearly. The topic should be focused—the tighter, the better.

There are a million Web sites devoted to music, for example, or to farming. The odds of drawing much of a crowd with such generic topics are slim— you're sure to be overwhelmed by other bigger and better established Web sites with more resources to devote to the project.

However, if your Web site is focused on something specific, such as Lithuanian folk music or llama raising, you're sure to pull in a devoted following of true, die-hard advocates of the topic. Figure 2.3 is a perfect example of a Web site with a tightly defined subject matter. The St. Augustine page at the University of Pennsylvania (**http://ccat.sas.upenn.edu/jod/ augustine.html**) is a scholarly site devoted completely to the study of St. Augustine. There are complete texts (including some in Latin), images, commentaries, and essays, all presented in a well-organized and appealing way. And it's not stuffy—you'll even find the lyrics to Sting's rock-and-roll ballad, "St. Augustine in Hell!" This site won't attract many punk rockers or rocket scientists. However, its intended audience—philosophers and theologians, both amateur and professional—are sure to not only find it, but to keep coming back.

FIG. 2.3

This page, devoted to the study of St. Augustine, is a perfect example of an HTML document that is focused, well-presented, and rich in content.

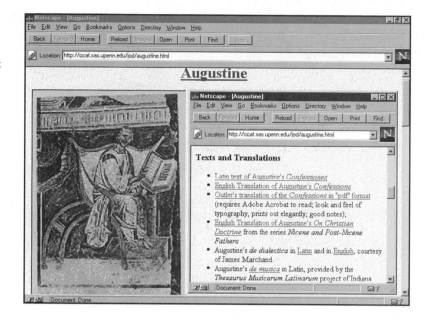

On the links

Here's another motto for you: "Think hyper!"

Almost every HTML document features hypertext links; They're what make HTML unique. But, I'm sure you've seen many Web sites which throw up a huge, unorganized list of links, some of which are more relevant to the topic at hand than others. A well-organized list of links—whether to associated Web pages or to a network database—can be a valuable asset to an HTML document.

For example, Scott Yanoff began his list of must-see sites on the Internet back before the World Wide Web existed. People would download his list of informative Gopher, FTP, and Telnet sites every month or grab it off their Usenet news feed when it was updated. With the advent of the Web, Yanoff added Web sites to his list and set up a site of his own to host the list (**http://www.spectracom.com/islist/**). It is, and always has been, one of the best topically organized lists of resources on the Net (see Figure 2.4). Take a look at his site, and try to do as good a job of organizing your own hypertext link lists.

FIG. 2.4

Scott Yanoff's topical list of Internet services is one of the most comprehensive and well-organized lists of resources on the Web.

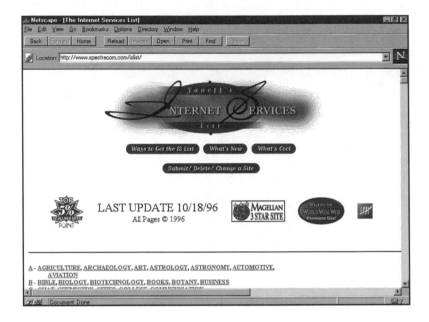

Timeliness

One of the reasons that people love the World Wide Web is because of its capability to deliver new information with an immediacy that can only be matched by other broadcast media, such as TV and radio. Whenever news breaks—whether it is a major world event, or just the release of the latest new software product—you can bet that the Web will have the information first. If you can keep the information on your site up-to-the-minute fresh, you're sure to attract loyal viewers.

Don't let your Web site lag behind. Keep it up to date. Always be on the lookout for new information and new links. Make sure to delete or update older information so that your site never, ever presents outdated or stale information.

There are hundreds of daily news sites on the Web that do an amazing job of posting the latest news items every day. Even if your site isn't news oriented, you can learn a few things by checking out how these sites keep up the pace. Figure 2.5 shows the Web site of the *Beloit Daily News*, one of the smaller newspapers keeping a daily presence on the Web—and doing an excellent job of it. Check out their site at **http://www.beloitdailynews.com/**.

FIG. 2.5

The *Beloit Daily News* is just one of hundreds of sites that present the latest news stories on the Web daily—or even hourly!

NOTE **For general news updated on a daily basis, you can't beat CNN's** Web pages at **http://www.cnn.com/**. For the best in computer-related daily news, check out c|net's site at **http://www.news.com/**.

Create a vortex

So your HTML documents should be appealing, focused, organized, and up to date. That's not too much to ask, is it? The whole idea is to create an information vortex that draws in your audience like a spider draws in flies.

You've got to strike a careful balance between form and content, between innovation and familiarity. People long for the new, innovative, and unique— but, conversely, they are more comfortable with the recognizable and familiar. Everything must work together to make your pages appealing.

Everything in your documents should be directed towards delivering your message. All should point to the center: your focus topic. Graphics should illustrate, links should be relevant, and design should set a mood.

There are people accomplishing this every day on the World Wide Web. For example, take a look at Figure 2.6, the Web site for the Rock and Roll Hall of

Fame at **http://www.rockhall.com**. The home page features a big, colorful, playful, clickable graphic menu that leads to fun and relevant areas of interest—from a tour of the museum itself to a list of the 500 top rock songs of all time. There's even a thoughtful link to the Cleveland home page. (This is a good tie-in because the Rock Hall is a tourist attraction, and potential visitors want to know about travel, hotels, restaurants, and other tourist sites in the area.)

Right up front are two very timely items: a link to Rock News and an item right below the menu showing what happened in rock-and-roll history on this date. The first thing you think when you check into this site is, "awesome!" But, all of the information is relevant and up front, so the site accomplishes its real goal: to entice people to visit the Rock and Roll Hall of Fame.

FIG. 2.6

The Rock and Roll Hall of Fame Web site is the perfect example of what an HTML document should be: entertaining, appealing, and focused with a clear goal in mind.

The wrong stuff

So what shouldn't you put into your HTML documents? That's easy—just turn everything we've said so far around.

Remember to focus. Don't try to be everything to everybody. This is the number-two problem of many personal sites on the World Wide Web. They haven't defined who or what they are there for. They spew out whatever pops up in whatever areas interest them at the moment. You might see graphics of motorcycles, rock bands, comic book characters, and computer screens all mixed up like a nightmare collage.

"Wait a minute," you protest, "you said that's the number-two problem of personal Web sites. What's number one?"

Even worse than a site that's burdened down with everything is one that contains nothing of interest at all. Many personal sites contain next to nothing: lists of CDs or comic books the person owns; pictures of his or her dog, gerbil, or fish; fuzzy photos of the site's owner goofing around with friends; and so on. Let's face it; except for a small circle of your very closest friends, nobody but nobody (not even your significant other) wants to know that much about you. So why put it up in public? It's a waste of bandwidth. It's boring!

What astounds me is many people are aware that it's mind-numbingly boring, and yet they put it up anyway! Some even seem to take pride in how boring they can make their sites, as shown by examples like the following page, appropriately titled "My Boring Life" (see Figure 2.7). Please don't ever put another site like this up on the Web. There are far too many of them already.

FIG. 2.7

There are already too many boring sites on the Web. Make sure your's isn't one of them.

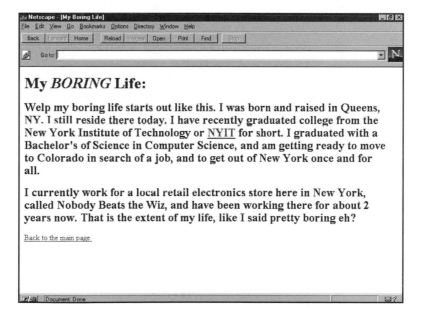

TIP **The number-one rule of writing is this: "Have something to say."** If a writer has a message, a story, or a cause, she never gets "writer's block." Apply the same rule to your HTML documents, and you'll never have to worry about what you should create.

Another thing you definitely don't want to do is to put up a page that consists of nothing but huge wads of unedited, unorganized links, such as the Web site shown in Figure 2.8. (And don't mistake alphabetical order for organization!) This site is like a library where the books are all stacked at random. It's almost worse than having none at all. People want useful links, but they also want to be able to find them easily.

FIG. 2.8
An unorganized list of random links is of no use to anyone. At least this site includes short descriptions!

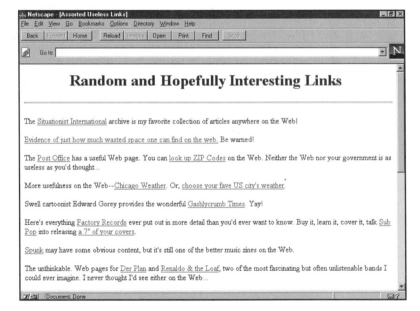

Everyone expects data in an HTML document—especially one on the Web—to be up to date and accurate. The worst thing you can do to your viewers is put up some purportedly useful data only to have it go stale. It's better to take your site down completely than to let it sit there with outdated, useless information.

Figure 2.9 is an example of a site past its prime. It features graphs of card prices for the collectable trading card game, "Magic: The Gathering." Prices for these cards fluctuate wildly, and when the data was current, this was a valuable service for card collectors. Unfortunately, the site is still up, and, as of this writing, the information is well over a year out of date. This is worse than useless, as someone is likely to consult these graphs and not notice that the information is outdated. They could make some bad decisions based on this old data. Don't ever do this to those who visit your site. If you can't keep it current, then take it down.

FIG. 2.9
The data in this graph is outdated and useless. Visitors to this site are going to be disappointed.

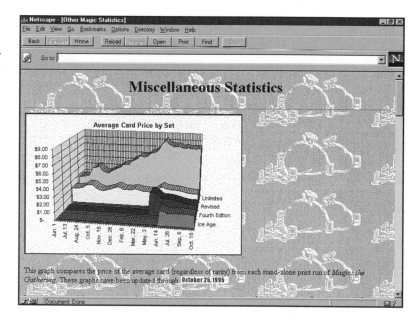

 NOTE Bad grammar and poor spelling are rampant on the Web. If a document is worth doing, it's worth doing well. No one is too hurried to use a spelling checker or grammar checker. People who read your documents will assume that bad English usage and misspellings mean that you don't know what you're talking about, and they'll move on.

Legal and moral issues

 CAUTION I am not a lawyer, and this section is not a legal guide. It is, rather, an overview of some of the legal issues to keep in mind when you are developing HTML documents. For advice on legal matters, consult an attorney.

When you're creating a private e-mail message, or a closed newsgroup post, you probably don't have to worry much about possible legal problems with your HTML documents. After all, your audience is all on the same team you are, and your communications are most likely governed by company policies and guidelines. However, when you create a site on the World Wide Web, you are subject to many of the same laws that govern printing, publishing, and broadcasting.

Be a legal eagle

The first amendment to the U.S. Constitution guarantees every American the right of free speech (and, of course, most other free nations have similar laws). This does not guarantee you the right to say anything you want with impunity. People who feel that you have treated them unfairly in public have legal recourse. You can be sued for libel and slander for anything you say on the Web, just as you could if you had printed it on paper. And in this litigious society, it is probably better to err on the side of caution than to strike out boldly and without forethought.

Controversy and debate online are fine, but if you're diplomatic and noninflammatory you'll not only avoid legal battles, you'll attract more sympathizers. After all, you're on the Web to share your ideas, not to entice someone to sue you. Before you post something questionable, consider the following: Even if you're sure you'd win, do you really want to spend your time sitting in court for months on end?

The right to privacy ties in closely with libel and slander issues. If you receive private information about any of your users—through a registration form, for example—you must be very, very careful about how it is used and who has access to it. Though there is no actual law guaranteeing U.S. citizens a right to privacy, there is a long-established legal precedent that says it is a basic right implied by the U.S. Constitution. It is best to keep all such information completely private, unless you have asked for and received specific permission to use it publicly.

Perhaps no laws are more openly flaunted on the Web than those concerning copyright and plagiarism. Everyone seems to steal text, graphics, programs, hypertext link lists, HTML code, and everything else from one another pretty freely and openly. However, the most recent U.S. copyright law says that all original creative works in any medium (including electronic) are automatically assigned to their creator when created. No registration is necessary (though it is a good idea, so that ownership can be proven if challenged). Again, it's best to not "borrow" anything at all from anyone else's site, unless you have written permission to do so.

No Web-related topic has gotten more press than the issue of adult material on the Web and its accessibility by minors. It is such a hot topic that Congress included tough anti-pornography language directed at the Internet in the Telecommunications Act of 1996. Although this law was quickly challenged in the courts, it has made many ISPs very, very nervous about the content of pages posted through their sites. If you plan to post adult material on your site, you certainly should at least make people enter through a disclaimer page. And make sure you have the permission of your ISP beforehand, or you could be kicked unceremoniously offline at the first hint of controversy.

Got you scared, now? You say you need advice? The Electronic Freedom Foundation is the champion of the rights of those online. If you have questions about copyrights, pornography, libel, or other legal issues online, the odds are good that you can find the answers on the EFF site at **http://www.eff.org** (see Figure 2.10).

FIG. 2.10
The Electronic Freedom Foundation home page features full coverage of the topic of legal issues online, including a lively discussion of the Telecommunications Act of 1996.

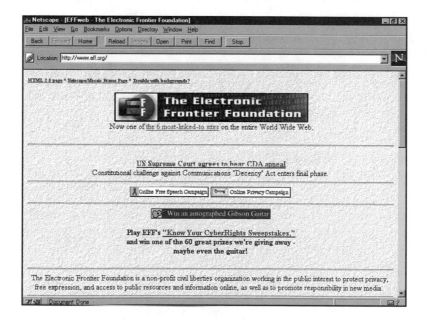

Electronic morality

Once past the legal issues, you might want to stop a moment and ponder the fine line between rights and responsibilities. Are you the guardian of society's mores? Is it up to you to try to bolster a civilization that is sagging under its own decaying weight? I happen to think the answer to that question is a resounding "Yes!"

I've always considered it better to be positive than negative, to build up rather than to tear down. With a forum as wide-ranging as the World Wide Web, anyone putting up a Web site has a huge potential audience, and therefore a potential to do great good or great harm.

Nonetheless, there are legitimate issues, worthy of open discussion, that are the subjects of controversial Web sites. Take tax reform, for instance. Many sides of this issue are represented in force on the Web (see Figure 2.11), and all draw their share of criticism, harassment, and hate mail. I'm sure those who have chosen to establish these sites consider the controversy all part of the territory. There are religious denominations, environmentalists, pro-choice and pro-life organizations, neo-Nazis, and other controversial groups on the Web who are constantly drawing fire from others. Before you establish a site that's destined to become the center of controversy, you should answer just one question: Can you take the heat? If the answer is "yes," then by all means go online with your views.

FIG. 2.11

All sorts of controversial sites, such as this tax reform newsletter page, exist on the Web. Before you set one up, make sure you're willing to do battle for your cause.

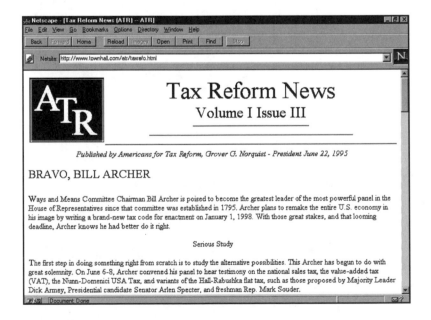

Sending your work out into the world

As noted in Chapter 1, "The Wide World of HTML Publishing," HTML isn't just for Web pages, anymore. People are using HMTL to create flashy e-mail and news postings, and even user interfaces for applications.

So what do you do with your HTML once you've written it? As you might expect, that depends on your application.

If your HTML pages are destined for the World Wide Web, you'll likely upload them to your ISP (Internet service provider). Finding an ISP to host your Web pages is a relatively simple task these days. If you're on an online service like America Online, you probably already have space available to you, whether you know it or not. Most local ISPs also include a few megabytes of space for hosting your pages, all as a part of your dial-up service contract. Chapter 15, "Putting Your Pages Online," provides detailed information on how you can get your Web site up and running.

If your HTML is destined to dress up e-mail or newsgroup posts, you'll need to use an e-mail or newsgroup program that allows attaching HTML to messages. Netscape Communicator's Messenger (for e-mail) and Collabra (for news) applications include this capability, as do many others.

Part II: Basic HTML

3

HTML Document Architecture

● **In this chapter:**

- ● **The required elements for an HTML document**

- ● **How to create relationships between documents**

- ● **The attributes associated with the *BODY* element**

- ● **How to add comments to your HTML source documents**

- ● **How to create a template for your own use**

HTML documents are easy to create, after a few basic rules are understood. The rules provide the structure that allows many different browsers on almost every computer platform to display a document. As an HTML author, you have the responsibility to follow these rules.

Starting with the basics

The most fundamental of all the tags used to create an HTML document is, not surprisingly, the <HTML> tag. This tag should be the first item in your document, and the corresponding end tag, </HTML>, should be the last. Together, these tags indicate that the material contained between them represents a single HTML document (see Listing 3.1). This is important because an HTML document is a plain text ASCII file. Without these tags, a browser or other program isn't able to identify the document format and interpret it correctly.

Listing 3.1

The simplest HTML document

```
<HTML>
<HEAD>
<TITLE>A Very Basic HTML Document</TITLE>
</HEAD>
<BODY>
This is where the text of the document would be.
</BODY>
</HTML>
```

 NOTE **While most of the recent browsers properly interpret a document** that is not contained within the <HTML> start and </HTML> end tags, it is still very important to use them. Many of the new uses for HTML documents, such as e-mail and UseNet postings, do not necessarily involve browsers, and the other programs are more likely to interpret an ASCII document as plain text without the hint that the <HTML> tag provides.

The </HTML> end tag is just as important as the start tag. It is becoming possible to include HTML documents within e-mail messages and news postings. Without </HTML>, the viewer does not know when to stop interpreting the text as HTML code.

The document heading

The document head container is not a required element, but a proper head can greatly increase the usefulness of a document. The purpose of the head is to provide information to the application that is interpreting the document. With the exception of the TITLE element, the elements within the HEAD element are not seen by the reader of the document, at least not directly.

Elements within the HEAD element do the following:

- Provide a title for the document.

- Lay out the relationships between multiple documents.

- Tell a browser to create a search form.

- Provide a method for sending special messages to a specific browser or other viewer.

Listing 3.2 shows an example of a document HEAD element.

Listing 3.2

A fairly detailed *HEAD* element

```
<HTML>
<HEAD>
<TITLE>General Officers of the US Army in the Civil War</TITLE>
<LINK HREF="mailto:rmeegan@ia.net" REV="made">
<BASE HREF="http://www.ia.net/~rmeegan/civil">
<ISINDEX PROMPT="Enter the desired name">
<META HTTP-EQUIV="EXPIRES" CONTENT="31 Dec 1997">
<META NAME="Last Modified" CONTENT="16 Dec 1996">
<META NAME="Keywords" CONTENT="Yankee, Grand Army of the
Republic,
➥War Between the States">
<META NAME="Description" CONTENT="A listing of the general
officers of the US
➥Army in the Civil WAR">
</HEAD>
<BODY BGCOLOR="NAVY" TEXT="WHITE" LINK="RED" VLINK="BLUE"
➥ALINK="GREEN">
<BASEFONT SIZE=3 FONT="Georgia, Century Schoolbook, Times New
➥Roman">
<H1><FONT COLOR="YELLOW">Union Generals of the American Civil
➥War</FONT></H1><BR>
```

continues

Listing 3.2

```
Continued

This listing contains the names of the general officers of the
➡Regular Army
  and of the Volunteer Army, as well as the date of their
  ➡appointment to the
 rank.<BR><BR>
 The names are taken from<BR>
<CITE>
Statistical Record by Frederick Phisterer<BR>
Published 1883, New York<BR><BR>
</CITE>
In all cases only the full rank is given. Many officers had a
➡<EM>brevet</EM>
 (or temporary) rank that was often one or two ranks higher
 ➡than the full rank.
 Remember also, that it was possible for an officer to have
 ➡rank in a state
 militia, the Volunteer Army, and the Regular Army; all at the
 ➡same time. With
 brevet ranks taken into account, it was possible for an
 ➡individual to have as
 many as six ranks simultaneously, depending upon who he was
 ➡dealing with.
</BODY>
</HTML>
```

The HEAD element is opened by the start tag, <HEAD>. This tag normally should immediately follow the <HTML> start tag. The end tag, </HEAD>, is used to close the element. The rest of the HEAD element tags are located within this container.

Naming your document

The TITLE element is the only required element of the heading. It is used to give your document a name. This title is generally displayed in the title bar of the browser. The TITLE should not be confused with the file name of the document; instead, it is a text string that is completely independent of the name and location of the file, which makes it highly useful. The file name is generally constrained by the operating system of the computer that the file is located on.

The TITLE element is delimited by a <TITLE> start tag and a </TITLE> end tag. The actual title is located between these tags. Do not enclose the title in quotation marks unless you want it to appear with the quotes. It is most common for the TITLE element to be all on one line.

The title text is a string of unlimited length that can include any text except for the few special characters that are restricted in HTML. In practice, it is a good idea to keep the length of the title fairly short so that it fits on the title bar. Another thought to keep in mind when making up a title is that many browsers use the title as the caption for the icon when the browser is minimized. Try to make the first few characters particularly meaningful.

 NOTE **The TITLE is normally used as the default name when a user** creates a bookmark to the document. To make this default as useful as possible, avoid having a title like Home Page or Index. Entries like this are nearly useless in a bookmark list.

Listing 3.3 is an example of a document TITLE. Figure 3.1 shows how Microsoft Internet Explorer uses the document TITLE as the title of the browser window.

Listing 3.3

An example of the *TITLE* element

```
<HTML>
<HEAD>
<TITLE>General Officers of the US Army in the Civil War</TITLE>
</HEAD>
<BODY>
</BODY>
</HTML>
```

FIG. 3.1
Titles provide your
readers with a way to
identify your docu-
ments.

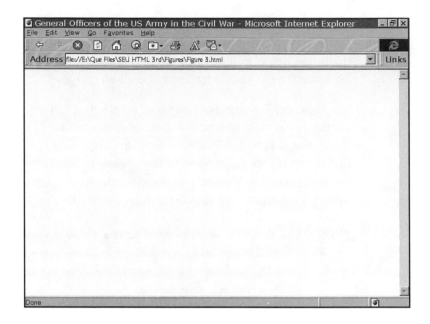

Indexing your document

One of the less commonly used HEAD elements is the <ISINDEX> tag. This tag
originally predated the <FORM> element and the advanced search engines that
are now available. The tag is used to inform the browser that a searchable
index of the document is maintained on the server. The browser creates a
prompt that allows the user to enter a word for which she would like to
search the document.

NOTE **If you aren't certain that your server supports this function or**
if you don't know how to implement it, you probably should avoid using
<ISINDEX>. Your readers are guaranteed to be frustrated by an index that
doesn't work.

Although powerful search tools are available, if your server supports this
feature, it is a very easy way to make large documents much more useable.
Documents such as catalogs and phone lists are good examples of where a
built-in index would be handy.

The attributes for the ISINDEX element are shown in Table 3.1.

Table 3.1 *ISINDEX* **attributes and their functions**

Attribute	Function
ACTION	Points to the search program to which the response should be passed
PROMPT	Defines a prompt to be used in place of the default prompt

Listing 3.2 shows how the <ISINDEX> tag is used in an HTML document. This document contains the names of General Officers in the Grand Army of the Republic in the American Civil War, sorted by seniority. The list could have been automatically generated from a database. Because there are more than 2,600 names on the list, it would be difficult to find a particular person just by scanning the list. Figure 3.2 shows how the browser opens a search text field that can be used to enter a desired name. The reader types the name and presses Enter, and the search program on the server locates the name in the document.

FIG. 3.2
The viewer displays a text box that allows the reader to enter a search text string when a document has the <ISINDEX> tag in the HEAD section.

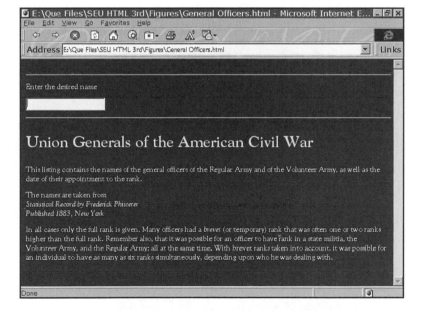

CAUTION **While testing the documents for this chapter, I discovered that** Netscape Navigator 3.0 does not display text and background colors correctly if an <ISINDEX> tag is present.

Creating a document hierarchy

HTML documents often have a relationship with other documents. This relationship is most frequently in terms of a link to another document. Links to other documents can be relative or absolute (see Listing 3.4). Each of these links poses its own problems. Absolute links can be long, cumbersome, and prone to breaking when the child document is moved. Relative links are easier to type and update, but they break when the parent document is moved. Both of these links are particularly vulnerable to breaking when a document is moved from one machine to another.

Listing 3.4

Absolute and relative links

```
<HTML>
<HEAD>
<TITLE>News Links</TITLE>
</HEAD>
<BODY>
<IMG SRC=/gifs/news.gif ALT="News">            <--- Relative
➥Link --->
<UL>
<BR><A HREF=http://www.cnn.com>CNN Interactive</A>
<BR><A HREF=http://www.usatoday.com>USA Today</A>
</UL>
<P>
<IMG SRC=//www.ia.net/~rmeegan/gifs/mags.gif ALT="mags">
➥<--- Absolute Link --->
<UL>
<BR><A HREF=http://www.infoworld.com>Infoworld Magazine</A>
<BR><A HREF=http://www.zdnet.com>Ziff-Davis Publications</A>
</UL>
<P>
</BODY>
</HTML>
```

This might sound unlikely, but consider that a long document might be downloaded to a user's machine so that he might read it when not online. Any links, such as a bibliography, would be unusable when the local copy was viewed. If the user wanted to link to other documents or images, he would first need to reopen the first document on the computer where it normally resides.

The document body

Although the nature of the World Wide Web appears to be changing in the direction of increasing active content, most people who view your documents will still be interested in your text. This will be especially true for documents that are created for corporate intranets and for documents that serve as online manuals and texts. Because of this, whether you are converting existing documents or creating new ones, you will spend much of your time working in the body.

Starting with the required elements

Before you can fill in your document, you need to lay out a basic working framework. HTML documents must follow a defined pattern of elements if they are to be interpreted correctly. Rather than retype the elements that are used in every HTML document, it is a good idea for you to create a template to use for each of your pages so that you are less likely to leave out an important detail. At the end of this chapter, we build a template that you can use as a starter. Until then, we'll use the example presented in Listing 3.5.

Listing 3.5

A basic HTML document

```
<HTML>
<HEAD>
<TITLE>This is an example document</TITLE>
</HEAD>
<BODY>
Enter body text here.
</BODY>
</HTML>
```

This example begins with the <HTML> tag, which, as you have read, is necessary for every HTML document. Next is the <HEAD> tag, which opens up the heading part of the document. This contains the TITLE element. We've titled the document "This is an example document." The heading is closed with the </HEAD> tag. Finally, the <BODY> tag follows. This is where you place the bulk of the material in your document. Remember to close the BODY element with the </BODY> tag and finish the page with the </HTML> tag.

Because HTML is a markup language, the body of your document is turned on with the start tag, <BODY>. Everything that follows this tag is interpreted according to a strict set of rules that tell the browser about the contents. The BODY element is closed with the end tag, </BODY>.

NOTE **Strictly speaking, it isn't absolutely necessary to use the <BODY>** start and end tags; HTML allows you to skip a tag if it is obvious from the context. However, it's still a good idea to use them. Some older browsers and other HTML programs can become confused without them and may not display the document correctly.

In the preceding basic document, the body text is a single line. In your document, you replace this line with the main text of your document. Unless you are using a special HTML editor, you must enter your text using a strict ASCII format. This limits you to a common set of characters that can be interpreted by computers throughout the world. The text that you enter here—whether for the first time or from an existing document—must be completely free of any special formatting. Note that some ASCII characters can only be added to the document using a special coding scheme. This is discussed later in this chapter in "Special characters."

NOTE **Most browsers consider all nonblank white space (tabs,** end-of-line characters, and so on) as a single blank. Multiple white spaces are normally condensed to a single blank.

Attributes of the *BODY* element

The BODY element supports a large number of attributes. These are all important for determining the general appearance of your document. Table 3.2 lists these attributes and their functions for your convenience, but we cover each of them in more detail.

Table 3.2 *BODY* attributes and their functions

Attribute	Function
ALINK	Defines the color of an active link.
BACKGROUND	Points to the URL of an image to use for the document background.
BGCOLOR	Defines the color of the document background.

Attribute	Function
BGPROPERTIES	If this is set to FIXED, the background image does not scroll.
LEFTMARGIN	Sets the width of the left margin in pixels.
LINK	Defines the color of an unvisited link.
TEXT	Defines the color of the text.
TOPMARGIN	Sets the width of the top margin in pixels.
VLINK	Defines the color of an already visited link.

Coloring your documents

The first small step toward creating a document is to define the colors that will be used for the various text components. If you do not specify any colors, the default colors are used. These are normally set by the reader on his viewer.

NOTE **Because you have no way of knowing which colors have been** selected as defaults by the reader, it is considered good HTML practice to set all of the colors, if you set any. This way, the same color isn't used for more than one component.

There is no simple rule that can be used to define a well-balanced palette, but remember that your readers must actually *read* your document. Try to maintain a high contrast between the text and the background and don't make the color differences too subtle.

Color definitions

Colors are defined in HTML using a hexadecimal coding system. The system is based upon the three components—red, green, and blue—which leads to the common name of RGB. Each of the components is assigned a hexadecimal value between 00 and FF (0 and 255 in decimal numbers). These three values are then concatenated into a single value that is preceded by a pound sign (#). An example of such a value is #800080, which is purple. Because few people can visualize colors based solely on a hexadecimal value, HTML 3.2 defines 16 standard color names, which are listed, along with their hexadecimal values, in Table 3.3.

Table 3.3   Standard colors and their values

Color	Value	Color	Value
Black	#000000	Silver	#C0C0C0
Maroon	#800000	Red	#FF0000
Green	#008000	Lime	#00FF00
Olive	#808000	Yellow	#FFFF00
Navy	#000080	Blue	#0000FF
Purple	#800080	Fuchsia	#FF00FF
Teal	#008080	Aqua	#00FFFF
Gray	#808080	White	#FFFFFF

The body color attributes

The BGCOLOR attribute is used for the document background color. If your document has a background image, the BGCOLOR should be as close to the primary color of the image as possible. This allows readers who may not be downloading images to see your text clearly. Many authors make this common mistake, which is particularly bad if the background image is primarily black and the text color that you selected was white. In this case, the reader of your document is greeted by the sight of what is apparently a blank page!

The TEXT attribute is the color used for the text in the document. Because most of your text appears in this color, it should be chosen to provide the reader with sufficient contrast. If you have elected to set the font, be aware that fonts with fine detail are often easier to read when they are dark against a bright background.

The LINK attribute is used by the browser for links that have not yet been followed. This color should be obviously different from the TEXT color so that readers can identify links.

The VLINK attribute is used to identify links that have already been visited. A common choice for VLINK is to use a darker version of the LINK color.

The ALINK attribute marks links that are currently active. This is a relatively recent development and is normally used for documents that have multiple frames. Quite frankly, choose your other colors first; the reader is least likely to see this color than any of the others.

Having seen all of the things that can be colored in an HTML document, you might wonder if the results justify the effort. If you are creating a static document—such as a manual or a textbook—you might be best off to let the reader set the colors that she wishes to use. On the other hand, if your document is a high-energy page with a lot of graphics, then it is certainly worth the time to find the right blend of colors.

Filling in the background

One popular way to dress up an HTML document is to add a background image. A background image is a graphics file that is visible under the document text. Using a background can help provide continuity to a document, or it can also serve to differentiate the various pages.

Most background images are small and are tiled across the viewer window like wallpaper. Images of textures are particularly popular for this purpose; bricks, marble, and cloth are often seen on HTML documents. Most of these serve only to fill in the blank space on the document, though. More interesting documents have a background that fits the theme of the page. Figure 3.3 shows an example of an astronomy page that uses a pattern of stars as the wallpaper.

FIG. 3.3

Using a background image that "fits" your document is a nice, professional touch.

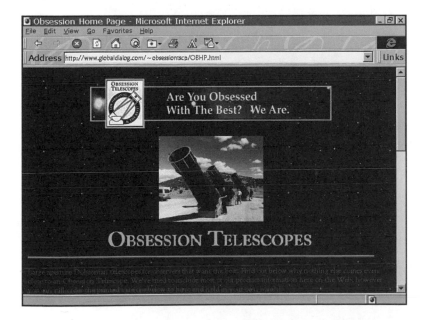

Other types of wallpaper that can make a document look good include a corporate logo or other image. These should be very subdued, almost monochrome, so as not to interfere with the foreground text. One way to accomplish this is to emboss an existing image using a graphics program. Chapter 14, "Graphics," discusses some of the tools available for creating these images. Figure 3.4 is an example of how this can be used.

FIG. 3.4
A company logo, embossed into a monochrome background, can give continuity to a collection of documents.

A background can also be created to watermark a document. This type of background can be used for an official seal or for a text message such as Draft or Confidential.

Background images look good, but they won't be seen by someone who's turned off the automatic loading of images. Remember the advice in the BGCOLOR section and set the background color to match the primary color of the image so that your page is readable even if the reader doesn't get to see the background.

NOTE **The BGPROPERTIES attribute is unique to Microsoft Internet** Explorer at this point. The only acceptable value for this attribute is FIXED. If BGPROPERTIES=FIXED, the background image does not scroll with the text. This is a nice effect with a wallpaper background and is useful if you've created a watermark background.

Setting the margins

The LEFTMARGIN and TOPMARGIN attributes are used to set the margins between your text and the edges of the viewer. There is no method provided to set either the right or bottom margin. This results from HTML documents being viewer independent. As an author, you don't know what size window the viewing software will have open.

The LEFTMARGIN sets the width of the space between the left edge of the viewer window and the left edge of the text. The width of the margin is specified in pixels. This attribute is most often used when the background image has a pattern on the left edge that you would like to keep clear of text. Listing 3.6 is an example of this use for a left margin, and Figure 3.5 shows how it looks in Internet Explorer.

Listing 3.6

A basic HTML document

```
<HTML>
<HEAD>
<TITLE>Demonstration of the LEFTMARGIN Attribute</TITLE>
</HEAD>
<BODY LEFTMARGIN="120" BACKGROUND="purplebg.jpg">
<H2>Note the handsome left border on this document.</H2>
<BR>
<H3>All of the text will line up so that it just barely clears
➥the
border. This creates a visual edge that really sets your
➥documents
apart from the rest.<H3>
</BODY>
</HTML>
```

CAUTION **Unfortunately, Netscape Navigator does not support the** LEFTMARGIN tag at this time. If you don't know that your readers will be using Internet Explorer, you should use a background image with colors that allow the text to be read, even if the border is overwritten.

FIG. 3.5

The LEFTMARGIN attribute can be used with a background image to create an attractive border for your text.

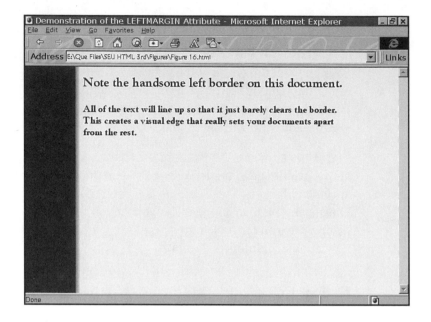

Note the handsome left border on this document.

All of the text will line up so that it just barely clears the border. This creates a visual edge that really sets your documents apart from the rest.

The TOPMARGIN attribute is used to set the height of the space between the top of the viewer window and the top of your text. This is normally used if the background image is particularly busy near the top. It can also be used simply to provide some space at the top of your document. Netscape Navigator 3.0 does not support this tag.

Commenting your HTML documents

It is possible to add comments to your HTML document that aren't seen by a reader. The syntax for this is to begin your comment with the <!-- tag and to end it with the --> tag. Anything located between the two tags is not displayed in the browser. This is a convenient way to leave notes for yourself or others. For example, you can enter a comment when new material is added to a document that shows the date of the new addition.

CAUTION   **Don't assume your comments can't be seen by your readers.**
Most browsers allow the source of your document to be viewed directly, including any comments that you have added.

On the other hand, don't try to use comments to "comment out" any HTML elements in production documents. Some browsers interpret any > as the end of the comment. In any case, the chances of an older browser becoming confused are pretty good, resulting in the rest of your document being badly scrambled. If you are going to use comments to cut out HTML elements while you are testing the document, you should remove them in the final release.

A new use of comments is to hide scripts from browsers that cannot recognize them.

The *ADDRESS* element

One of the most important elements for your documents is the ADDRESS element. This is where you identify yourself as the author of the document and (optionally) let people know how they can get in touch with you. Any copyright information for the material in the page can be placed here as well. The address element is normally placed at either the top or bottom of a document.

The ADDRESS element consists of text enclosed by an <ADDRESS> start tag and an </ADDRESS> end tag. The text within an ADDRESS element is normally displayed in italics.

Listing 3.7 is an example of one such address element, and Figure 3.6 shows how it looks.

Listing 3.7

Using the *ADDRESS* element

```
<HTML>
<HEAD>
<TITLE>Amateur Astronomy on the World Wide Web</TITLE>
<META NAME="Keywords" CONTENT="Astronomy, Telescope,
➡Stargazing">
<META NAME="Description" CONTENT="Amateur Astronomy resources
➡available on the Web">
</HEAD>
<BODY BGCOLOR="WHITE" TEXT="BLACK" LINK="RED" VLINK="GREEN"
➡ALINK="YELLOW" >
</HEAD>
<BODY>
<FONT SIZE=3 FACE="Verdana, Arial, Helvetica">
<BR>
<H1>Amateur Astronomy on the World Wide Web</H1>
<HR>
<H2>Magazines</H2>
```

continues

Listing 3.7

Continued

```
<OL>
<LI><A HREF=http://www.astronomy-mall.com/Astronomy-Mall/
➥?190,54>The Astronomy Mall</A> - A place to find many amateur
➥astronomy companies.
<LI><A HREF=http://www.skypub.com>Sky On-line</A> - Publishers
➥of <I>Sky and Telescope</I> and <I>CCD</I> magazines.
</OL>
<HR>
<ADDRESS>
Created by Robert Meegan<BR>
Last Modified on 16 Dec 1996
</ADDRESS>
</BODY>
</HTML>
```

 NOTE **A very important addition to the address is to indicate the date** you created the document and the date of the last revision. This helps people determine if they have already seen the most up-to-date version of the document.

FIG. 3.6
The *ADDRESS* element is used to identify the author or maintainer of the document.

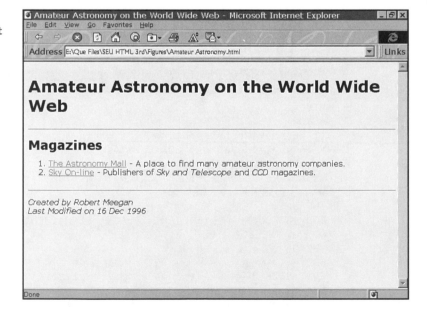

Creating a document template

Now, let's build a basic document template that you can use with your documents. This template allows you to start converting some of your existing documents to HTML. In the following chapters, you will see how to expand upon this template.

Let's begin with the required tags: <HTML>, <HEAD>, </HEAD>, <BODY>, </BODY>, and </HTML>. You also need to include the TITLE element, as this is a required element in HTML 3.2. Finally, put in a dummy line of text to remind yourself where to put the text. This gives you Listing 3.8.

Listing 3.8

A first pass at a basic document template

```
<HTML>
<HEAD>
<TITLE> A Basic Document Template </TITLE>
<HEAD>
<BODY>
Put the body text in here.
</BODY>
</HTML>
```

This would certainly suffice for a basic document, but you can do a lot better without much effort. First, let's add a simple gray textured background to the document, which changes the <BODY> tag to the following:

```
<BODY BACKGROUND="greybg.jpg">
```

Earlier in the chapter you read that if you add a background image to a document, you should set the colors so that the reader can see your text. First, set the BGCOLOR attribute to GRAY. This is the closest match to the background. We'll also set the TEXT to BLACK, and LINK, ALINK, and VLINK to BLUE, GREEN, and RED, respectively. These additions change the <BODY> tag to the following:

```
<BODY BACKGROUND="greybg.jpg" BGCOLOR="GRAY", TEXT="BLACK",
  LINK="BLUE", ALINK="GREEN", VLINK="RED">
```

You should have an ADDRESS element for the document, so add the following:

```
<ADDRESS>Created by Robert Meegan<BR>
Created on 16 December 1996</ADDRESS>
```

Of course, you'll want to put your own name in the ADDRESS.

When all of these are added to the first pass of the template, you get Listing 3.9.

Listing 3.9

Your final basic document template

```
<HTML>
<HEAD>
<TITLE> A Basic Document Template </TITLE>
<HEAD>
<BODY BACKGROUND="greybg.jpg" BGCOLOR="GRAY", TEXT="BLACK",
 LINK="BLUE", ALINK="GREEN", VLINK="RED">
Put the body text in here.
<ADDRESS>Created by Robert Meegan<BR>
Created on 16 December 1996</ADDRESS>
</BODY>
</HTML>
```

The results of this template can be seen in Figure 3.7.

FIG. 3.7
The results of the basic document template opened Netscape Navigator.

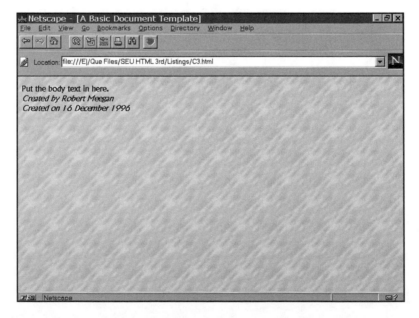

As you learn more about HTML, your template will grow and become more sophisticated. Until then, this simple document should prove to be sufficient for most purposes.

Document Formatting

● **In this chapter:**

● **Organize your HTML text into paragraphs**

● **Add structure to your document with headers**

● **Divide your document by using horizontal lines**

● **Use preformatted text to lay out text yourself**

● **Create a specialized document template**

Now that you've learned the basics of creating an HTML document, the next step is to expand upon that knowledge and make documents that are interesting to read. All published material has a structure; even something as visually flat as the stock quotations in the newspaper have been carefully designed to provide a maximum amount of information in an easy-to-use fashion. Imagine how many people would bother to look at these pages if they were formatted in a continuous stream of letters and numbers that filled the page from top to bottom and margin to margin.

The documents that you create have the same requirements. Whether you are writing Web pages, or developing HTML-based hypertext books, you will need to format your work so that a reader can quickly skim the text to find the sections in which he or she is interested.

Breaking text into paragraphs

Your old English teacher taught you to break your writing up into paragraphs that expressed complete thoughts, and an HTML document shouldn't be an exception. Unfortunately, line and paragraph breaks are a little more complicated in HTML than you might expect.

As a markup language, HTML requires that you make no assumptions about your reader's machine. The readers of your document can set whatever margins and fonts they want to use. This means that text wrapping must be determined by the viewer software, as it is the only part of the system that knows about the reader's setup. Line feeds in the original document are ignored by the viewer, which then reformats the text to fit the context. This means that a document that may be perfectly legible in your editor (see Figure 4.1) is badly mashed together in the viewer, as shown in Figure 4.2.

FIG. 4.1

Line feeds separate the paragraphs in the editor.

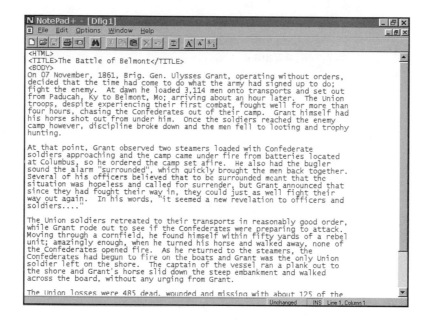

FIG. 4.2

The viewer ignores the line feeds and runs the text together.

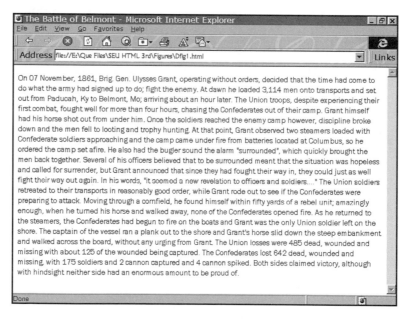

The proper way to break text into paragraphs is by using paragraph elements. Place a paragraph start tag, <P>, at the beginning of each new paragraph, and the viewer will know to separate the paragraphs. Adding a paragraph end tag, </P>, is optional, as it is normally implied by the next start tag that comes along. Still, adding the </P> tag at the end of a paragraph can help to protect your documents against viewers that don't precisely follow the HTML 3.2 standard.

 NOTE **Seriously consider using the beginning and ending paragraph tags.** As style elements, which give you more control over the <P> tag, become more prevalent, this syntax becomes more important.

Figure 4.3 shows what the document looks like in the editor after the paragraph tags have been added. You can see the tags were added to the start of each paragraph and that the line feeds are still in the document. Because the viewer ignores the line feeds anyway, it is best to keep them in the source document to make it easier to edit later.

FIG. 4.3

If you want to separate paragraphs, you need to use the <P> tag.

Paragraph tags—

```
NotePad+ - [Dfig3]
File  Edit  Options  Window  Help

<HTML>
<TITLE>The Battle of Belmont</TITLE>
<BODY>
<P>On 07 November, 1861, Brig. Gen. Ulysses Grant, operating without orders,
decided that the time had come to do what the army had signed up to do;
fight the enemy.  At dawn he loaded 3,114 men onto transports and set out
from Paducah, Ky to Belmont, Mo; arriving about an hour later.  The Union
troops, despite experiencing their first combat, fought well for more than
four hours, chasing the Confederates out of their camp.  Grant himself had
his horse shot out from under him.  Once the soldiers reached the enemy
camp however, discipline broke down and the men fell to looting and trophy
hunting.

<P>At that point, Grant observed two steamers loaded with Confederate
soldiers approaching and the camp came under fire from batteries located
at Columbus, so he ordered the camp set afire.  He also had the bugler
sound the alarm "surrounded", which quickly brought the men back together.
Several of his officers believed that to be surrounded meant that the
situation was hopeless and called for surrender, but Grant announced that
since they had fought their way in, they could just as well fight their
way out again.  In his words, "it seemed a new revelation to officers and
soldiers...."

<P>The Union soldiers retreated to their transports in reasonably good order,
while Grant rode out to see if the Confederates were preparing to attack.
Moving through a cornfield, he found himself within fifty yards of a rebel
unit; amazingly enough, when he turned his horse and walked away, none of
the Confederates opened fire.  As he returned to the steamers, the
Confederates had begun to fire on the boats and Grant was the only Union
soldier left on the shore.  The captain of the vessel ran a plank out to
the shore and Grant's horse slid down the steep embankment and walked
across the board, without any urging from Grant.

<P>The Union losses were 485 dead, wounded and missing with about 125 of the

                                         Unchanged    INS  Line 1, Column 1
```

When you look at the document in Figure 4.4, you can see the viewer separated the paragraphs correctly by adding a double-spaced line between them.

FIG. 4.4
With paragraph elements, the text becomes much easier to read.

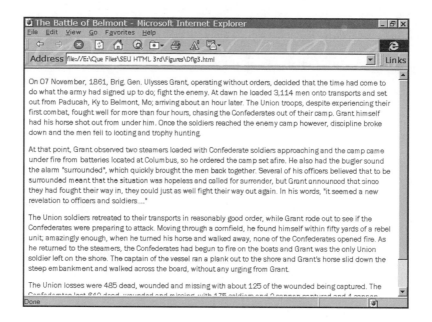

NOTE In some HTML documents, you will see a paragraph start tag, <P>, used repeatedly in order to create additional white space. This is not supported in HTML, and most current viewers will ignore all of the <P> tags after the first one.

The paragraph element has one attribute that is supported by both Netscape Navigator and Microsoft Internet Explorer. This is the ALIGN attribute. The possible values for the ALIGN attribute and their functions are listed in Table 4.1. The default value, if the ALIGN attribute is not used, is for left alignment.

Table 4.1 *ALIGN* values and their functions

Attribute	Function
LEFT	Aligns the text with the left margin of the viewer. The right edge is ragged.
CENTER	Centers the text between the viewer margins.
RIGHT	Aligns the text with the right margin of the viewer. The left edge is ragged.

Adding and preventing line breaks

As you have seen, HTML does all of the formatting at the viewing software rather than at the source. This has the advantage of device independence. But what do you do if you have a reason to break up a line of text at a certain point?

The way to end a line where you want is to use the *line break tag*, <BR>. This forces the viewer to start a new line, regardless of the position in the current line. Unlike the paragraph element, the line break does not double space the text. Because the line break element is not a container, it does not have an end tag.

One reason you might want to force line breaks is to show off your poetic muse, as shown in Listing 4.1.

Listing 4.1

**A limerick showing the use of the *
* tag**

```
<HTML>
<HEAD>
<TITLE>Creating an HTML Document</TITLE>
</HEAD>
<BODY>
<P>A very intelligent turtle<BR>
Found programming UNIX a hurdle<BR>
The system, you see,<BR>
Ran as slow as did he,<BR>
And that's not saying much for the turtle.<BR>
<CITE>Mercifully anonymous</CITE>
</BODY>
</HTML>
```

When this source is viewed in Figure 4.5, you can see how the line break element works.

 **CAUTION** You might think you can use multiple line breaks to provide extra white space in your document. Some browsers will condense multiple line breaks (multiple <BR> or <P> tags) to a single line break, however.

FIG. 4.5

Use line breaks to force a new line in the viewer.

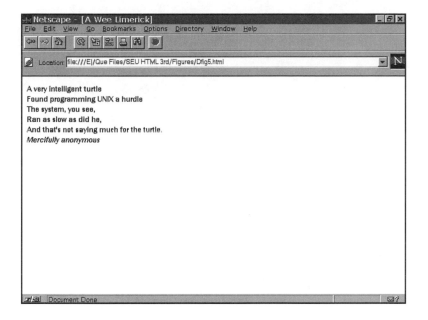

You need to be careful when using line breaks; if the line has already wrapped in the viewer, your break may appear after only a couple of words in the next line. This is particularly the case if the viewer that you test your documents on has wider margins than your reader's viewer. Figure 4.6 shows an example where the author saw that the break was occurring in the middle of the quotation, so she added a <BR>. Unfortunately, when displayed on a screen with different margins, the word "actually" ends up on a line by itself.

Just as there are instances in which it is convenient to break a line at a specified point, there are also times when you would like to avoid breaking a line at a certain point. Any text between a <NOBR> start tag and the associated end tag is guaranteed not to break across lines.

NOTE **This can be very useful for items such as addresses, where an** unfortunate line break can cause unexpected results. Don't overuse the <NOBR> element, however. Text can look very strange when the natural line breaks have been changed.

FIG. 4.6
Careless use of line breaks can produce an unexpected result.

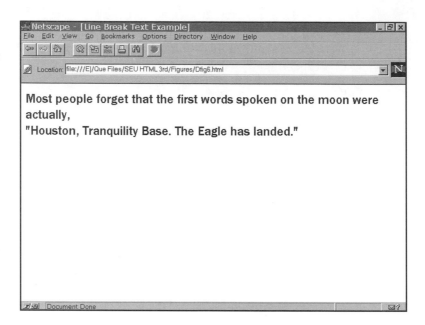

>
> **TIP**   **If you think you might need a break inside of a <NOBR> element,** you can suggest a breaking point with a <WBR> tag (soft line-break). The viewer will only use the <WBR> if it needs it.

Creating a text outline

So far, your HTML document probably looks a little dull. To make it more interesting, the first thing that you need to do is add a little more structure to it. Users of the Web want to be able to quickly scan a document to determine whether or not it has the information they are looking for. The way to make this scanning easier is to break the document up into logical sections, each covering a single topic.

After you have broken up the document, the next step is to add meaningful headers to each section, enabling your reader to quickly jump to the material of interest.

Adding headings

Headings in HTML provide an outline of the text that forms the body of the document. As such, they direct the reader through the document and make your information more interesting and usable. They are probably the most commonly used formatting tags that you will find in HTML documents.

The heading element is a *container* and must have a start tag (<H1>) and an end tag (</H1>). HTML has six levels of headings: H1 (the most important), H2, H3, H4, H5, H6 (the least important). Each of these levels will have its own appearance in the reader's viewer, but you have no direct control over what that appearance will be. This is part of the HTML philosophy: you, as the document writer, have the responsibility for the content, while the viewer has the responsibility for the appearance. See the example in Listing 4.2.

Listing 4.2

An HTML document showing the use of headings

```
<HTML>
<HEAD>
<TITLE>Creating an HTML Document</TITLE>
</HEAD>
<BODY>
<H1>Level 1 Heading</H1>
<H2>Level 2 Heading</H2>
<H3>Level 3 Heading</H3>
<H4>Level 4 Heading</H4>
<H5>Level 5 Heading</H5>
<H6>Level 6 Heading</H6>
</BODY>
</HTML>
```

 NOTE **Although it is not absolutely necessary to use each of the heading** levels, as a matter of good practice you should not skip levels because it may cause problems with automatic document converters. In particular, as new Web indexes come online, they will be able to search Web documents and create retrievable outlines. These outlines may be confusing if heading levels are missing.

Figure 4.7 shows how these headings look when they are displayed in Microsoft Internet Explorer.

FIG. 4.7
Here are the six
heading levels as they
appear in Internet
Explorer.

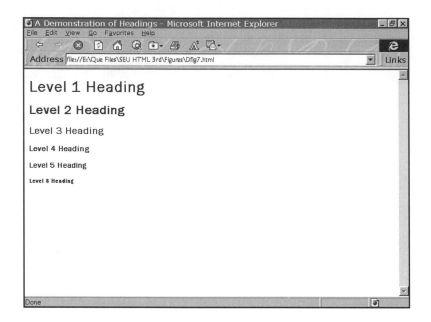

NOTE **Remember that forgetting to add an end tag will definitely mess** up the appearance of your document. Headings are containers and require both start and end tags. Another thing to remember is that headings also have an implied paragraph break before and after each one. You can't apply a heading to text in the middle of a paragraph to change the size or font. The result will be a paragraph broken into three separate pieces, with the middle paragraph in a heading format.

The best way to use headings is to consider them the outline for your document. Figure 4.8 shows a document in which each level of heading represents a new level of detail. Generally, it is good practice to use a new level whenever you have two to four items of equal importance. If more than four items are of the same importance under a parent heading, however, try breaking them into two different parent headings.

Headings can use the ALIGN attribute, just as the <P> tag does. This is important to remember, because not all viewers will show all headings left-aligned. Figure 4.9 shows the use of the ALIGN attribute in a heading.

FIG. 4.8

Headings provide
an outline of the
document.

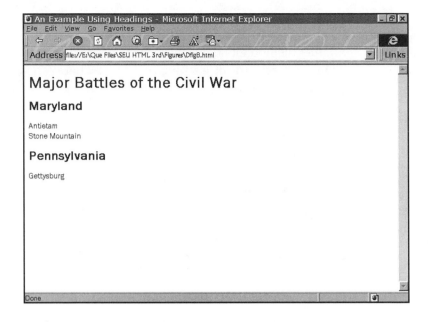

FIG. 4.9

Headings can be
aligned on the left or
right or in the center.

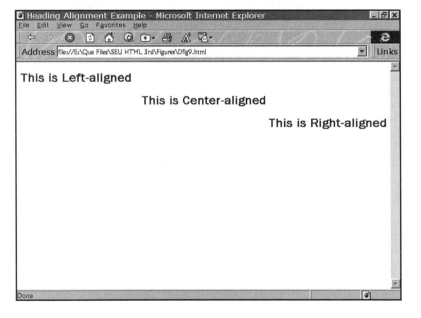

Adding horizontal lines

Another method for adding divisions to your documents is the use of horizontal lines. These provide a strong visual break between sections and are especially useful for separating the various parts of your document. Many viewers use an "etched" line that presents a crisp look and adds visual depth to the document.

You can create a horizontal line by using the horizontal rule element, <HR>. This tag draws a shaded horizontal line across the viewer's display. The <HR> tag is not a container and does not require an end tag. There is an implied paragraph break before and after a horizontal rule.

Listing 4.3 shows how horizontal rule tags are used, and Figure 4.10 demonstrates their appearance in the Netscape Navigator viewer.

Listing 4.3

An HTML document showing the use of horizontal rules

```
<HTML>
<HEAD>
<TITLE>Manned Space Craft</TITLE>
</HEAD>
<BODY>
<H1 ALIGN=CENTER>Manned Space Craft</H1>
<BR>
<H2 ALIGN=LEFT>Soviet</H2>
Vostok<BR>
Voskhod<BR>
Soyuz<BR>
<HR>
<H2 ALIGN=LEFT>American</H2>
Mercury<BR>
Gemini<BR>
Apollo<BR>
Shuttle<BR>
<HR >
</BODY>
</HTML>
```

Table 4.2 lists the attributes of the <HR> tag. Listing 4.4 is similar to Listing 4.3, but shows how some of the attributes are used. Figure 4.11 shows the results as seen in Internet Explorer.

FIG. 4.10
Most viewers interpret the <HR> tag as an etched line.

Listing 4.4

The use of attributes in horizontal rules

```
<HTML>
<HEAD>
<TITLE>Manned Space Craft</TITLE>
</HEAD>
<BODY>
<H1 ALIGN=CENTER>Manned Space Craft</H1>
<BR>
<H2 ALIGN=LEFT>Soviet</H2>
Vostok<BR>
Voskhod<BR>
Soyuz<BR>
<HR WIDTH=50% SIZE=6 ALIGN=LEFT COLOR=RED>
<H2 ALIGN=LEFT>American</H2>
Mercury<BR>
Gemini<BR>
Apollo<BR>
Shuttle<BR>
<HR WIDTH=50% SIZE=6 ALIGN=LEFT COLOR=NAVY>
</BODY>
</HTML>
```

Table 4.2 HR attributes and their functions

Attribute	Function
ALIGN	Can be set to LEFT, CENTER, or RIGHT.
WIDTH	Can be entered in pixels or as a percentage of the viewer window width. If a percentage is desired, add a percent time to the number.
SIZE	The height of the ruled line in pixels.
NOSHADE	If this attribute is present, the viewer will not use a three-dimensional effect.
COLOR	Specifies the color of the ruled line. An RGB hexadecimal value or a standard color name can be used.

FIG. 4.11
The attributes of the
<HR> tag can make
the rules more
attractive.

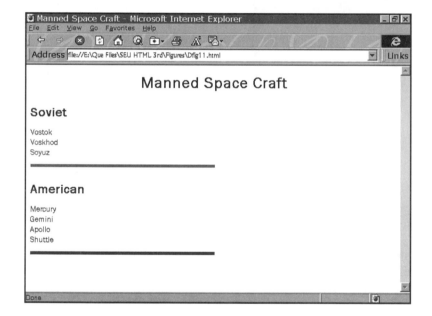

 TIP **The additional attributes that have been added in HTML 3.2 are**
very useful. Documents created using early versions of HTML often used a
graphic image to provide a more colorful and obvious break. Of course,
these would not appear in viewers that had image loading turned off. Even
if the viewer was loading images, a color bar was another file that had to be
copied and maintained. The new <HR> attributes allow you much more
flexibility in the creation of your documents at virtually no loss of speed or
ease of maintenance.

Horizontal rules should be reserved for instances when you want to represent a strong break in the flow of the text. Some basic guidelines for adding rules is that they should never come between a heading and the text that follows the heading. They should also not be used to create "white-space" in your document.

Using preformatted text

Is it absolutely necessary to use paragraph and line break elements for formatting text? Well, not really; HTML provides a container that can hold preformatted text. This is text that gives you, the author, much more control over how the viewer displays your document. The trade-off for this control is a loss of flexibility.

The most common and useful of the preformatting tags is the <PRE> container. Text in a <PRE> container is basically free-form with line feeds causing the line to break at the beginning of the next clear line. Line break tags and paragraph tags are also supported. This versatility enables you to create such items as tables and precise columns of text. Another common use of the <PRE> element is to display large blocks of computer code (C, C++, and so on) that would otherwise be difficult to read if the browser reformatted it.

Text in a <PRE> container can use any of the physical or logical text formatting elements. You can use this feature to create tables that have bold headers or italicized values. The use of paragraph formatting elements, such as <Address> or any of the heading elements, is not permitted however. Anchor elements, which are described in Chapter 7, "Creating Document Links," can be included within a <PRE> container.

The biggest drawback to the <PRE> container is that any text within it is displayed in a monospaced font in the reader's viewer. This tends to make long stretches of preformatted text look clunky and out of place.

Figure 4.12 shows an example of some preformatted text in an editor. You can use the editor to line up the columns neatly before adding the character formatting tags. The result of this document is shown in Figure 4.13.

TIP   **HTML 3.2 introduces HTML tables. If you are not converting** existing documents, the HTML tables are much more attractive than are the ones that you can create by using the <PRE> element. See Chapter 9, "Creating Tables," for more information on this topic.

CAUTION   **Tab characters move the cursor to the next position, which is an** integer multiple of eight. The official HTML specification recommends that tab characters not be used in preformatted text because they are not supported in the same way by all viewers. Spaces should be used for aligning columns.

FIG. 4.12
Preformatted text can be used to line up columns of numbers.

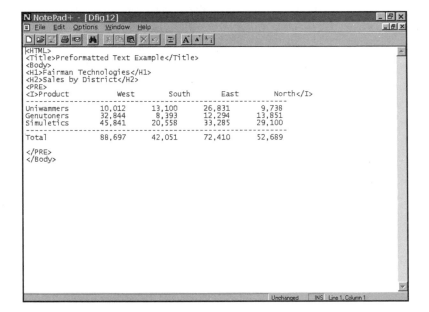

TIP   **There are other preformatted container classes, but these have** been declared as obsolete. The <XMP> and <LISTING> elements give you the capability to create text that is already laid out. There are some disadvantages to these in that other HTML elements are not permitted inside of them. Viewers are not allowed to recognize any markup tags except the end tag. Unfortunately, many viewers don't comply with this standard properly, and the results can be unpleasant.

The difference between the two elements are that <XMP> text must be rendered in a font size that permits at least 80 characters on a line and <LISTING> requires a font that permits 132 characters.

You should avoid using the <XMP> and <LISTING> elements unless it is absolutely necessary. Because they have been declared obsolete, viewers are not required to support them any longer. You will be more certain of what your readers are seeing if you use the <PRE> element instead.

FIG. 4.13
A preformatted table can be used in a document.

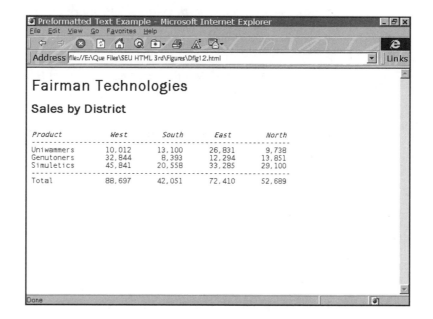

NOTE If you want to show actual HTML code in a preformatted section, or you just want to use the < or > characters, you need to use the &lt and &gt codes, like this: &ltPRE&gt.

Layout tips

Understanding the HTML tags that you can use is a different matter than understanding how to use them effectively. Thus, here are a few tips that you should consider when using the tags you learned about in this chapter:

- *Use equal spacing* Try to keep the spacing between elements consistent. That is, make sure the same amount of space is above and below each of your paragraphs. Readers will perceive uneven spacing as sloppiness on your part.

- *Avoid right and center justification* Don't right or center justify the main body of text. Right- and center-justified text is harder to read than left-justified text.

- *Don't go overboard with indents* Proper indentation depends on the size of the font you're using. A larger font requires a deeper indent and vise versa.

- *Use <NOBR> with <WBR> to maintain control of line breaks* Sometimes, you want to control exactly where the browser will break a line if it needs to. <NOBR> turns off line breaks while <WBR> provides hints to the browser that suggests a spot for a line break if necessary.

- *Consider dividing a page that uses <HR>* If you find yourself using rules to divide a Web page into individual topics, consider splitting that Web page up into individual pages so each page remains focused on a single topic.

- *Give plenty of space to artwork* The images and tables in your HTML document should have enough white space around them so that they're set apart from the text. You don't want them to appear cramped.

- *Use headings to organize your text* Headings give readers a visual road map that helps them locate the information in which they're interested. Use them liberally.

A specialized template

Using what we we've learned in this chapter, we can create a more sophisticated template. Building upon the template that we laid out at the end of Chapter 3, let's use some of the features of this chapter to build a template that can be used for glossaries and related documents.

The first step is to bring the existing template into our editor. Once we've loaded it, we can make the appropriate changes to the elements that are already present. These can be seen in Listing 4.5.

Listing 4.5

The glossary template with the first changes

```
<HTML>
<HEAD>
<TITLE>Glossary</TITLE>
<HEAD>
<BODY BACKGROUND="greybg.jpg" BGCOLOR="GRAY", TEXT="BLACK",
LINK="BLUE", ALINK="GREEN", VLINK="RED">
<ADDRESS>Created by Author<BR>
Created on Date</ADDRESS>
</BODY>
</HTML>
```

Now, we can add a title to the page and bracket the text with some horizontal rules. We make the decision that the terms to be defined will be level-two headings, left-aligned, and that the definitions themselves will be normal text. These decisions lead to Listing 4.6, which is a template that can now be saved and used anytime you need a glossary document. This same template would also work for a phone list or a catalog.

Listing 4.6

The final glossary template

```
<HTML>
<HEAD>
<TITLE>Glossary</TITLE>
<HEAD>
<BODY BACKGROUND="greybg.jpg" BGCOLOR="GRAY", TEXT="BLACK",
LINK="BLUE", ALINK="GREEN", VLINK="RED">
<H1 ALIGN=CENTER>Glossary</H1>
<HR ALIGN=CENTER WIDTH=50% SIZE=5 COLOR=NAVY>
<H2 ALIGN=LEFT>Term 1</H2>
Type the definition for term 1 here.
<H2 ALIGN=LEFT>Term 2</H2>
Type the definition for term 2 here. And so on...
<HR ALIGN=CENTER WIDTH=50% SIZE=5 COLOR=NAVY>
<ADDRESS>Created by Author<BR>
Created on Date</ADDRESS>
</BODY>
</HTML>
```

An example of how this template could be used is shown in Figure 4.14.

FIG. 4.14

An example using the glossary template.

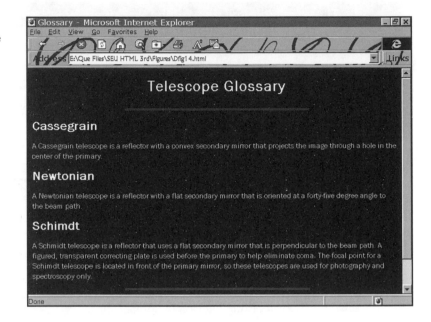

5

Text Formatting

● **In this chapter:**

● **Logical formatting makes your documents portable across multiple platforms and browsers**

● **Format your text by using HTML text-formatting tags**

● **Take control of the fonts you use**

● **Create documents that are easy to read**

You've now seen how to create an HTML document and how to perform basic document formatting. The next step is exercising control over how the text looks. With the arrival of HTML 3.2, a document author now has a tremendous amount of discretion over the text formatting. You won't find quite as much detail as you might expect in the latest word processor, but you'll be amazed at how much there is.

Text formatting

Once you've created your document, much of the hard work is done. The text that you've written is neatly broken into paragraphs, headings are in place, and the miscellaneous items such as the title and the author information has been added. At this point you could walk away satisfied, but something still seems to be missing.

One of the primary things that separate documents created on a word processor from those produced on a typewriter is the idea of text formatting. Word processors give the author control over how her text will look. She can choose the font that she likes in the appropriate size, and she can apply one or more of a myriad of options to the text. In HTML, you have this same capability. Your only real restrictions involve the importance of viewer independence.

Logical formatting

One of the ideas behind HTML is that documents should be laid out in a logical and structured manner. This gives the users of the documents as much flexibility as possible. With this in mind, the designers of HTML created a number of formatting elements that are labeled according to the purpose they serve rather than by their appearance. The advantage of this approach is that documents are not limited to a certain platform. Although they may look different on various platforms, the content and context will remain the same.

These logical format elements are as follows:

- `<CITE>`   The citation element is used to indicate the citation of a quotation. It can also be used to indicate the title of a book or article. An italic font is normally used to display citations.

```
<CITE>Tom Sawyer</CITE> remains one of the classics of
➥American literature.
```

- <CODE>   The code element is used to indicate a small amount of computer code. It is generally reserved for short sections, with longer sections noted by using the <PRE> tag described later. Code normally appears in a monospaced font.

```
One of the first lines that every C programmer learns
➥is:<BR><CODE>puts("Hello World!");</CODE>
```

- <EM>   The emphasis element is used to indicate a section of text that the author wants to identify as significant. Emphasis is generally shown in an italic font.

```
The actual line reads, "Alas, poor Yorick. I knew him,
➥<EM>Horatio</EM>."
```

- <KBD>   The keyboard element is used to indicate a user entry response. A monospaced typewriter font is normally used to display keyboard text.

```
To run the decoder, type <KBD>Restore</KBD> followed by
➥your password.
```

- <SAMP>   The sample element is used to indicate literal characters. These normally are a few characters that are intended to be precisely identified. Sample element text normally is shown in a monospaced font.

```
The letters <SAMP>AEIOU</SAMP> are the vowels of the
➥English language.
```

- <STRONG>   The strong element is used to emphasize a particularly important section of text. Text using strong emphasis is normally set in a bold font.

```
The most important rule to remember is <STRONG>Don't
➥panic</STRONG>!
```

- <VAR>   The variable element is used to indicate a dummy variable name. Variables are normally viewed in an italic font.

```
The sort routine rotates on the <VAR>I</VAR>th element.
```

Note that all of these elements are containers, and as such, they require an end tag. Figure 5.1 shows how these logical elements look when seen in the Netscape viewer.

FIG. 5.1

Samples of the logical format elements are displayed in Netscape.

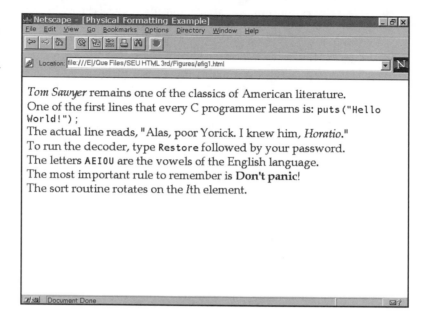

You have probably noticed that a lot of these format styles use the same rendering. The most obvious question to ask is why use them if they all look alike?

The answer is these elements are logical styles. They indicate what the intention of the author was, not how the material should look. This is important because future uses of HTML may include programs that search the Web to find citations, for example, or the next generation of Web viewers may be able to read a document aloud. A program that can identify emphasis would be able to avoid the deadly monotone of current text-to-speech processors.

The *<BLOCKQUOTE>* element

You may have the opportunity to quote a long piece of work from another source in your document. To indicate that this quotation is different from the rest of your text, HTML provides the <BLOCKQUOTE> element. This container functions as a body element within the body element and can contain any of the formatting or break tags. As a container, the <BLOCKQUOTE> element is turned off by using the end tag.

The normal method used by most viewers to indicate a <BLOCKQUOTE> element is to indent the text away from the left margin. Some text-only viewers may indicate a <BLOCKQUOTE> by using a character, such as the "greater than" sign, in the leftmost column on the screen. Because most viewers are now graphical in nature, the <BLOCKQUOTE> element provides an additional service by enabling you to indent normal text from the left margin. This can add some visual interest to the document.

Listing 5.1 shows how a <BLOCKQUOTE> is constructed, including some of the formatting available in the container. The results of this document when read into Netscape can be seen in Figure 5.2.

Listing 5.1

Construction of a *<BLOCKQUOTE>*

```
<HTML>
<TITLE>BLOCKQUOTE Example</TITLE>
<BODY>
<BLOCKQUOTE>
Wit is the sudden marriage of ideas which before their union
were not
perceived to have any relation.
</BLOCKQUOTE>
<CITE>Mark Twain</CITE>
</BODY>
</HTML>
```

FIG. 5.2

This is the appearance
of the document in
Netscape.

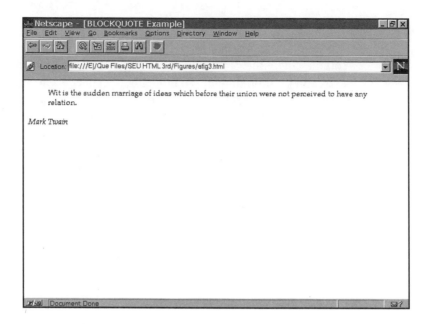

Physical format elements

Having said that HTML is intended to leave the appearance of the document
up to the viewer, I will now show you how you can have limited control over
what the reader sees. In addition to the logical formatting elements, it is
possible to use physical formatting elements that will change the appearance
of the text in the viewer. These physical elements are as follows:

- <B> The bold element uses a bold font to display the text.

      This is in <B>bold</B> text.

- <I> The italic element renders text by using an italic font.

      This is in <I>italic</I> text.

- <TT> The teletype element displays the contents with a monospaced
  typewriter font.

      This is in <TT>teletype</TT> text.

- `<U>` The underline element causes text to be underlined in the viewer.

    `This text is <U>underlined</U>.`

- `<STRIKE>` The strikethrough element draws a horizontal line through the middle of the text.

    `This is a <STRIKE>strikethough</STRIKE> example.`

- `<BIG>` The big print element uses a larger font size to display the text.

    `This is <BIG>big</BIG> text.`

- `<SMALL>` The small print element displays the text in a smaller font size.

    `This is <SMALL>small</SMALL> text.`

- `<SUB>` The subscript element moves the text lower than the surrounding text and (if possible) displays the text in a smaller size font.

    `This is a <SUB>subscript</SUB>.`

- `<SUP>` The superscript element moves the text higher than the surrounding text and (if possible) displays the text in a smaller size font.

    `This is a <SUP>superscript</SUP>.`

If the proper font isn't available, the reader's viewer must render the text in the closest possible manner. Once again, each of these is a container element and requires the use of an end tag. Figure 5.3 shows how these elements look in Internet Explorer.

These elements can be nested, with one element contained entirely within another. On the other hand, overlapping elements are not permitted and can produce unpredictable results. Figure 5.4 gives some examples of nested elements and how they can be used to create special effects.

FIG. 5.3
Samples of the physical format elements are shown in Internet Explorer.

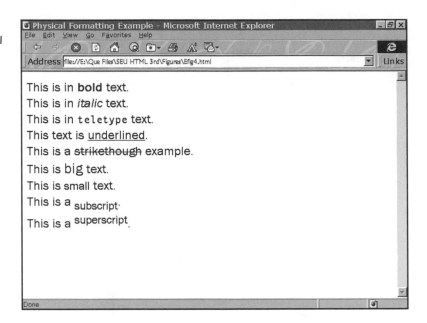

FIG. 5.4
Logical and physical format elements can be nested to create additional format styles.

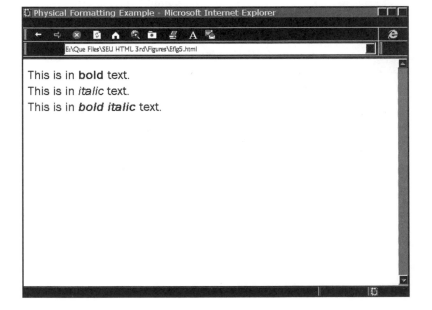

TIP **There is a tag available only in Netscape Navigator that has** acquired a particularly bad reputation: the <BLINK> tag is notorious in HTML circles. Unless you want people to speak ill of your documents, it's best to avoid this tag.

Fonts

One of the nicest features of HTML 3.2 is that you, as document author, now have the ability to control the appearance of the text in your documents. This capability was restricted entirely to the reader in previous versions of HTML. The problem with this ability is that you can only use fonts that exist on you readers' machines. So how do you know what your user might have available?

Unfortunately, you don't. If you are building documents to be used on a intranet, your organization should set standards as to which fonts should be found on every machine. As long as this is a reasonable set, it will be easy to maintain and you will be able to choose any of the standard fonts for your document. If you are developing for the Web, however, you have a more serious problem. In practice, you really don't know what fonts your readers might have. Even the most basic selection depends greatly upon the hardware that your readers are using. There are no really graceful ways around this problem at the present, although several companies are looking into ways of distributing font information with a document.

 NOTE **If you are developing for the Web and you would like to use some** different fonts, you should be aware that Microsoft has several fonts available for free download on their Web site. These fonts are available in both Windows and Macintosh formats. If you decide to use any of these fonts in your documents, you might want to put a link to the Web page where your readers can download the fonts, if they don't already have them.

http://www.microsoft.com/truetype/fontpack/default.htm

The *FONT* element

The method that HTML uses for providing control over the appearance of the text is the FONT element. This element is new to HTML 3.2 and may not be supported by all viewers, but both Microsoft and Netscape make full use of it. The FONT element is a container that is opened with the <FONT> start tag and closed with the </FONT> end tag. Unless attributes are assigned in the start tag, there is no effect of using a FONT element.

The FONT element can be used inside of any other text container and it will modify the text based upon the appearance of the text within the parent container.

NOTE **Netscape Navigator 3.0 does not support the FACE or COLOR** attributes of BASEFONT. This support will likely appear in later versions, but to be strictly compatible, you probably would want to avoid them at this time.

The final version of Netscape Navigator 4.0 will provide Web developers the ability to temporarily download a font with a Web page, so that the user sees it as the developer intends. This eliminates the problem with using a font on a Web page that the user doesn't have installed.

The *FACE* attribute

The FACE attribute allows you to specify the font that you would like the viewing software to use when displaying your document. The parameter for this attribute is the name of the desired font. This name must be an exact match for a font name on the reader's machine, or the viewer will ignore the request and use the default font as set by the reader. Capitalization is ignored in the name, but spaces are required. Listing 5.2 shows an example of how a font face is specified and Figure 5.5 shows the page in Microsoft Internet Explorer.

Listing 5.2

An example of *FONT FACE* selection

```
<HTML>
<HEAD>
<TITLE>Font Selection Example</TITLE>
</HEAD>
<BODY>
<FONT FACE="Tolkien">
This is an example of font selection. </FONT>
</BODY>
</HTML>
```

Since you don't know for certain what fonts the user might have on his system, the face attribute allows you to list more than one font, with the names separated by commas. This is especially useful, since nearly identical fonts often have different names on Windows and Macintoshes. The font list will be parsed from left to right and the first matching font will be used. Listing 5.3 shows an example where the author wanted to use a sans serif font for his text.

FIG. 5.5

The FACE attribute of the FONT element lets you select the font in which the text will be displayed.

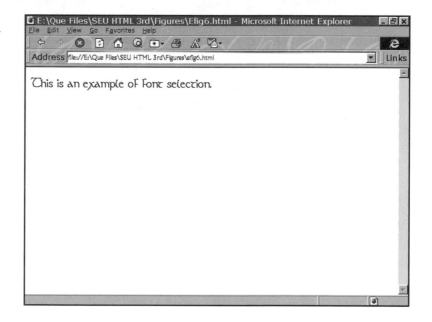

Listing 5.3

FONT FACE selection can use a list of acceptable choices

```
<HTML>
<HEAD>
<TITLE>Font Selection Example</TITLE>
</HEAD>
<BODY>
<FONT FACE="Verdana", "Arial", "Helvetica">
This is an example of font selection. </FONT>
</BODY>
</HTML>
```

In this example, the author wanted to use Verdana as his first choice, but listed Arial and Helvetica as alternatives.

The *SIZE* attribute

The SIZE attribute of the FONT element allows the document author to specify character height for the text. Font size is a relative scale from 1 though 7 and is based upon the "normal" font size being 3. The SIZE attribute can be used in either of two different ways: the size can be stated absolutely, with a statement like SIZE=5, or it can be relative, as in SIZE=+2. The second method is more commonly used when a BASEFONT size has been specified. Listing 5.4 shows how the font sizes are specified and Figure 5.6 shows how they would look.

Listing 5.4

An example of *FONT SIZE* selection

```
<HTML>
<HEAD>
<TITLE>Font Size Example</TITLE>
</HEAD>
<BODY>
<FONT SIZE=1>Size 1</FONT><BR>
<FONT SIZE=-1>Size 2</FONT><BR>
<FONT SIZE=3>Size 3</FONT><BR>
<FONT SIZE=4>Size 4</FONT><BR>
<FONT SIZE=+2>Size 5</FONT><BR>
<FONT SIZE=6>Size 6</FONT><BR>
<FONT SIZE=+4>Size 7</FONT><BR>
</BODY>
</HTML>
```

FIG. 5.6

Text size can be specified with the SIZE attribute of the FONT element.

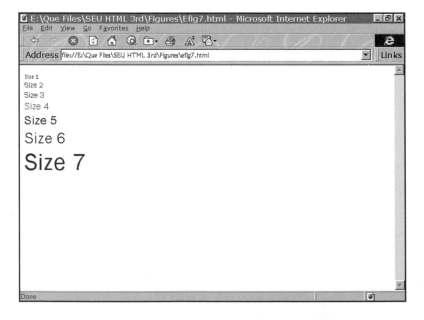

The *COLOR* attribute

Text color can be specified in the same manner as the face or the size. The COLOR attribute accepts either a hexadecimal RGB value or one of the standard color names. Listing 5.5 is an example of how colors can be specified.

Listing 5.5

An example of *FONT COLOR* selection

```
<HTML>
<HEAD>
<TITLE>Font Color Example</TITLE>
</HEAD>
<BODY>
<FONT COLOR="#FF0000">This text is red</FONT><BR>
<FONT COLOR="GREEN">This text is green</FONT><BR>
</BODY>
</HTML>
```

The *<BASEFONT>* tag

The <BASEFONT> tag is used to establish the standard font size, face, and color for the text in the document. The choices made in the <BASEFONT> tag remain in place for the rest of the document, unless they are overridden by a FONT element. When the FONT element is closed, the BASEFONT characteristics are returned. BASEFONT attributes can be changed by another <BASEFONT> tag at any time in the document. Note that BASEFONT is a tag and not a container. There is no </BASEFONT> end tag.

BASEFONT uses the FACE, SIZE, and COLOR attributes just as the FONT element does.

Listing 5.6 is an example of the <BASEFONT> tag. Figure 5.7 shows how the example looks in Internet Explorer.

Listing 5.6

An example of the *<BASEFONT>* tag

```
<HTML>
<HEAD>
<TITLE>BASEFont Example</TITLE>
</HEAD>
<BODY>
This text is before the BASEFONT tag.<BR>
<BASEFONT SIZE=6 FACE="GEORGIA">
This text is after the BASEFONT tag.<BR>
Size changes are relative to the BASEFONT <FONT SIZE=-3>SIZE</
FONT>.<BR>
</BODY>
</HTML>
```

FIG. 5.7

The <BASEFONT> tag can be used to control the text characteristics for the entire document.

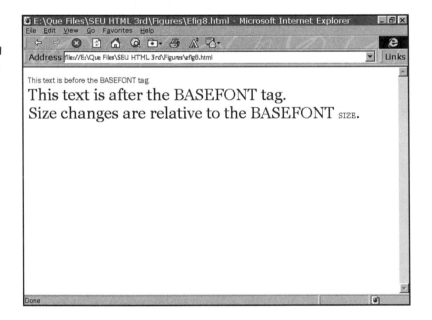

Text formatting tips

Now that you have all of the tools to format your text, you need to decide how you are going to use them. It is possible to use so many different fonts, sizes, and formats that your document will be unpleasant to read. Figure 5.8 is a bad example of how a document can use too many formats.

FIG. 5.8
The ability to select formats should not be overused.

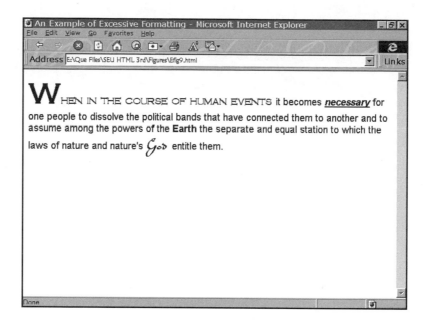

The following are general tips to keep in mind as you format your documents:

- Most documents should use only two or three different font faces.

- In general, if the body text is in a serif font, such as Times New Roman, the headings should be a sans serif font, such as Arial.

- Italics are much less intrusive than are bold characters, which should be reserved for very important points.

- Don't overuse underlining. When long strings of text are underlined, the user's eyes easily get confused.

- The size of headings should decrease with the decreasing importance of the heading. This provides your readers with a quick and easy way to scan your documents.

Graphics Formatting

● **In this chapter:**

● **Use appropriate images in your HTML files**

● **Choose the most appropriate graphics file format**

● **Easily add images to your HTML documents**

● **Learn the tricks of the trade**

Images can make your HTML document more compelling than text alone. Imagine an HTML document that contains some fairly dry material, such as the specification for the techno-widget that you invented, for example. If you only put text in this document, the document would seem quite dull. On the other hand, a few well-placed graphics can break up the text, making it seem more readable, and make the document more visually appealing.

Images can often convey your message better than text alone. Can you picture this book without any figures? It wouldn't convey its message as well. Remember the old cliché that a picture is worth a thousand words? Beyond that, without figures you probably would have put this book right back onto the shelf because it wouldn't look very appealing. I wouldn't blame you, either.

Up to this point, you've learned about the basic HTML required to add text to your document and how to format that text. This chapter stuffs your toolkit with another tool, inline images, that lets you convey your message better and create a more visually attractive Web page. In this chapter, you learn how to add those images to your HTML documents. You also learn several tips and tricks that you need to know when using images in HTML.

Understanding the issues

You need to carefully consider each image that you add to your HTML documents. Yes, you should carefully consider the design and contents of each image, but, in this section, you learn about other issues. For example:

- Does the image add enough value to the Web page?

- Can I borrow an image? What about copyrights?

- What about offensive or pornographic images?

What should I know when using inline images?

Before adding images to your HTML documents, you need to understand the issues. That doesn't mean you should avoid using images—you shouldn't. If you understand the issues, however, you're better able to choose appropriate images. Just keep these points in mind as you add each image to your document:

- **Graphics files are slow to download**. The average user with a 14.4K modem can wait several seconds or even several minutes while a graphics file downloads.

- **Search engines don't know what to do with images**. The search engines, such as AltaVista and Excite, can't index your images. Thus, if you depend heavily on images, your Web page isn't as likely to be hit upon by these search engine's users.

- **Many users don't have graphical browsers.** Thousands of folks are still using Lynx, for example, which is a UNIX based text-only browser. As well, Internet Explorer and Netscape users might disable inline images in order to open Web pages faster.

- **Images aren't always internationalized.** Such a big word, internationalized. Folks in cultures other than yours might not understand the significance or meaning of an image. Since HTML documents published on the Web have a world-wide audience, internationalized images might be important.

- **Color images aren't always portable**. A color image that looks good on your computer might not look quite as good on another user's computer. Thus, you need to pay particular attention to how you use colors in an image.

Do I have to worry about an image's copyright?

The growth in electronic publishing has given rise to a startling new crime wave. Many people, who are perfectly honest in all of their day-to-day dealings, think nothing of using a clever graphic that they found on the Web. After all, once they download it, the image has lost all of its ties to the original author. Regardless, the copyright laws apply to electronic images just as much as they do to works like this book. If you use an image that has been copyrighted, the author can sue for damages.

How can you tell if a graphic has been copyrighted? It's not as easy as looking for a little copyright symbol in the image. Here are some tips to help you tell if an image is copyrighted, though:

- Look at the original document that contained the image for a copyright notice.

- If you borrowed the image from clip art or an image library, look in the library's document for a copyright notice.

- If you scanned the image from a magazine or book, you can bet the image is copyrighted.

- If you downloaded an image from a commercial site, such as an online magazine, the image is probably copyrighted.

 NOTE **Images that are obviously commercially oriented are usually** copyrighted. These include images of people, logos, cartoon characters, and other unique images. As well, interesting decorations, such as bullets or horizontal rules, probably come from a clip art library, which grants rights to use those images only to the purchaser of the library.

Can you plead ignorance if you're busted using a copyrighted image? Nope. You have the total responsibility for determining whether or not an image is copyrighted. Since this is not always practical, the best advise is to only use images that either you're completely certain are not copyrighted, those that you have been granted the right to use, or those for which you hold the copyright.

 ***CAUTION*** **Changing a copyrighted work does not revoke the copyright. The** copyright holder has rights to all derived works. This means that you cannot download an image, change it in some fashion, and then freely use the new version.

As you can see, copyright law is a tricky thing. Your best bet is to assume that all images are copyrighted unless proven otherwise. If you have any questions or if you're developing a high-profile Web site, you should probably contact an attorney who specializes in copyright law.

Can I get into trouble for pornographic images?

Maybe. A simple rule of thumb is that you should avoid pornographic images. From a practical point of view, a Web site that has pornographic images on it is likely to be overwhelmed with traffic. As a result you may run afoul of your Internet service provider, who is almost certainly not going to be pleased with hundreds of megabytes of downloads from a single Web page.

There are a couple of legal aspects to this issue, as well:

- Most pornography has been scanned from published sources and is in violation of the copyright laws. These publishers are among the most aggressive plaintiffs in pursuit of legal damages.

- A variety of states and countries have laws regarding what is obscene. Since the Web is a world-wide medium, you might violate laws that you don't even know exist.

 *CAUTION* **The information you read in this section is common sense. This** information doesn't replace your legal council, however, in cases where you have real questions about pornographic images.

Picking the right graphics file format

You'll find dozens of graphics file formats that you can use to store images, such as: GIF, JPEG, PCX, WMF, and so on. When creating images for use in an HTML document, however, you're better off sticking with those file formats that most browsers understand: GIF or JPEG.

Each file format has certain trade offs. While one file format downloads faster, for example, the other format maintains more image detail. This section helps you pick the right file format by describing these trade offs. First, it briefly describes each file format. Then, it compares the speed, color depth, "loss-y-ness," and browser support of each file format.

If you want to get right to the bottom-line, I recommend that you use GIF. It's widely supported by most Web browsers (whereas PNG is not). It's interlaced, which lets users view an image before it's finished downloading. It does transparency, too, so you can create great-looking imagemaps with transparent backgrounds.

Formats

Chapter 14, "Graphics," describes each file format you read about here in great detail. For your convenience, however, the following sections contain an overview of each file format.

GIF

The most common file format on the Web is GIF (CompuServe Graphical Interchange Format) or more specifically, GIF89A. This format was developed for CompuServe. It's been through a number of revisions and now includes many important features that you learn about in Chapter 14, including:

- It uses a lossless compression scheme, so images don't lose detail when they're compressed.

- It supports transparent backgrounds, so you can create images with transparent regions.

- It's an interlaced file format (see Figure 6.1), so the user can view the image before the browser has finished downloading it.

- It's widely supported by most browsers, so most users can view this file format inline.

GIF has recently made the headlines. GIF, like several other compressed file formats, uses an algorithm known as *LZW*, which is patented by Unisys. In late 1994, Unisys announced that, in order to protect their rights, anyone producing software that used GIF would need a license from Unisys. This requirement is on the developers of that software and does not affect end users. In fact, the Unisys press release specifically states that using GIF on a Web page is acceptable and doesn't require a license.

FIG. 6.1
An interlaced GIF allows a user to start viewing an image before the browser has finished downloading it.

Interlaced image, which is partially loaded

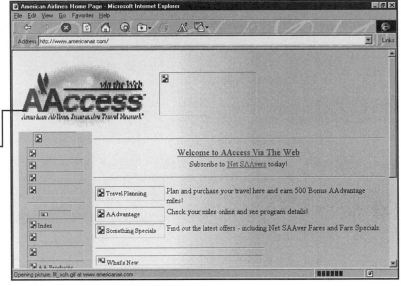

JPEG

Another popular format for graphics is the JPEG format. This was developed by the Joint Photographics Expert Group to provide a standard "lossy" compression scheme for photographic images. Here's an overview of JPEG:

- It uses a lossy compression scheme, so images lose detail when they're compressed.

- It produces smaller images than GIF, so they download faster.

- It supports 16.7 million colors, so it reproduces photographic images very well.

- It loses detail around sharp edges, so it's not suitable for images that contain sharp images or text.

PNG

The Portable Network Graphics (PNG) format was developed as a result of the confusion and concern that followed the Unisys/CompuServe GIF announcement. Early in 1995 a group of graphics programmers started to develop a new lossless format that would avoid the licensing issues of GIF, while resolving some of the technical problems that GIF has. The new format, PNG, (pronounced "ping") was released in March 1995.

Since that time, PNG has become ever more common and will probably replace GIF completely within the next few years. It provides better compression and supports a larger number of colors than does GIF. At this time, add-ins are available to give PNG display capabilities to both Netscape Navigator and Microsoft Internet Explorer.

BMP

A bitmap (BMP) file is a format commonly encountered in the Windows and OS/2 operating systems. These files are completely uncompressed and take inordinate amounts of time to download. Only Internet Explorer supports BMP files, and I recommend *very* strongly that you avoid using this format.

File speed

When choosing a graphics file format, the most important issue to keep in mind is download speed versus image quality. If you're going to use an image in your Web page, you obviously want to store that image in a format that downloads as quickly as possible. On the other hand, you trade image quality for faster download speeds.

The best possible choices are GIF, PNG, or JPEG. BMP files aren't compressed at all, thus it is the slowest of all file formats to download. GIF, PNG, and JPEG all provide an acceptable experience when compared to the variety of other formats available on the Web:

- GIF and PNG files are larger than JPEG files, but GIF and PNG files decode faster and maintain more image detail.

- JPEG files download faster than GIF and PNG, but they decode slower and maintain less image detail.

 TIP **GIF does an extremely good job compressing images that contain** only a handful of colors. Thus, with an image that uses only a few colors, GIF compresses better than JPEG.

Colors

GIF supports 256 colors. JPEG supports 16.7 million colors. Thus, if color depth is not important, or you're using a limited number of colors in an image, you can be comfortable using GIF. On the other hand, if you want to maintain a photographic quality color depth, then you might consider using JPEG.

Loss

Lossy compression schemes cause an image to lose detail when the graphics program saves it. This is how these schemes compress the file so much. Lossless compression schemes, on the other hand, don't cause an image to lose any detail at all. Table 6.1 describes each file format's compression scheme.

Table 6.1   Compression schemes

Format	Scheme	Description
GIF	Lossless	GIF compresses without losing any detail. Thus, if you're concerned more with maintaining detail than download speed, use GIF.
PNG	Lossless	PNG also compresses without losing any detail. PNG is a good alternative to GIF, except that it's not directly supported by most Web browsers.
JPEG	Lossy	JPEG causes an image to lose detail when you save it. If you're concerned more with file size than with detail, however, use JPEG.
BMP	N/A	BMP provides no compression. You should avoid this file format for that reason.

 Browser support

You really don't want readers to have to install a helper application to view the images in your HTML documents. Thus, you should stick with those file formats that are directly supported by the most popular browsers. These formats include GIF and JPEG. PNG is not yet supported by a majority of the Web browsers, so you should shy away from this format for now.

Adding inline images to your HTML document

Putting an image in an HTML document is incredibly easy. You use the <IMG> tag with its SRC attribute. Add the following tag to your HTML document at the location in which you want to display the image. Then, replace *filename* with the URL of the image you want to display.

```
<IMG SRC="filename">
```

By default, the browser displays the image inline. Thus, the browser displays it immediately to the right of any text or any other object that immediately precedes the image. Take a look at Listing 6.1, for example. It shows the same image three different times. Each time, the image is shown inline. That is, the browser displays the image immediately to the right of any text preceding it as shown in Figure 6.2.

Listing 6.1

Using the *<IMG>* tag

```
<HTML>
<HEAD>
  <TITLE>Using the IMG tag</TITLE>
</HEAD>
<BODY>
  <P>
    <IMG SRC="book.gif">
    This text immediately follows the image.
  </P>
  <P>
    This text is interrupted
    <IMG SRC="book.gif">
    by the image.
  </P>
  <P>
    In this case, the image appears inline after this text.
    <IMG SRC="book.gif">
  </P>
</BODY>
</HTML>
```

FIG. 6.2
You can insert an image anywhere in an HTML document that you like.

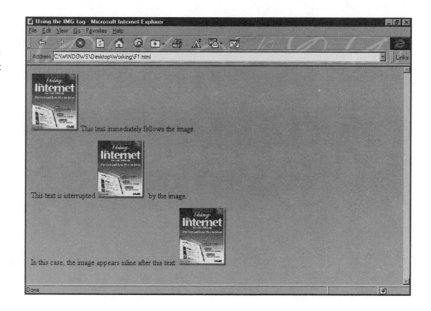

 TIP **Consider storing all of your images in a single directory off your** Web site's root folder. Then, you can use relative paths in combination with the <BASE> tag to access your images without specifying a full URL.

Aligning text with an inline image

By default, when you insert an image inline with text, the text is aligned with the bottom of the image. Chances are good that you won't like this default alignment. You can change it, though, using the <IMG> tag's ALIGN attribute. Table 6.2 describes each value you can assign to this attribute.

Table 6.2   Values for the *ALIGN* attribute

Value	Description
TOP	Aligns the text with the top of the image.
MIDDLE	Aligns the text with the middle of the image.
BOTTOM	Aligns the text with the bottom of the image.

Listing 6.2 shows you an HTML document that inserts three images, each of which uses one of the alignment values shown in Table 6.2. Figure 6.3 shows the resulting Web page.

Listing 6.2

Using the *<IMG>* tag's *ALIGN* attribute

```
<HTML>
<HEAD>
  <TITLE>Using the IMG tag's ALIGN attribute</TITLE>
</HEAD>
<BODY>
  <P>
    <IMG SRC="book.gif" ALIGN=TOP>
    This text is aligned with the top of the image.
  </P>
  <P>
    <IMG SRC="book.gif" ALIGN=MIDDLE>
    This text is aligned with the middle of the image.
  </P>
  <P>
    <IMG SRC="book.gif" ALIGN=BOTTOM>
    This text is aligned with the bottom of the image.
  </P>
</BODY>
</HTML>
```

FIG. 6.3

By default, the baseline of the text is aligned with the bottom of an inline image.

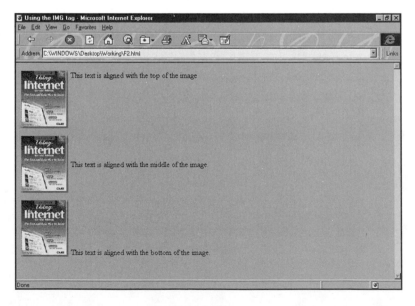

Positioning an image on the Web page

By default, the browser displays images inline. That is, it displays an image immediately to the right of the previous content. Text does not wrap around it, either. You can display an image on the left- or right-hand side of the Web page, however, allowing the surrounding content to flow around the image. This type of image is called a *floating* image.

You create a floating image by using the <IMG> tag's ALIGN attribute. This is the same attribute you use to align the surrounding text with an image. Table 6.3 describes each value you can assign to this attribute.

Table 6.3   Values for the *ALIGN* attribute

Value	Description
LEFT	Displays image on left-hand side and surrounding content flows around the image.
RIGHT	Displays image on the right-hand side of the window and surrounding content flows around the image.

Listing 6.3 shows you an HTML document that inserts two images, each of which uses one of the alignment values shown in Table 6.3. Figure 6.4 shows the resulting Web page.

Listing 6.3

Using the *<IMG>* tag's *ALIGN* attribute

```
<HTML>
<HEAD>
  <TITLE>Using the IMG tag's ALIGN attribute</TITLE>
</HEAD>
<BODY>
  <P>
    <IMG SRC="book.gif" ALIGN=LEFT>
    This text will wrap around the right-hand and bottom of
    ➡the image.
    This text will wrap around the right-hand and bottom of
    ➡the image.
    This text will wrap around the right-hand and bottom of
    ➡the image.
```

continues

Listing 6.3

Continued

```
      This text will wrap around the right-hand and bottom of
      ➥the image.
      This text will wrap around the right-hand and bottom of
      ➥the image.
      This text will wrap around the right-hand and bottom of
      ➥the image.
      This text will wrap around the right-hand and bottom of
      ➥the image.
      This text will wrap around the right-hand and bottom of
      ➥the image.
      This text will wrap around the right-hand and bottom of
      ➥the image.
      This text will wrap around the right-hand and bottom of
      ➥the image.
      This text will wrap around the right-hand and bottom of
      ➥the image.
      This text will wrap around the right-hand and bottom of
      ➥the image.
</P>
<P>
      <IMG SRC="book.gif" ALIGN=RIGHT>
      This text will wrap around the left-hand and bottom of
      ➥the image.
      This text will wrap around the left-hand and bottom of
      ➥the image.
      This text will wrap around the left-hand and bottom of
      ➥the image.
      This text will wrap around the left-hand and bottom of
      ➥the image.
      This text will wrap around the left-hand and bottom of
      ➥the image.
      This text will wrap around the left-hand and bottom of
      ➥the image.
      This text will wrap around the left-hand and bottom of
      ➥the image.
      This text will wrap around the left-hand and bottom of
      ➥the image.
      This text will wrap around the left-hand and bottom of
      ➥the image.
      This text will wrap around the left-hand and bottom of
      ➥the image.
      This text will wrap around the left-hand and bottom of
      ➥the image.
      This text will wrap around the left-hand and bottom of
      ➥the image.
      This text will wrap around the left-hand and bottom of
      ➥the image.
```

```
                    This text will wrap around the left-hand and bottom of
                  ➥the image.
                </P>
                </BODY>
                </HTML>
```

FIG. 6.4

By default, the baseline of the text is aligned with the bottom of an inline image.

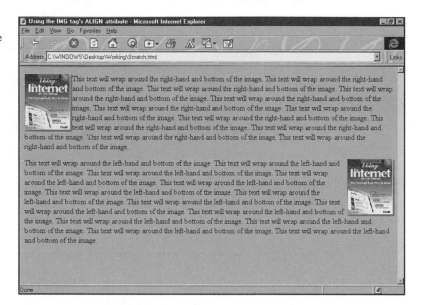

Giving the browser size hints

Providing the browser a size hint means that you explicitly state the height and width of the image within the `<IMG>` tag. This has two benefits that make this a must:

- **Size hints help users who've disabled inline image**. If a user has disabled inline images, and you're not using size hints, she will see a small icon in place of the image. Thus, the Web page will not be formatted quite like you expect. Size hints cause the browser to display an empty box that is the same size as the image.

- **Size hints make the Web page render faster**. A browser displays the HTML document first. Then, it displays the image. If you provide size hints for your inline images, the browser can display the formatted HTML document while it finishes downloading the images. Thus, the user sees the Web page faster.

You use the `<IMG>` tag's `HEIGHT` and `WIDTH` attributes to provide size hints to the browser. You set the `HEIGHT` attribute to the exact height and the `WIDTH` attribute to the exact width in pixels that you want to reserve for the image. Listing 6.4 shows what an HTML document looks like that sets the height and width of an image. Figure 6.5 shows what this HTML document looks like when inline images are disabled.

Listing 6.4

Using *HEIGHT* and *WIDTH* to give size hints

```
<HTML>
<HEAD>
  <TITLE>Using HEIGHT and WIDTH to give size hints</TITLE>
</HEAD>
<BODY>
<IMG SRC="book.gif" WIDTH=320 HEIGHT=240>
</BODY>
</HTML>
```

FIG. 6.5
Without size hints, all you'd see in this image is a small box with an icon in it.

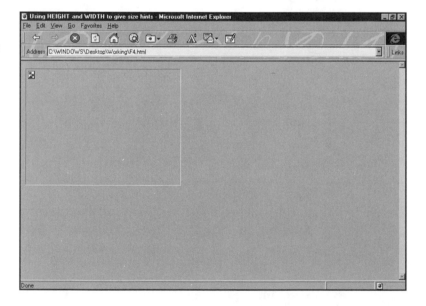

If the size you specify by using the `HEIGHT` and `WIDTH` attributes isn't the same as the actual size of the image as determined in your favorite graphics editor, the browser scales the image. The following sections describe the result of scaling the image down and scaling the image up.

Scaling an image down

Scaling the image down means the actual image is larger than the space you reserved for it by using the HEIGHT and WIDTH attributes. In this case, the browser shrinks the image so that it fits in the reserved space.

You can easily distort an image if you're not careful how you specify its size. For example, if you decrease the image's height by 50 percent and the width by 25 percent, the image will look funny in the browser (see Figure 6.6).

FIG. 6.6
Equally scaling an image's height and width is also known as maintaining the image's aspect ratio.

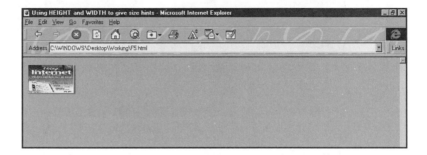

CAUTION **Specifying a height and width that's smaller than the actual** image height and width doesn't save any download time. The browser still downloads the entire image before it scales it to fit the reserved area.

Scaling an image up

Scaling the image up means the actual image is smaller than the space you reserved for it by using the HEIGHT and WIDTH attributes. In this case, the browser enlarges the image so it fits in the reserved space.

Just like with scaling an image down, you have to be concerned with maintaining an image's aspect ratio when you scale it up.

Unlike scaling an image down, however, you also have to worry with pixelation. That is, when you enlarge an image, the image's contents are expanded to fill the area. Where are the additional details coming from, though? The browser makes each pixel bigger so that it fills more space. This effect is sometimes very unattractive, as shown in Figure 6.7.

Providing alternative text

So, you've dumped a bunch of images into your HTML document. What about those folks who aren't viewing images? You can provide alternative text to them that, at least, tells them about the image. You do that with the <IMG> tag's ALT attribute, like this:

```
<IMG SRC="filename" ALT="Description">
```

If the user's browser isn't displaying images, they'll see the alternative text in the image's place. For those users whose browser is displaying images, they'll see the alternative text until the browser is ready to display the image. Better yet, if you combine alternative text with size hints, they'll see a box that's correctly sized with the alternative text within its borders.

Listing 6.5 is an HTML document that uses alternative text to provide a description of the image. Figure 6.8 shows you what this document looks like in a browser that's not displaying inline images.

Listing 6.5

Using the *ALT* attribute

```
<HTML>
<HEAD>
  <TITLE>Using the ALT attribute</TITLE>
</HEAD>
<BODY>
<IMG SRC="book.gif" WIDTH=320 HEIGHT=240 ALT="A picture of my
➡latest book's cover">
</BODY>
</HTML>
```

FIG. 6.8
Internet Explorer displays the image's alternative text in a pop-up window when the mouse pointer lingers over the image for more than a few seconds.

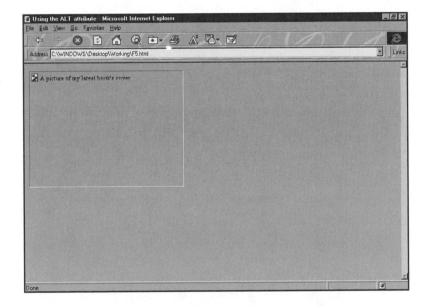

Framing an image with a border

By default, the user's browser will display a border around each inline image that you're using as an anchor. You have a lot of control over that border and the white-space around the image.

You set the <IMG> tag's BORDER attribute to the width of the border in pixels. If you want the border to be 10 pixels in width, set this attribute to 10. Listing 6.6 shows an HTML document with three images, each of which has a different border width. Figure 6.9 shows the result in the browser.

Listing 6.6

Using the *BORDER* attribute

```
<HTML>
<HEAD>
  <TITLE>Using the BORDER attribute</TITLE>
</HEAD>
<BODY>
<A HREF=""><IMG SRC="book.gif" BORDER=0></A>
<BR>
<A HREF=""><IMG SRC="book.gif" BORDER=5></A>
<BR>
<A HREF=""><IMG SRC="book.gif" BORDER=10></A>
</BODY>
</HTML>
```

FIG. 6.9
If you don't want the browser to draw a border around an image, set the BORDER attribute to 0.

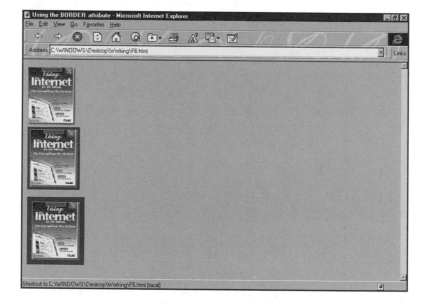

Giving an image space

You might not like how the text surrounding an image is crowding it. If so, you can use the VSPACE and HSPACE attributes to add vertical and horizontal space around the image, respectively. You set each of these attributes to the amount of space, in pixels, you want to allow between the surrounding content and the image. Listing 6.7 shows you an example of an image, which adds additional space around the image to separate it from the text. Figure 6.10 shows you the result.

Listing 6.7

Using the *VSPACE* and *HSPACE* attributes

```
<HTML>
<HEAD>
  <TITLE>Using the BORDER attribute</TITLE>
</HEAD>
<BODY>
<IMG SRC="book.gif" VSPACE=20 HSPACE=20 ALIGN=LEFT>
This text will wrap around the image.
This text will wrap around the image.
This text will wrap around the image.
This text will wrap around the image.
This text will wrap around the image.
This text will wrap around the image.
This text will wrap around the image.
This text will wrap around the image.
This text will wrap around the image.
This text will wrap around the image.
This text will wrap around the image.
This text will wrap around the image.
This text will wrap around the image.
This text will wrap around the image.
This text will wrap around the image.
This text will wrap around the image.
This text will wrap around the image.
This text will wrap around the image.
This text will wrap around the image.
This text will wrap around the image.
This text will wrap around the image.
This text will wrap around the image.
This text will wrap around the image.
This text will wrap around the image.
This text will wrap around the image.
This text will wrap around the image.
This text will wrap around the image.
This text will wrap around the image.
This text will wrap around the image.
This text will wrap around the image.
This text will wrap around the image.
</BODY>
</HTML>
```

FIG. 6.10
Adding additional white space around an image keeps it from looking too cramped.

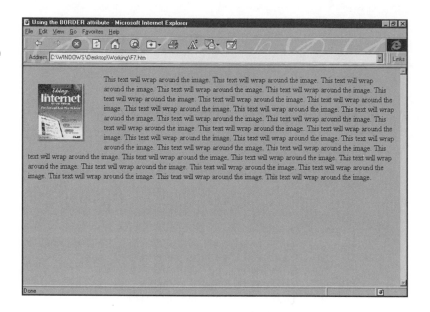

Using an image as an anchor

Chapter 7, "Creating Document Links," describes how to use an image as a link to another resource. It's easy, however. You enclose an image within the <A> tag as shown here:

```
<A HREF="http://www.mysite.com"><IMG SRC="image.gif"></A>
```

Creating Document Links

● In this chapter:

● **Hypertext and hypermedia are the basic concepts behind the Web**

● **Link the text and graphics on your Web page to another document or file on the Internet**

● **Link your Web page to other Internet resources, such as Gopher, FTP, e-mail, and UseNet news**

● **Use the <BASE> tag in your HTML file**

B y now, you've noticed the references to other chapters that are scattered all through this book. They serve a similar purpose as links on a Web page—albeit a little low-tech. They refer you to other places in this book that might be useful or interesting to read. Without these references, you would have to resort to flipping through the pages looking for what you need.

Links on a Web page are even more vital. You have all the pages of this book right in front of you. At least you would know where to start looking. On the other hand, you have no idea where to find all the Web pages on the Internet. And there are too many to keep track of anyway. Therefore, links are the only reasonable way to go from one Web page to another related Web page.

Understanding hypertext and hypermedia

Hypertext is a term you'll frequently hear associated with the Web. A hypertext document is a document that contains links to other documents—allowing you to jump between them by clicking the links. It's also a term associated with help files and other types of documents that are linked together. For example, if you've published a report that cites several sources, you can link the references of those sources to related works. Likewise, if you're discussing the migratory habits of the nerd-bird, you can provide links to Web pages where nerd-birds are known to frequent.

Hypermedia is based upon hypertext but it contains more than text. It contains multimedia such as pictures, videos, and audio, too. In hypermedia documents, pictures are frequently used as links to other documents. You can link a picture of Edinburgh to a Web site in Edinburgh, for example. There are countless types of multimedia you can include on a Web page, and some of those can serve as links to other Internet documents and resources. Figure 7.1 shows you can example of a hypermedia document.

FIG. 7.1
Hypermedia docu-
ments contain much
more than just text;
they contain graphics,
sounds, and video, too.

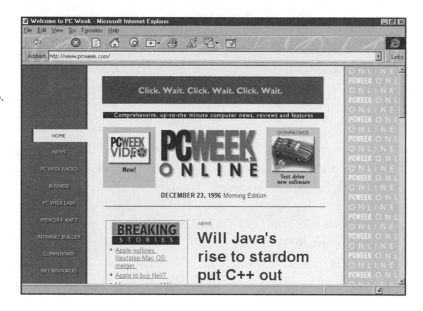

Understanding links

A link really has two different parts. First, there's the part you see on the Web page—called an *anchor*. There's also the part that tells the browser what to do if you click that link—called the *URL reference*. When you click a link's anchor, the browser loads the file or document given by the link's corresponding URL reference. You'll learn about both parts of a link in the following sections.

Anchors

A link's anchor can be a word, group of words, or a picture. Exactly how an anchor looks in the browser depends largely on what type of anchor it is, how the user has configured the browser to display links, and how you created it. There are only a few types of anchors though: text and graphical. You'll learn about both types in this section.

Text anchors

Most text anchors look somewhat the same. A text anchor is one or more words the browser underlines to indicate it represents a link. The browser also displays a text anchor using a different color than the rest of the text around it (the color and appearance of links are under the author's and user's control).

Figure 7.2 shows a Web page that contains three text anchors. In particular, notice how the text anchors on this Web page are embedded in the text. That is, they aren't set apart from the text, like the references in this book, but are actually an integral part of it. Clicking one of these links will load a Web page that is related to the link. You'll find many text anchors used this way. The HTML for the first text link looks a bit like the following (you'll learn more about the <A> tag later in this chapter):

```
<A HREF="vero.html">Vogon Earth Reconnaissance Office</A>
```

FIG. 7.2
You'll find Vogon's Hitch-Hiker's Guide to the Galaxy Page at **http://www. metronet.com/ ~vogon/hhgttg. html**.

Graphical anchors

A graphical anchor is similar to a text anchor. When you click a link's graphical anchor, the browser loads the Web page that the link references. Graphical anchors aren't underlined or displayed in a different color, but you can display a border around them. And no two graphical anchors need to look the same, either. It depends entirely on the picture that you choose to use.

Versatility is the strong suit of graphical anchors. You can use them for a variety of reasons. Here are some examples of the ways you'll find graphical anchors used on a Web page:

- *Bullets.* Graphical anchors are frequently used as list bullets. You can click the picture to go to the Web page described by that list item. Frequently, the text in the list item is also a link. You can click either the picture or the text.

- *Icons.* Many Web sites use graphical anchors in a similar manner to Windows 95. They are common on home pages and represent a variety of Web pages available at that site. Figure 7.3 shows a Web site that uses graphical anchors in this manner. The HTML for the icon on the left side of this Web page that says `What's New!` might look a bit look the following (you'll learn how to create graphical anchors later in this chapter):

```
<A HREF="whatsnew.htm"><IMG SRC="whatsnew.gif" BORDER=0></A>
```

FIG. 7.3
GolfWeb's home page uses graphical anchors to represent a variety of the pages you can load.

Graphical anchors used as icons

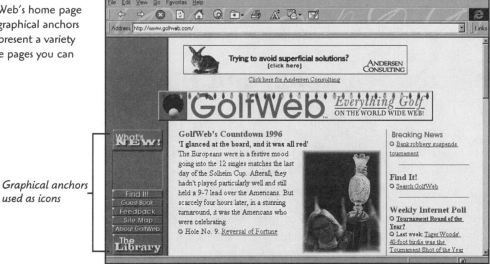

URL references

The other part of a link is the URL reference. This is the address of the Web page the browser will load if you click the link. Every type of link, whether it uses a text or graphical anchor, uses either a relative or absolute reference. You'll learn about each type in this section.

Relative references

An URL reference to a file on the same computer is also known as a *relative reference*. It means that the URL is relative to the computer and directory from which the browser originally loaded the Web page. If the browser loads a page at **http://www.mysite.com/page**, for example, then a relative reference to **/picture** would actually refer to the URL **http://www.mysite.com/page/picture**. Relative references are commonly used to refer to Web pages on the same computer.

The primary reason you use a relative reference is convenience. It's much simpler to just type the file name, instead of the entire URL. It also makes it easier for you to move Web pages around on the server. Since the URL references are relative to the Web page's computer and directory, you don't have to change all the links in the Web page every time the files move to a different location.

Absolute references

An URL reference that specifies the exact computer, directory, and file for a Web page is an *absolute reference*. Whereas relative references are common for links to Web pages on the same computer, absolute references are necessary for links to Web pages on other computers.

Linking to documents and files

Now that you have the terminology down (anchors, links, relative references, and so on), you're ready to start adding links to your own Web pages. It's truly very simple. You have to tell the browser what element in the HTML file is the anchor and the address of Internet document or resource to which you're linking. You do both things with one tag: <A>.

The following example shows you what the <A> tag looks like. This is its simplest form used for linking to another Web page on the Internet. It's only attribute is HREF, which specifies the URL to which you're linking. The URL can be any valid absolute or relative reference, such as **http://www.server.com/home/index.htm**. Since the <A> tag is a container, you must put the closing </A> tag on the other side of the anchor. That is, the opening <A>

tag tells the browser where the anchor (text or graphical) starts and the closing </A> tag tells the browser where the anchor ends.

```
<A HREF=URL>Anchor</A>
```

The following bit of HTML shows you how to add a text anchor to your HTML file. In this example, HREF references my home page on the Internet. The anchor, which is underlined in the Web browser, is Jerry Honeycutt's. The text before and after the <A> container isn't part of the anchor and is therefore not underlined. For that matter, nothing will happen when the user clicks the text outside of the container. On the other hand, when the user clicks Jerry Honeycutt's, the browser will load my home page in the browser. Figure 7.4 shows what this anchor looks like in Internet Explorer.

```
While you're here, why don't you visit
<A HREF="http://rampages.onramp.net/~jerry">Jerry
➡Honeycutt's</A> homepage
```

FIG. 7.4
You can control the appearance of links by using the <BODY> tag, as described in Chapter 3, "HTML Document Architecture."

NOTE **The examples you've seen thus far all use absolute references.** You can also use relative references. Relative references can get a bit out of hand, however, if you store different Web pages in different directories. You'll have a difficult time remembering exactly in which directory an HTML file is stored and thus how to formulate the relative reference.

To remedy this problem, you can add the <BASE> tag to the top of your HTML file. In the absence of the <BASE> tag, all relative references are based upon the URL of the current HTML file. Adding the <BASE> tag provides an URL on which all relative references in the HTML file are based. It affects relative references in every HTML tag, including the <A> tag, <IMG> tag, and so on.

continues

continued

Thus, if you add

```
<BASE HREF="http://www.server.com">
```

to your HTML file, all relative references are based upon that address, instead of the address of the current HTML file. In this case, the relative reference "images/face.gif" resolves to **http://www.server.com/images/face.gif**.

Note that the <BASE> tags original intention was to provide the URL of the document in which it's found. This allows folks who are viewing the document out of context to locate the document on the Internet. It works perfectly well for the purpose of dereferencing relative URLs, however, and is documented by W3C in this manner.

TIP **Some browsers support tooltip style help for links. That is, when** the user holds the mouse over a link for a certain period of time, the browser will display the contents of the <A> tags TITLE attribute in a small pop-up window. Thus, if you want to provide additional information about the link to the user, assign it to the TITLE attribute, like this:

```
<A HREF="page.html" TITLE="Go to page.html">.
```

The previous example showed you how to create a text anchor. Creating a graphical anchor isn't much different. Instead of enclosing text in the <A> container, you put an image. Consider the following HTML, which is very similar to the previous example. Figure 7.5 shows what it looks like. The HREF references my home page, but, instead of using a text anchor, it uses the <IMG> tag to create a graphical anchor. When the user clicks anywhere on the picture, the browser opens the Web page referred to by the <A> tag.

```
<A HREF="http://rampages.onramp.net/~jerry"><IMG
➡SRC="photo.gif"></A>
```

FIG. 7.5
If you don't want to display a border around the image, you can add the BORDER attribute to the <IMG> tag, and set its value to 0.

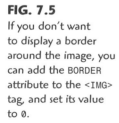

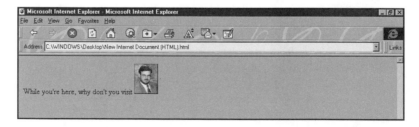

Internal links

As well as providing links to other HTML files, you can link to an anchor within the current document. For example, you can provide a Table of Contents for the current Web page at the top of the page. You can then link each entry to a different section within the current Web page.

There are two steps to do this. First, you must create an anchor in the HTML file that indicates the location to which you're linking. For example, if you want to provide a link to the middle portion of your Web page, you'd create an anchor in the middle and give it a name using the NAME attribute. You name the anchor so that you can refer to that name in your link. Note that since you're only naming an anchor, instead of creating a link, you don't set the HREF attribute. You still have to use the opening and closing <A> tags, but the browser docsn't highlight the contents of the <A> tag because you're not using it as a link. The following is what the named anchor looks like:

```
<A NAME=MIDDLE>Middle Section in Web Page</A>
```

After you've created the named anchor, you create a link to it. You use a special notation to link to that anchor. Instead of setting the HREF attribute to the URL of another Web page, you set it to the name of the anchor. You prefix the anchor's name with a pound sign (#), though. Consider the following example. The HREF attribute refers to the named anchor shown in the previous example. The name is prefixed with the pound sign to indicate to the browser that you're making an internal link. When the user clicks Jump to the middle, the browser will align the anchor in the previous example to the top of the browser window.

```
<A HREF="#MIDDLE">Jump to the middle</A>
```

 NOTE **Some browsers will not move the named anchor to the top of the** browser window if the anchor is already displayed in the window. That is, if your internal link is at the top of the Web page, and the named anchor appears somewhere in the middle of the Web page, when the user clicks the internal link, the browser will do nothing.

Files, plug-in content, and so on

When the user clicks a link to another Web page, the browser opens that Web page in the browser window. On the other hand, if the user clicks a link to a different type of document, it downloads the document to the user's computer and then decides what to do with it. One of two things will happen as a result:

- The browser will know how to handle the file, which is the case with many graphics formats, and will display the file in the browser window. For example, if you create a link to a GIF file and the user clicks that link, the browser will download the GIF file, clear the current Web page from the browser window, and display the GIF file in the window as shown in Figure 7.6. In some cases, however, the browser can use a plug-in to display the file in the browser window without actually opening a separate window, even though the browser itself doesn't know what to do with the file.

FIG. 7.6

Linking to a file, such as a GIF file, is not the same thing as inserting or embedding that file in your Web page.

- The browser will not know how to handle the file, which is the case for a variety of documents and many types of plug-in content. In this case, the browser will download the file and look for a helper application that knows what to do with it. If it finds one, it'll launch the helper application and pass it the downloaded file. For example, if the user clicks a link to an AVI video, the browser will download the file, find a helper application to play AVI files, and launch that file in the application. In most cases, the application will display the file in a separate window, as shown in Figure 7.7.

FIG. 7.7
You can cause the browser to play AVI files inline by embedding them, instead of linking to them.

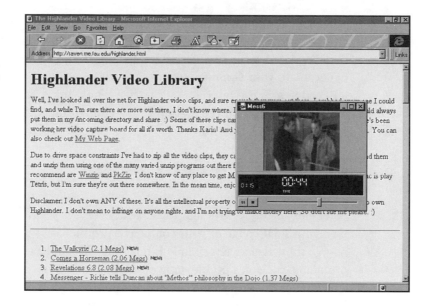

TIP **Digital Infoworks sells a product call Cyberlinks that you can use** to create links in any OLE-enabled product, such as WordPad. This means you can create hypertext links in your documents just like you can in your Web pages. For more information, see **http://www.pioneersys.com**.

Linking to other Net resources

The World Wide Web is a popular part of the entire Internet, but many others resources are available. These resources can take various shapes, from the peanut gallery that is UseNet news, to personal e-mail, to the capability to access other computers through telnet. Although you can create your own versions of these resources using forms (see Chapter 11, "Forms"), most of the time you wouldn't want to do so. For example, you could easily create a page with many HTML form tags, text elements, and a submit button for e-mail, but simply creating a link to e-mail with a particular address would be easier. This way, you can more easily update the page because you don't have to worry about which forms to read. Also, sometimes browsers have built-in support for some of the other resources, giving the user faster response time.

You especially want to create links to other resources on the Net if you're already using a resource. If you already have a Gopher site with information that's updated automatically, why rebuild it to fit the Web? Just adding a hyperlink to your Gopher site makes more sense. Similarly, if you're running a BBS that's on the Internet, putting in a telnet link to it makes more sense. There's no reason for re-creating or even mirroring your BBS through forms for the Web.

Creating a link to e-mail

You'll most likely want to put in an e-mail link when you want people to give you feedback on a particular topic. Whatever it is you want comments on— be it your home page or your company's product—if you want to know what people think use an e-mail link. E-mail links are also useful for reporting problems, such as a problematic or missing link. Typically, the Webmaster of a particular site should put these types of links to himself or herself. You really have no reason not to put in a link to your e-mail address.

Creating a link to an e-mail address is similar to creating a link to another home page. The only difference is the reference for your anchor element. Normally, you put a link to a home page around some text as in the following:

```
<A HREF="http://www.mycom.com/myhome.html">Go to my home
➥page</A>.
```

Linking to e-mail is just as simple. Instead of entering **http://**, which specifies a Web address, enter **mailto:** to specify an e-mail address. And instead of specifying an URL, put in your full e-mail address. The preceding example now looks like this:

```
<A HREF="mailto:me@mycom.com">Send me E-mail</A>.
```

The link created with the preceding HTML will look like any other hypertext link. You can easily mix and match hyperlinks to different resources, and they'll all look the same (see Figure 7.8). When this link is selected, the browser opens its own e-mail interface for the user. Each interface is different, but most of them automatically get your e-mail address and real name and prompt you for a subject.

FIG. 7.8
E-mail links look just like regular hypertext links.

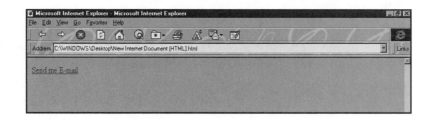

Creating a link to UseNet news

UseNet is one of the best, or worst, resources on the Net, depending on whom you ask. Anybody with an opinion can tell you what he or she thinks. They may not know what they're talking about, but they'll let you know their opinion. UseNet is the ultimate embodiment of the freedom of speech, letting everybody say anything they want.

Creating a link to a UseNet newsgroup is pretty simple; this kind of link is also just a derivative of the basic hypertext link. As you did with the e-mail link, you need to modify two parts in the anchor reference. When you're creating a UseNet link, enter **news:** instead of **http://**. Likewise, instead of specifying a particular URL, you put in a specific newsgroup, as follows:

```
For more information, see
<A HREF="news:news.newusers.questions">
➥news.newusers.questions</A>.
```

As you can see in Figure 7.9, the UseNet news hyperlink looks identical to other links. When a user selects such a link, the browser tries to access the user's UseNet news server. If the news server is available to that person, the browser goes to the specified newsgroup. The user can then read as much as he or she likes in that particular group.

FIG. 7.9
UseNet news links allow you to make a point to people interested in your topic.

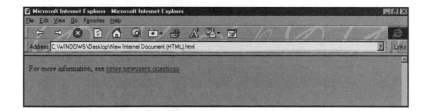

Making FTP available on your site

Another popular activity is accessing an FTP site. FTP, or file transfer protocol, allows users to copy files from other computers (the FTP site) onto their own computers. This popular method allows companies to distribute their demonstration software or patches to their products.

You create a link to an FTP site the same way you create other links, and they look the same, too (see Figure 7.10). You enter **ftp://** instead of the usual **http://**, and you change the URL address to *//sitename/path*. Simply put, the site name looks the same as the URL address. You need to make sure the site name you specify points to a machine that accepts anonymous FTP connections. FTP links are almost always supported by the browser natively. You can create A typical FTP link as follows:

```
You can get the FAQ <A HREF="ftp://ftp.mysite.com/pub/
➥FAQ">here</A>.
```

FIG. 7.10
An FTP link allows many people to access a particular file.

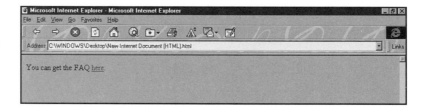

If you don't specify a particular file name, the browser will list the files in the directory you specified. This is particularly useful if you want the user to have access to multiple files. Programs available on multiple machines or large files broken up into several chunks typically fall into this category.

Linking your home page to a Gopher site

Before there was the World Wide Web, there was something known as Gopher. It was originally designed by the University of Minnesota (the Golden Gophers) as a way of making information that was spread out easily available. Gopher has probably been the Internet resource most affected by the Web, often being superseded by it. The biggest difference between Gopher and the Web is that it is very difficult for individual people to create their own Gopher sites.

Although Gopher sites are not as prevalent as they once were, they still have a strong following. You can typically find Gopher sites at places that dispense a lot of automated information. Although the site could have easily been converted to HTML, it simply hasn't bothered to. This conversion of Gopher data into usable HTML code is typically the work of a programmer and often not worth the effort. Putting in an HTML link to a Gopher site allows people browsing your page easy access to a great deal of information.

You can create a link to a Gopher site by modifying the same two elements of the anchor reference. Change the **http://** to **gopher://**, and change the URL to **//sitename**. The site name must be a valid Internet host name address. The link created looks like every other type of hypertext link, and built-in support is provided by most Web browsers. A Gopher site link usually looks something like the following:

```
For more information, go <A HREF="gopher://
➥gopher.mysite.com">here</A>.
```

Just like FTP, Gopher is a Net resource that is built into HTML. Consequently, most Web browsers will support any links to a Gopher site internally. That is, you don't need a Gopher-specific application to go to a Gopher site, the browser will take care of it for you. But just like FTP, the built-in support for Gopher is often very bland (see Figure 7.11).

FIG. 7.11
There's only so much a Web browser can do to liven up the text-based Gopher resource.

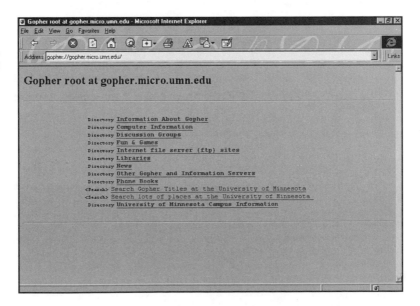

Accessing remote computers with telnet links

The capability to access other computers is not something new to the Web; it's been around for a long time. This access has always been achieved with a UNIX program called telnet, which doesn't stand for anything in particular. Telnet allowed people to try to log on to a remote machine, much the same way as some people access their Internet providers. The Web allows for support of accessing remote machines through a telnet link to a remote computer.

Usually, people trying to get on a secure system are the people for whom you want to provide a telnet link. People who provide access to a private, Internet-accessible BBS will most likely want to put in a telnet link. Also, companies that offer a BBS for customer support may want to make use of link to a telnet site. Generally speaking, for most home pages, you have little or no reason to include a link to a remote site.

As you might have guessed, creating a telnet link to a remote site requires modifying the anchor reference element. You change the **http://** to **telnet://**. You also need to change the URL part of the anchor reference to hostname. Hypertext links that refer to telnet sites look the same as other links. A typical telnet link takes the following form:

```
Click <A HREF="telnet://wais.mysite.com">here</A> to access
→our BBS.
```

NOTE **Most Web browsers do not support telnet activity natively. They** typically depend on an external application to talk correctly to the remote machine. If you put in a link to telnet to another site, be sure to also include some reference to a telnet client.

Even though telnet is a rather simple Net resource, it also has some problems. Among the many problems are issues of how to display the remote session and how to interpret keypresses. As simple as these problems may appear, they're hard to implement in a Web browser. For these reasons, most Web browsers don't have support for telnet. Rather, they leave it up to the individual person to find a telnet program and set it up (see Figure 7.12).

FIG. 7.12
Most Web browsers don't support the telnet links internally, so you need another program to access these links.

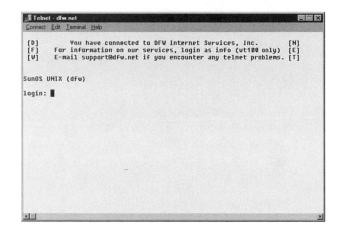

 TIP **Some Web browsers allow something extra in the anchor** reference. Simply add the user name you want the person to logon as, followed by the "@" sign, before the site name. So that instead of:

```
Access my <A HREF="telnet://mysite.com/">system!</A>
```

You can have

```
Access my <A HREF="telnet://john@mysite.com/">system!</A>
```

On those browsers that support this, the Web browser will pop up a little notice. This notice tells the user what logon name should be used to access the system.

Creating Lists

● **In this chapter:**

● Create numbered, bulleted, menu, directory, and definition lists

● Create a custom-list format

You can organize information for presentation in many different ways. One of the most effective formats is the list. Lists are both functional and easy to read; they can define sequential procedures, relative importance, available decision options, collections of related data, and data ordering. We see lists everywhere and every day. From restaurant menus to encyclopedias to phone books, lists are a fundamental way that we organize and disseminate information.

HTML provides container elements for creating lists in HTML documents. The basic list types available are numbered, bulleted, menu, directory, and definition. You can mix these types to create a variety of display and organizational effects, too.

Creating an ordered list

A basic list in HTML consists of a list-identifier container plus the standard list items tag. (In HTML, all list items use one tag, <LI>, while the lists themselves are differentiated by their container tags.) An ordered list, also called a numbered list, is used to create a sequential list of items or steps. When a Web browser sees the tag for an ordered list, it sequentially numbers each list item by using standard numbers, such as 1, 2, 3, and so on.

Using the <OL> tag

Ordered (or numbered) lists begin with the <OL> tag, and each item uses the standard <LI> tag. If needed, you can create a list heading by using the <LH> tag. Close the list with the </OL> tag to signal the end of the list to the browser. List containers provide both a beginning and ending line break to isolate the list from the surrounding text; it's not necessary (except for effect) to precede or follow the list with the paragraph <P> tag.

NOTE **Lists support internal HTML elements. One of the most useful** elements is the paragraph tag (<P>), which enables you to separate text in a list item. Other useful tags include both logical and physical style tags (such as <EM> and <I>) and HTML entities. Headings are not appropriate for use in lists; although they're interpreted correctly, their forced line breaks make for an ugly display. SGML purists also object to them because heading tags are meant to define relationships in paragraphs, not lists.

Listing 8.1 shows how you can use the OL list container. Pay particular attention to include closing tags, especially in nested lists. You can use leading blanks and extra lines to make your list code easier to read, but Web browsers ignore them. Figure 8.1 shows how Netscape Navigator interprets this HTML code.

Listing 8.1

Ordered list example

```
<HTML>
<HEAD>
<TITLE>ordered List Example</TITLE>
</HEAD>
<BODY>
<OL>
        <LH><EM>Colors of the Spectrum:</EM><BR>
        <LI>Red
        <LI>Orange
        <LI>Yellow
        <LI>Green
        <LI>Blue
        <LI>Indigo
        <LI>Violet
</OL>
</BODY>
</HTML>
```

FIG. 8.1
Web browsers display internal HTML elements according to their defined usage.

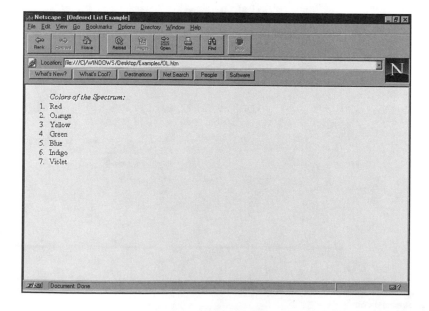

TIP   **The line break tag, <BR>, after the list header is not necessary for**
Netscape Navigator, but it is necessary for Microsoft's Internet Explorer,
which will otherwise put the first list item on the same line as the header.

It is also possible to nest ordered lists, creating a document that looks more
like an outline. Listing 8.2 shows the HTML code for such a list, which is
rendered in Figure 8.2.

Listing 8.2

Nested ordered list example

```
<HTML>
<HEAD>
<TITLE>Nested Ordered List Example</TITLE>
</HEAD>
<BODY>
<OL>
        <LH><EM>Planets of the Solar System:</EM><BR>
        <LI>Mercury
        <OL>
                <LI>57.9 million kilometers from the sun
                <LI>no satellites
        </OL>
        <LI>Venus
        <OL >
                <LI>108 million kilometers from the sun
                <LI>No satellites
        </OL>
        <LI>Earth
        <OL>
                <LI>149.6 million kilometers from the sun
                <LI>one satellite: The Moon
        </OL>
        <LI>Mars
        <OL>
                <LI>227.9 million kilometers from the sun
                <LI>two satellites
                <OL>
                        <LI>Phobos
                        <LI>Deimos
                </OL
        </OL>
</OL>
</BODY>
</HTML>
```

FIG. 8.2
Sublists are automatically indented to create an outline effect.

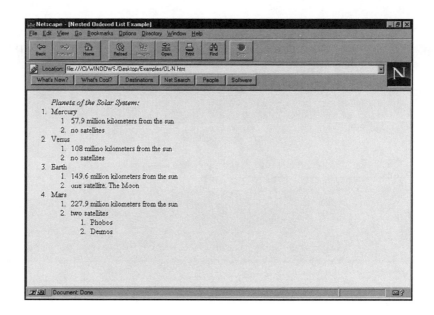

TIP **Use indentations and blank lines to organize your data when**
creating HTML documents. Web browsers don't care how the text is aligned
or run together, but you will appreciate the extra effort when rereading and
editing the HTML code.

New HTML 3.2 <OL> attributes

HTML 3.2 defines a handful of new attributes for the <OL> tag, which were previously Netscape extensions. Now that these attributes have gained more acceptance, they're part of the HTML 3.2 specification.

These attributes give you control over the appearance of the item markers and the beginning marker number. Table 8.1 lists these new attributes and their functions.

Table 8.1 New HTML 3.2 attributes for <OL>

Attribute	Description
COMPACT	Render the list in a more compact form.
TYPE=A	Sets markers to uppercase letters.
TYPE=a	Sets markers to lowercase letters.
TYPE=I	Sets markers to uppercase Roman numerals.
TYPE=i	Sets markers to lowercase Roman numerals.
TYPE=1	Sets markers to numbers.
START=*n*	Sets beginning value of item markers in the current list.

Varying the marker style enables you to create distinctions between numbered lists in the same document. Listing 8.3 shows how an HTML document incorporates these new attributes, and Figure 8.3 shows how these attributes can enhance a document.

Listing 8.3

Nested ordered list example using type

```
<HTML>
<HEAD>
<TITLE>Nested Ordered List Example Using Type</TITLE>
</HEAD>
<BODY>
<OL>
        <LH><EM>Planets of the Solar System:</EM><BR>
        <LI>Mercury
        <OL TYPE=A>
                <LI>57.9 million kilometers from the sun
                <LI>no satellites
        </OL>
        <LI>Venus
        <OL TYPE=A>
                <LI>108 million kilometers from the sun
                <LI>No satellites
        </OL>
        <LI>Earth
        <OL TYPE=A>
                <LI>149.6 million kilometers from the sun
                <LI>one satellite: The Moon
```

```
</OL>
<LI>Mars
<OL TYPE=A>
        <LI>227.9 million kilometers from the sun
        <LI>two satellites
        <OL>
                <LI>Phobos
                <LI>Deimos
        </OL
    </OL>
</OL>
</BODY>
</HTML>
```

FIG. 8.3
Controlling the appearance of lists is useful for both functional and aesthetic purposes.

Ordered list uses uppercase Roman numerals

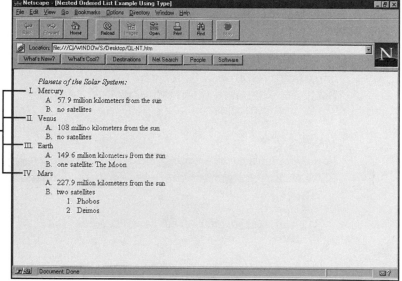

Q&A *I'm creating a list of items, and I need to interrupt the list for a regular paragraph of text. How can I make the list pick up where it left off and continue numbering the items sequentially?*

The HTML 3.2 specification includes an attribute to the <OL> tag called START. Ideally then, you could pick up, say, at item seven by specifying <OL START=7>.

The number 7 is just an example. Put whatever value you want the numbering to start with.

Creating an unordered list

HTML also supports the unordered or bulleted list: a list of items that does not define a specific structure or relationship among the data.

Using the *<UL>* tag

Unordered lists (bulleted lists) use the <UL> container tag. Just like ordered lists, bulleted lists provide beginning and ending line breaks and support internal HTML elements and sublists. Also, like ordered lists, they require closing tags; include the </UL> tag to signal the end of the list to the browser. Web browsers support and automatically indent sublists, and some will also vary the bullet icon based on the relative level of the list. These icons vary depending on the client software viewing the HTML document.

Listing 8.4 shows how to use the <UL> list container. Again, to make the HTML document easier to read, you can include leading blanks and extra lines, but Web browsers will ignore them. Figure 8.4 shows how Netscape Navigator will render this HTML code.

Listing 8.4

Nested unordered list example

```
<HTML>
<HEAD>
<TITLE>Nested Unordered List Example</TITLE>
</HEAD>
<BODY>
<UL>
        <LH><EM>Planets of the Solar System:</EM><BR>
        <LI>Mercury
        <UL >
                <LI>108 million kilometers from the sun
                <LI>no satellites
        </UL>
        <LI>Venus
        <UL >
                <LI>108 million kilometers from the sun
                <LI>No satellites
        </UL>
        <LI>Earth
        <UL>
                <LI>149.6 million kilometers from the sun
                <LI>one satellite: The Moon
```

```
                         </UL>
                         <LI>Mars
                         <UL>
                                 <LI>227.9 million kilometers from the sun
                                 <LI>two satellites
                                 <UL>
                                         <LI>Phobos
                                         <LI>Deimos
                                 </UL
                         </UL>
                 </UL>
                 </BODY>
                 </HTML>
```

FIG. 8.4
Web browsers
automatically indent
sublists and apply the
corresponding markers.

Different bullet types

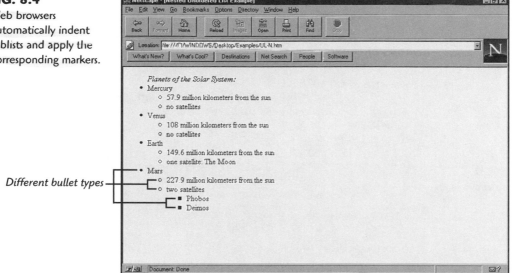

New HTML 3.2 *<UL>* attributes

Like the <OL> tag, HTML 3.2 has adopted some of Netscape's extensions for
the <UL> tag. You can manually control the appearance of item markers as
either circles, squares, or discs. This feature is meant to give you more
control over the look of bulleted lists.

You use the TYPE attribute to change the bullet used in the list. Its value can
be one of disc, square, or circle. Listing 8.5 demonstrates its use in an
HTML document, which is rendered by Netscape Navigator in Figure 8.5.

Listing 8.5

Nested unordered list example using type

```
<HTML>
<HEAD>
<TITLE>Nested Unordered List Example Using Type</TITLE>
</HEAD>
<BODY>
<UL TYPE=SQUARE>
        <LH><EM>Planets of the Solar System:</EM><BR>
        <LI>Mercury
        <UL TYPE=CIRCLE>
                <LI>108 million kilometers from the sun
                <LI>no satellites
        </UL>
        <LI>Venus
        <UL TYPE=CIRCLE>
                <LI>108 million kilometers from the sun
                <LI>No satellites
        </UL>
        <LI>Earth
        <UL TYPE=CIRCLE>
                <LI>149.6 million kilometers from the sun
                <LI>one satellite: The Moon
        </UL>
        <LI>Mars
        <UL TYPE=CIRCLE>
                <LI>227.9 million kilometers from the sun
                <LI>two satellites
                <UL TYPE=DISC>
                        <LI>Phobos
                        <LI>Deimos
                </UL
        </UL>
</UL>
</BODY>
</HTML>
```

 NOTE **Besides the new attributes for the <OL> and <UL> elements, HTML**
3.2 also provides extensions for individual list items. The extensions are
based on those available to the list container that the item is in (ordered or
unordered). Ordered lists pass on the capability to change the current TYPE
of list items and also the VALUE they begin with—by using the VALUE tag,
you can begin a list with a value other than one, or change the numbering

within a list. This would be another good way to continue a list that has been interrupted by some other type of HTML object. (All subsequent items adopt the extension changes until the list closes.) You can modify unordered list items with the TYPE extension; all subsequent items in the container use the new item marker.

FIG. 8.5
It's easy to control the display of bullet markers for your Netscape Navigator audience.

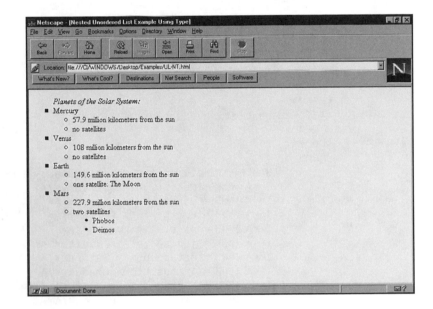

Like the <OL> tag, <UL> also supports the COMPACT attribute, which causes the browser to render the list in a more compact form.

Creating menu lists

You can create menu lists with another list type supported by HTML and Web browsers. The distinction here is primarily for HTML identification; most browsers' default display for the <MENU> container is very similar to the font and style used for the unordered list container. The value of this element is enhanced if you select a distinct screen format for the menu paragraph in a Web browser's preferences. The container might also be more functional in future versions of HTML and its client software, enabling browsers and other applications to identify the menu sections in your documents.

As with the previous lists, menu lists provide beginning and ending line breaks and can include other HTML elements in a menu container. The anchor element is the most likely HTML element to use in this type of list; it is used to link the menu listings to other document resources or Internet applications. Listing 8.6 shows typical uses for the <MENU> container.

Listing 8.6

Menu list example

```
<HTML>
<HEAD>
<TITLE>Menu Listing Example</TITLE>
</HEAD>
<BODY>
<MENU>
        <LH><EM>Planets of the Solar System:</EM><BR>
        <LI><A HREF="mercury.htm">Mercury</A>
        <LI><A HREF="venus.htm"> Venus </A>
        <LI><A HREF="earth.htm"> Earth </A>
        <LI><A HREF="mars.htm"> Mars </A>
        <LI><A HREF="jupiter.htm"> Jupiter </A>
        <LI><A HREF="saturn.htm"> Saturn </A>
        <LI><A HREF="uranus.htm"> Uranus </A>
        <LI><A HREF="neptune.htm"> Neptune </A>
        <LI><A HREF="pluto.htm"> Pluto </A>
</MENU>
</BODY>
</HTML>
```

Again, the current implementation of <MENU> by most Web browsers doesn't provide a visual distinction between menu and unordered lists. Netscape Navigator displays menu lists and unordered lists identically (see Figure 8.6), while Microsoft Internet Explorer displays them identically except it omits the bullets in the latter.

 NOTE **Menu items (and other list types) can contain hypertext links to** other documents or Internet resources. Use the <A> container to create the links, as follows:

`<A HREF="home.htm">Jump to My Home Page</A>`

Click the text, `Jump to My Home Page`, and the browser retrieves the document HOME.HTM.

FIG. 8.6
The <MENU> tag hasn't changed much since it was incorporated into HTML 2.0.

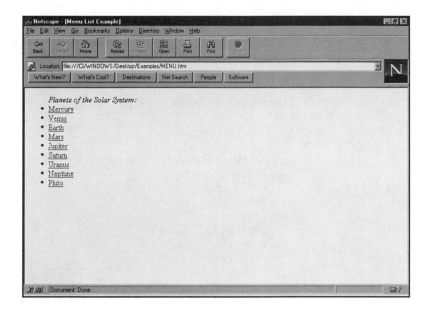

Creating directory lists

The <DIR> element functions much like the <MENU> element; it provides HTML identification to the section of text that has more potential usefulness than real functional value right now. Similar to <MENU>, <DIR> containers display with the same default settings as unordered lists. As browsers and other applications begin to support <DIR> as it's intended, it'll become more common.

The intended use for the <DIR> container limits items to 24 characters and displays the items in rows (like file directories in UNIX, or in DOS using the /W parameter). Current browsers don't support this interpretation. The <DIR> element also isn't intended to include other HTML elements, browsers interpret them correctly. When using <DIR>, remember to close the container with the ending </DIR> tag. Listing 8.7 shows typical uses of the <DIR> container.

Currently, browsers don't provide, by default, any unique display attributes for the <DIR> element. As with menu lists, Netscape Navigator and Microsoft Internet Explorer render directory lists just like unordered lists (Microsoft Internet Explorer without the bullets). My version of NCSA Mosaic also renders them as unordered lists, though in a different font and style.

Listing 8.7

Dir list example

```
<HTML>
<HEAD>
<TITLE>Dir List Example</TITLE>
</HEAD>
<BODY>
<DIR>
        <LH><EM>Colors of the Spectrum:</EM><BR>
        <LI>Red
        <LI>Orange
        <LI>Yellow
        <LI>Green
        <LI>Blue
        <LI>Indigo
        <LI>Violet
</DIR>
</BODY>
</HTML>
```

Creating definition lists

Definition lists, also called glossary lists, are a special type of list in HTML. They provide a format like a dictionary entry, with an identifiable term and indented definition paragraph. This format is especially useful when listing items with extensive descriptions, such as catalog items or company departments. The <DL> element provides both a beginning and ending line break. In the <DL> container, the <DT> tag marks the term and the <DD> tag defines the paragraph. These are both open tags, meaning they don't require a closing tag to contain text.

The standard format of a definition list is as follows:

```
<DL>
<DT>Term
<DD>Definition of term
</DL>
```

The <DT> tag's text should fit on a single line, but it will wrap to the next line without indenting if it runs beyond the boundary of the browser window. The <DD> tag displays a single paragraph, continuously indented one or two spaces beneath the term element's text (depending on how the browser interprets a definition list).

The HTML 3.2 specification provides an important optional attribute for <DL>: COMPACT. This attribute is supposed to be interpreted as a list with a different style, presumably with a smaller font size or more compact for character spacing. This could be useful for embedded definition lists (those inside other definition, numbered, or bulleted lists), or for graphic effect. Most browsers, however, ignore the attribute, displaying the definition list to the standard format.

Definition lists can include other HTML elements. The most common are physical and logical styles and other list containers. Although Web browsers can correctly interpret elements, such as headings, this is bad HTML; their forced line breaks are not pretty to look at, and heading tags are usually meant to define relationships in paragraphs—not within lists. Listing 8.8 shows examples of how you can create definition lists.

Figure 8.7 shows how this document displays in Netscape Navigator. Other browsers may format this text differently.

TIP **In Netscape Navigator, use a horizontal rule, <HR>, on a <DD>** tagged line in a definition list. The rule indents with the rest of the <DD> lines, providing an easy-to-read separator for your definition text.

Listing 8.8

Definition list example

```
<HTML>
<HEAD>
<TITLE>Definition List Example</TITLE>
</HEAD>
<BODY>
<DL>
        <DT>Mercury
        <DD>The smallest of the planets and the one nearest the
        ➥sun,
        having a sidereal period of revolution about the sun of
        ➥88.0
        days at a mean distance of 58.3 million kilometers (36.2
        million miles) and a mean radius of appropriately 2,414
        kilometers (1,500 miles).

        <DT>Venus
        <DD>The second planet from the sun, having an average
        ➥radius
```

continues

Listing 8.8

Continued

```
                of 6,052 kilometers (3,760 miles), a mass 0.815 times
                ➥that of
                Earth, anda sidereal period of revolution about the sun
                ➥of
                224.7 days at a mean distance of approximately 100.1
                ➥million
                kilometers (67.2 million miles).

                <DT>Earth
                <DD>The third planet from the sun, having a sidereal
                ➥period
                of revolution about the sun of 365.26 days at a mean
                ➥distance
                of approximately 149 million kilometers (92.96 million
                ➥miles),
                an axial rotation period of 23 hours 56.07 minutes, an
                ➥average
                radios of 6,374 kilometers (3,959 miles), and a mass of
                approximately 29.11 x 10^24 kilograms (13.17 x 10^24
                ➥pounds).
        </DL>
        </BODY>
        </HTML>
```

FIG. 8.7
Definition lists, appear
much the same as
dictionary entries and
enable easy reading of
each term.

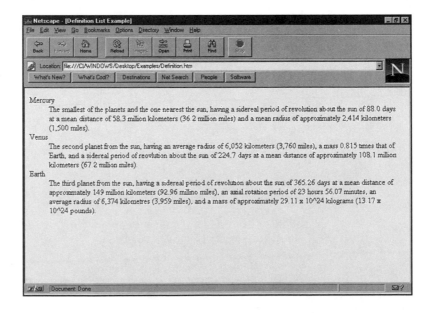

Combining list types

There are times when it's necessary to use sublists of more than one type within a single list. For instance, you may have a numbered list that includes a list as one of the numbered elements. Instead of just creating an ordered sublist, which numbers each of its items, you might prefer to display an unordered list to differentiate the sublist (while avoiding ordering the information as well). HTML supports embedded combinations of all of the list types. Listing 8.9 shows a sample of combined lists.

Listing 8.9

Combined list example

```
<HTML>
<HEAD>
<TITLE>Combined List Example</TITLE>
</HEAD>
<BODY>
<OL>
        <LH><EM>Planets of the Solar System:</EM><BR>
        <LI>Mercury
        <UL>
                <UL>
                        <LI>Roman god of commerce, travel, and
                        ➥thievery
                        <LI>Dictionary Definition
                        <DL>
                                <DT>Mercury
                                <DD>The smallest of the planets
                                ➥and the one
                                nearest the sun, having a
                                sidereal period of
                                revolution about the sun of 88.0
                                ➥days at a
                                mean distance of 58.3 million
                                ➥kilometers (36.2
                                million miles) and a mean radius
                                ➥of appropriately
                                2,414 kilometers (1,500 miles).
                        </DL>
                </UL>
        </UL>
        <LI>Venus
        <UL>
                <UL>
```

continues

Listing 8.9

Continued

```
                        <LI>Roman goddess of sexual love and
                        ➥physical beauty
                        <LI>Dictionary Definition
                        <DL>
                                <DT>Venus
                                <DD>The second planet from the
                                ➥sun, having an average radius
                                ➥of 6,052 kilometers (3,760
                                ➥miles), a mass 0.815 times that
                                ➥of Earth, and a sidereal period
                                ➥of revolution about the sun of
                                ➥224.7 days at a mean distance
                                ➥of approximately 100.1 million
                                ➥kilometers (67.2 million
                                ➥miles).
                        </DL>
                </UL>
        </UL>
</OL>
</BODY>
</HTML>
```

In Listing 8.9, I used three list types: numbered, bulleted, and definition. The primary list is a numbered list of planets. Each planet has a bulleted sublist indicating the Roman god after whom it was named, followed by its dictionary definition. I'm relying on the user's browsers to indent embedded lists; if I want to force more indentation, I can embed the lists inside additional, empty lists. For instance, instead of the following:

```
<OL>
        <LI>Small example list
        <LI>That I want to indent more
</OL>
```

I can force more indentation by using:

```
<OL><OL>
        <LI>Small example list
        <LI>That I want to indent more
</OL></OL>
```

Because the primary difference between list types involves either the list item markers or the format of the elements—and not the actual text representation itself—combined lists tend to display very well. Figure 8.8 shows how the samples in Listing 8.9 display in a typical Web browser.

FIG. 8.8
Embedded list types inherit certain formatting characteristics from the original list styles.

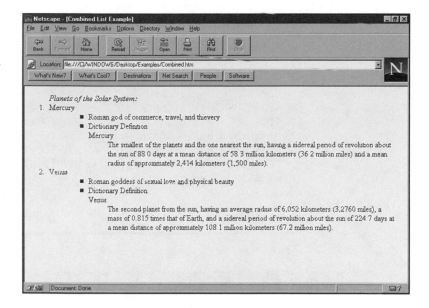

Manually formatting lists

It is possible to create your own custom bullets with a little manual effort in your HTML code. Consider the HTML code shown in Listing 8.10.

The <UL> and </UL> tags are used to instruct the Web browser to set up the formatting and indentation to support an unordered list. However, no <LI> tags are used: because you don't want the standard bullets, you can't use the standard list-item tag. Instead, each item in the list is specified similar to the following example:

```
<IMG SRC="cube.gif" ALIGN=TOP>Red<BR>
```

The <IMG> tag is used to specify and align the graphic you want to use as your bullet, followed by the list item. Because you're not using the standard <LI> tag to set off each item, you need to use the <BR> tag to insert a line break after each one. This HTML code is rendered as shown in Figure 8.9.

Listing 8.10

Manual list example

```
<HTML>
<HEAD>
<TITLE>Manual List Example</TITLE>
</HEAD>
<BODY>
<IMG SRC="BulletSquiggle.gif" ALIGN=TOP><em>Colors of the
Spectrum:</EM><BR>
<UL>
        <IMG SRC="BulletCheck.gif" ALIGN=TOP>Red<BR>
        <IMG SRC="BulletCheck.gif" ALIGN=TOP>Orange<BR>
        <IMG SRC="BulletCheck.gif" ALIGN=TOP>Yellow<BR>
        <IMG SRC="BulletCheck.gif" ALIGN=TOP>Green<BR>
        <IMG SRC="BulletCheck.gif" ALIGN=TOP>Blue<BR>
        <IMG SRC="BulletCheck.gif" ALIGN=TOP>Indigo<BR>
        <IMG SRC="BulletCheck.gif" ALIGN=TOP>Violet<BR>
</UL>
</BODY>
</HTML>
```

FIG. 8.9

With a little added work, nonstandard formatting and bullets can be used on your Web pages.

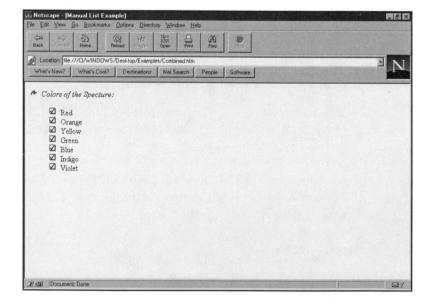

Creating Tables

● In this chapter:

● **Which table tags does HTML 3.2 support?**

● **Create tables in your HTML documents**

● **Learn about alternatives to using tables**

● **Apply the design techniques you learn here**

As a tool for government, commercial, educational, and personal Web applications, HTML has many needs and expectations to meet. It's the language behind the most popular resource on the Internet and, as such, is required to support a greater range of uses today than perhaps its original creators had first imagined. For example, you might design a corporate Web site similar to a marketing brochure, while you'd design a government publication to present static data in tabular form. In most cases, you can use tables to better present these types of Web pages (my technical writing professor would be proud).

In print publications, tables are a basic design element. They're used to present data in rows and columns. They make comparative analysis more understandable. They're also used (albeit invisibly) to divide the printed page into sections for layout purposes. Tables should be a basic design element in your Web pages, too.

On the Web, tables have been used for a while now, thanks to Netscape and subsequently Microsoft, but they've never been an official part of the HTML standard. With HTML 3.2, however, all that changes. Tables are now a formally defined part of HTML. This chapter shows you how to use HTML 3.2 tables to organize content on your Web page or even to help lay out your Web page.

Introducing tables

HTML 3.2 defines tables in much the same way it defines list containers. The <TABLE> element is the container for the table's data and layout.

HTML tables are composed row by row: you indicate a new row with the <TR> (table row) tag; and you separate the data with either the <TH> (table header) or <TD> (table data) tags. Think of the <TR> tag as a line break, signaling that the following data starts a new table row. Table headers are generally shown in bold and centered by WWW browsers, and table data is shown in the standard body-text format. Whereas you can think of a row as a line in a table, a cell represents each box within the table.

Understanding the basic tags

The HTML for a basic table is shown in Listing 9.1. All of the HTML 3.2 table elements used are supported by the latest versions of the most popular Web browsers: Netscape Navigator, Microsoft Internet Explorer, and NCSA Mosaic. This table, as rendered by Internet Explorer, is shown in Figure 9.1.

Listing 9.1

A basic table

```
<HTML>
<HEAD>
<TITLE>Basic Table Examples</TITLE>
</HEAD>
<BODY>
<TABLE BORDER>
  <TR>
    <TH>Colors</TH><TH>Of</TH><TH>The Rainbow</TH>
    <TR>
      <TD>Red</TD><TD>Orange</TD><TD>Yellow</TD>
    </TR>
    <TR>
      <TD>Green</TD><TD>Blue</TD><TD>Violet</TD>
    </TR>
</TABLE>
<HR>
<TABLE BORDER>
  <CAPTION>My Favorite Groups</CAPTION>
  <TR><TH>Rock</TH><TD>Pink Floyd</TD>
                  <TD>Led Zepplin</TD>
                  <TD>The Doobie Brothers</TD></TR>
  <TR><TH>Soft</TH><TD>Simon and Garfunkel</TD>
                  <TD>Peter, Paul, & Mary</TD>
                  <TD>Neil Young</TD></TR>
  <TR><TH>New Age</TH><TD>Enya</TD>
                  <TD>Clannad</TD>
                  <TD>Steamroller</TD></TR>
</TABLE>
</BODY>
</HTML>
```

The basic HTML table tags shown in Figure 9.1 and Figure 9.2 are as follows:

- **<TABLE></TABLE>**—These HTML tags are the containers for the rest of the table data.

- **<TR></TR>**—Each row in the table is contained by these tags. You can optionally leave off the closing </TR> tag.

- **<TD></TD>**—Defines a cell. Table data is contained within these tags. You can also nest additional tables within a single cell. You can optionally leave off the closing </TD> tag.

FIG. 9.1
Most of the HTML 3.2 table tags are supported by the most popular Web browsers.

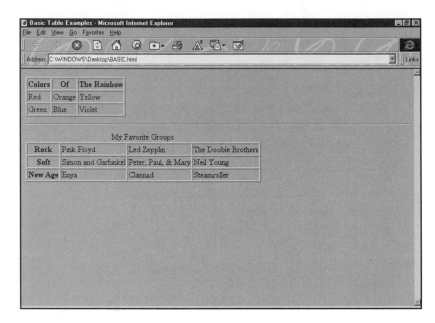

- `<TH></TH>`—These table header tags are used to define headers, usually in the first row or column of the table. You can optionally leave off the closing `</TH>` tag.

In addition to the basic tags shown here, some other characteristics should be noted from the example shown in Figures 9.1 and 9.2:

- **BORDER attribute**—By using the BORDER attribute of the `<TABLE>` tag, borders are put around the table. You set the value of this attribute to the number of pixels wide you want the border, like this: `BORDER=1`. If you set this attribute to 0, the browser will not display a border.

- **ALIGN attribute**—The `ALIGN` attribute can be specified in the `<TABLE>` tag with possible values of `LEFT`, `RIGHT`, and `CENTER` (the default is `LEFT`).

- **Table heads**—In most browsers, table heads enclosed by the `<TH></TH>` tags are emphasized and centered.

- **Table data**—In most browsers, table data enclosed by the `<TD></TD>` tags are shown in the normal font and are left-justified.

 NOTE **If you're concerned about browsers displaying your header text** correctly (as emphasized text, preferably in a bold font), you can use style tags to force the issue. Be careful what you wish for, though: If you want an italicized font but the browser automatically formats the text bold, you can wind up with bold italicized headers.

Cells do not necessarily have to contain data. To create a blank cell, either create an empty cell (for instance, <TD></TD>), or create a cell containing nothing visible (<TD> </TD>). Note that   is an HTML entity, or special character, for a nonbreaking space. Though you would think these two methods would produce the same result, as you will see later in this chapter, in the section "Empty Cells and Table Appearance," different browsers treat them differently.

It's not really necessary to create blank cells if the rest of the cells on the row are going to be blank; the <TR> element signals the start of a new row, so the Web browsers automatically fill in blank cells to even out the row with the rest of the table.

TIP Tables are necessarily uniform with equal numbers of cells in each row and in each column. No "L-shaped" tables (or worse!) are allowed.

Aligning table elements

It is possible, through the use of the ALIGN and VALIGN attributes, to align table elements within their cells in many different ways. These attributes can be applied in various combinations to the <CAPTION>, <TR>, <TH>, and <TD> table elements. The possible attribute values for each of these elements are as follows:

- <CAPTION>—The ALIGN attribute can be specified for this element with possible values of TOP and BOTTOM (the default is TOP); this places the table caption above or below the table.

- <TR>—The ALIGN attribute can be specified for this element with possible values of LEFT, RIGHT, and CENTER (the default is LEFT for table-data elements and CENTER for table-header elements), and the VALIGN attribute with possible values of TOP, BOTTOM, MIDDLE, and BASELINE (the default is MIDDLE). If specified, this will give the default alignment for all the table elements in the given row, which can be overridden in each individual element. The BASELINE element applies to all elements in the row and aligns them to a common baseline.

- **<TH>**—The ALIGN attribute can be specified for this element with possible values of LEFT, RIGHT, and CENTER (the default is CENTER), and the VALIGN attribute with possible values of TOP, BOTTOM, and MIDDLE (the default is MIDDLE).

- **<TD>**—The ALIGN attribute can be specified for this element with possible values of LEFT, RIGHT, and CENTER (the default is LEFT), and the VALIGN attribute with possible values of TOP, BOTTOM, and MIDDLE (the default is MIDDLE).

These alignments are illustrated by the HTML document shown in Listing 9.2 and rendered by Microsoft Internet Explorer in Figure 9.2.

Listing 9.2

Table alignments

```
<HTML>
<HEAD>
<TITLE>Table Alignments</TITLE>
</HEAD>
<BODY>
<TABLE BORDER>
  <CAPTION ALIGN=BOTTOM>A Really Ugly Table</CAPTION>
  <TR>
    <TH></TH><TH>##########</TH><TH>##########</TH>
    <TH>##########</TH>
  </TR>
  <TR ALIGN=RIGHT>
    <TH>Row 1</TH><TD>XX<BR>XX</TD><TD ALIGN=CENTER>X
    </TD><TD>XXX</TD>
  </TR>
  <TR VALIGN=BASELINE>
    <TH ALIGN=LEFT>Second Row</TH><TD>XXX<BR>XXX</TD><TD>XXX</
TD>
    <TD>XXX<BR>XXXXX<BR>XXX</TD>
  </TR>
  <TR ALIGN=LEFT>
    <TH>This Is<BR>The Bottom Row of <BR>The Table</TH>
    <TD VALIGN=BOTTOM>XXXXX</TD>
    <TD VALIGN=TOP>XXX<BR>XXXXX</TD>
    <TD VALIGN=MIDDLE>XXXXX</TD>
  </TR>
</TABLE>
</BODY>
</HTML>
```

FIG. 9.2
Table element
alignment can be
specified row by row or
for each individual
element in the table.

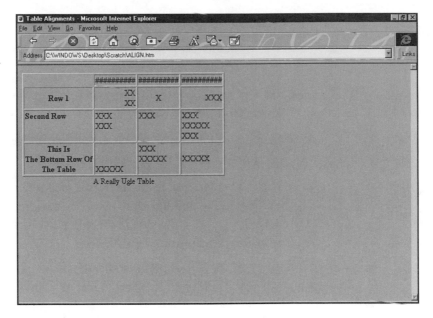

Although this table is pretty ugly, it illustrates the capabilities of the different
ALIGN and VALIGN attributes, as follows:

- **Table Caption:** <CAPTION ALIGN=BOTTOM> places the caption underneath
  the table—overriding the default value, which would put the caption on
  top.

- **"Row 1":**

  - The <TR ALIGN=RIGHT> sets a default horizontal alignment to the right
    margin for each element in the row.

  - The <TD ALIGN=CENTER> in the third column overrides the default set
    in the <TR> element for just this table element.

- **"Second Row":**

  - The <TR VALIGN=BASELINE> aligns all of the cells in the row vertically
    so that their baselines match.

  - The <TH ALIGN=LEFT> in the first column overrides the default table
    header alignment and aligns the table header along the left side.

- **"This Is The Bottom Row Of The Table":**

  - The `<TR ALIGN=LEFT>` sets a default horizontal alignment to the left margin for each element in the row.

  - The `<TD VALIGN=BOTTOM>` in the second column vertically aligns the element on the bottom of the row.

  - The `<TD VALIGN=TOP>` in the third column vertically aligns the element on the top of the row.

  - The `<TD VALIGN=MIDDLE>` in the fourth column vertically aligns the element in the middle of the row. Because this is the default behavior (and hasn't been overridden in the `<TR>` element for this row), this attribute isn't necessary.

 NOTE **Sitting down with your favorite text editor and hacking out the** HTML for a table isn't always the best way to do it. There comes a time when a piece of paper and a no. 2 pencil are the best design tools you can use.

Take a look at Figure 9.3. It shows a sketch for a table that has two rows and four columns. The first two columns of the first row are joined, and the last two columns of the last row are joined.

To make your HTML coding job easier, you can hand write a `<TABLE>` tag above the table and a `</TABLE>` tag below the figure. Then, hand write a `<TR>` at the beginning of each row, and a `</TR>` tag at the end of each row. Last, hand write a `<TD>` and `</TD>` within each cell. If a cell is spanned, then write the number of cells it spans next to the `<TD>` tag and indicate if it spans rows or columns. Figure 9.4 shows you an example of such a sketch.

With your marked-up sketch in hand, you're ready to write the HTML. Start at the top and work towards the bottom of the sketch in a left to right fashion. Type each tag as you encounter it. If you noted that a cell is spanned, be sure to add the `ROWSPAN` or `COLSPAN` attribute to the `<TD>` tag. The following code shows you the HTML that results from the previous sketch. (Note that indenting the code can help clarify the row and column breaks.)

```
<TABLE>
<TR>
        <TD COLSPAN=2> </TD>
        <TD> </TD>
        <TD> </TD>
</TR>
```

```
<TR>
        <TD> </TD>
        <TD> </TD>
        <TD COLSPAN=2> </TD>
</TR>
</TABLE>
```

FIG. 9.3
Laying out your table before you start writing the HTML code is the easiest way to design your tables.

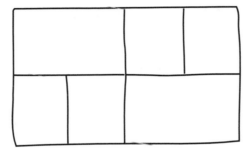

FIG. 9.4
After you mark up your sketch with tags, start at the top and work your way to the bottom, left to right.

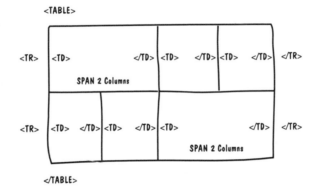

Working with advanced tables

There are more sophisticated things that can be done with tables, both by using additional table attributes and by different uses of some of the ones you already know about.

Creating borderless tables

As mentioned previously, the BORDER attribute to the <TABLE> element is what gives the borders around the table elements. Even though this attribute is off by default, for most conventional tables—those used to organize information in a tabular format—borders are usually used to accentuate the organization of the information. Consider the HTML document shown in Listing 9.3 and rendered in Figure 9.5. In this case, the organization of the information is much easier to see in the version that includes borders.

Listing 9.3

Table borders

```
<HTML>
<HEAD>
<TITLE>Table Borders</TITLE>
</HEAD>
<BODY>
<TABLE BORDER>
   <TR><TH>FRUITS</TH><TH>VEGETABLES</TH><TH>WHOLE GRAINS</TH>
</TR>
   <TR><TD>Apple</TD><TD>Broccoli</TD><TD>Barley</TD></TR>
   <TR><TD>Orange</TD><TD>Cauliflower</TD><TD>Wheat Berries
</TD></TR>
   <TR><TD>Kiwi</TD><TD>Sugar Snap Pea</TD><TD>Millet</TD></TR>
   <TR><TD>Pineapple</TD><TD>Bell pepper</TD><TD>Quinoa</TD>
</TR>
</TABLE>
<HR>
<TABLE>
   <TR><TH>FRUITS</TH><TH>VEGETABLES</TH><TH>WHOLE GRAINS</TH>
</TR>
   <TR><TD>Apple</TD><TD>Broccoli</TD><TD>Barley</TD></TR>
   <TR><TD>Orange</TD><TD>Cauliflower</TD><TD>Weat Berries
</TD></TR>
   <TR><TD>Kiwi</TD><TD>Sugar Snap Pea</TD><TD>Millet</TD></TR>
   <TR><TD>Pineapple</TD><TD>Bell pepper</TD><TD>Quinoa</TD>
</TR>
</TABLE>
</BODY>
</HTML>
```

However, HTML tables can be used in other ways, rather than for the simple tabular display of data. They give an HTML author great flexibility in presenting information, grouping it, and formatting it along with other information. Consider the HTML document shown in Listing 9.4 and rendered in Figure 9.6. In this case, the use of a borderless table allows the descriptive text of the image to be displayed alongside the image.

FIG. 9.5
In many cases, borders accentuate the organization of the information.

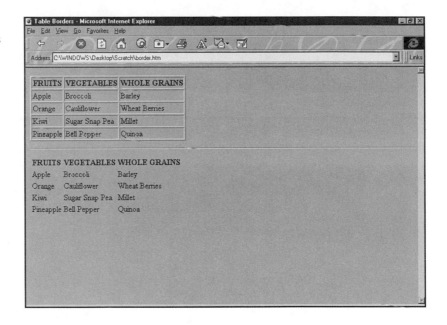

Listing 9.4

Table borders

```
<HTML>
<HEAD>
<TITLE>Table Borders</TITLE>
</HEAD>
<BODY>
<TABLE>
  <TR>
    <TD><IMG SRC="lion.gif"></TD>
    <TD>
The rampant lion is a symbol from Scottish heraldy. It
symbolizes
A duty and willingness to defend one's ideals and values, such
as
aret&ecirc. The color of the lion, White, is for the purity of
the
brotherhood of PEZ, void of the negativity associated with some
fraternities. This White symbolizes how PEZ is a practice of
the
pure theory of brotherhood. This brotherhood has its roots in
common
ties and support rather than hazing and the like.
    </TD>
  </TR>
```

continues

Listing 9.4

Continued

```
</TABLE>
</BODY>
</HTML>
```

FIG. 9.6
Side-by-side presenta-
tion of information
elements can be
achieved by using
HTML tables.

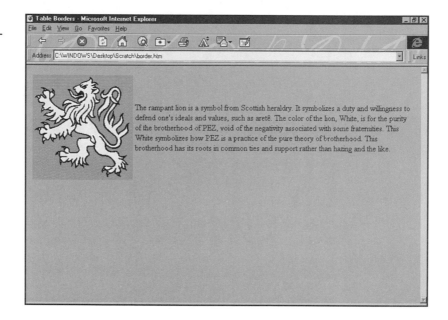

Spanning rows and columns

Rows and columns can be spanned—combined with adjacent cells—to create larger cells for the data. For instance, in a table with five rows and five columns, the first row could be spanned across all five columns to create a banner header for the whole table. In the same table, each of the columns could have elements that spanned multiple rows. It would be possible, through spanning, to create rectangular table elements that span both multiple rows and columns, up to the full size of the table.

To span two adjacent cells on a row, use the ROWSPAN attribute with <TH> or <TD>, as follows:

```
<TD ROWSPAN=2>
```

To span two adjacent cells in a column, use the COLSPAN attribute with <TH> or
<TD>, as follows:

```
<TD COLSPAN=2>
```

 TIP **Don't forget to close your table data with the </TABLE> closing**
tag.

Listings 9.5 and 9.6 show an HTML document that makes use of row-and-
column spanning. This example is shown in Figure 9.7, which shows some of
the trouble you can get yourself into with row-and-column spanning. The
table shown on the left is formatted correctly. However, HTML will allow you
to overlap rows and columns if you aren't careful with your spanning, and the
results of this can (and usually will) be unpredictable.

Listing 9.5

Row and column spanning

```
<HTML>
<HEAD>
<TITLE>Row and Column Spanning</TITLE>
</HEAD>
<BODY>
<TABLE BORDER>
  <TR><TH COLSPAN=3>DC nationals</TH><TR>
  <TR><TH>Offense</TH><TH>Defense</TH><TH>Goalie</TH></TR>
  <TR>
    <TD>Husmann</TD><TD>O'Donnell</TD><TD ROWSPAN=5>Weinberg
</TD>
  </TR>
  <TR>
    <TD COLSPAN=2>Popplewell</TD>
  </TR>
  <TR>
    <TD>McGilly</TD><TD>Longo</TD>
  </TR>
  <TR>
    <TD>Donahue</TD><TD>Seymour</TD>
  </TR>
  <TR>
    <TD>Camillo</TD><TD>Walsh</TD>
  </TR>
</TABLE>
</BODY>
<HTML>
```

Listing 9.6

Row and column spanning

```
<HTML>
<HEAD>
<TITLE>Row and Column Spanning</TITLE>
</HEAD>
<BODY>
<TABLE BORDER>
  <TR><TH COLSPAN=3>DC nationals</TH><TR>
  <TR><TH>Offense</TH><TH>Defense</TH><TH>Goalie</TH></TR>
  <TR>
    <TD>Husmann</TD><TD>O'Donnell</TD>
    <TD ROWSPAN=5>
      Weinberg<BR>Weinberg<BR>Weinberg<BR>
      Weinberg<BR>Weinberg<BR>Weinberg<BR>
    </TD>
  </TR>
  <TR>
    <TD COLSPAN=2>Popplewell</TD>
  </TR>
  <TR>
    <TD>McGilly</TD><TD>Longo</TD>
  </TR>
  <TR>
    <TD>Donahue</TD><TD>Seymour</TD>
  </TR>
  <TR>
    <TD>Camillo</TD><TD COLSPAN=2>Walsh Walsh Walsh</TD>
  </TR>
</TABLE>
</BODY>
<HTML>
```

NOTE **When you create larger cells in an HTML table, you might find** your cell data acts a bit unruly: not breaking properly, wrapping text when it shouldn't, and crowding too close to the cell divisions. Like other HTML documents, tables support internal HTML elements, such as
 (to create a line break in the data), hypertext link anchors, inline images, and even forms.

Use an HTML table in the same manner you would a spreadsheet: for data display, for creating data layouts (such as inventory lists or business invoices), and for calculation tables (when combined with a CGI script that can take your form input and generate output data that's displayed in your HTML table). The uses for tables are limited only by your data and your creativity.

FIG. 9.7
If you aren't careful, you can overlap rows and columns when using spanning, which tends to give ugly results.

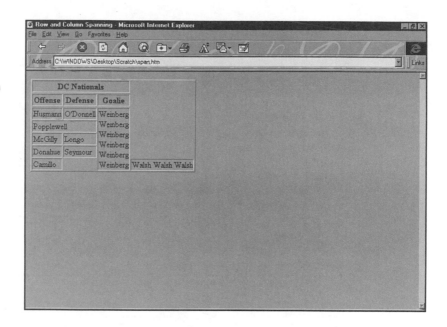

Understanding empty cells

As mentioned earlier, there is sometimes a difference between an empty cell in a table and one with nothing visible in it. This is particularly true with Netscape Navigator and Internet Explorer, which will display the two differently. Consider the HTML document shown in Listing 9.7, which shows two tables. In the top table, there are several empty table cells—cells with only white space in them—which Netscape Navigator will not treat as data. In the lower table, these same cells have something in them: the HTML entity ** **, which is a nonbreaking space (an invisible character).

As shown in Figure 9.8, Internet Explorer will display these two tables differently. As you can see here, now it is mainly an aesthetic difference.

Listing 9.7

Table example: empty cells

```
<HTML>
<HEAD>
<TITLE>Table Example: Empty Cells</TITLE>
</HEAD>
```

continues

Listing 9.7

Continued

```
<BODY>
<TABLE BORDER>
  <TR><TD>Amaranth</TD><TD>        </TD><TD>Buckwheat</TD></TR>
  <TR><TD>Barley  </TD><TD>Rye  </TD><TD>          </TD></TR>
  <TR><TD>Quinoa  </TD><TD>Wheat</TD><TD>          </TD></TR>
</TABLE>
<HR>
<TABLE BORDER>
  <TR><TD>Amaranth</TD><TD> </TD><TD>Buckwheat</TD></TR>
  <TR><TD>Barley  </TD><TD>Rye  </TD><TD>      </TD></TR>
  <TR><TD>Quinoa  </TD><TD>Wheat</TD><TD>      </TD></TR>
</TABLE>
<BODY>
<HTML>
```

FIG. 9.8
Internet Explorer will display tables with empty cells differently from those that contain invisible characters.

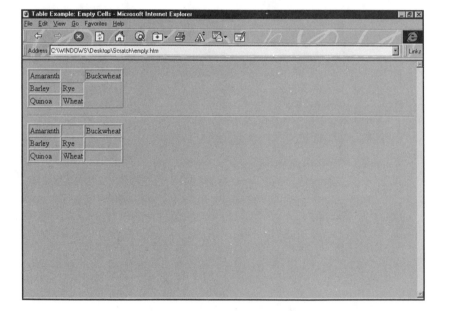

Controlling table layout

HTML 3.2 introduces several attributes that you can use to increase the degree of control you have on how tables are displayed. These attributes were once Netscape enhancements, supported by Internet Explorer, but are now a part of the HTML 3.2 standard. Listing 9.8 shows the HTML document for these attributes, which are rendered by Internet Explorer in Figure 9.9.

Listing 9.8

Formatting example

```
<HTML>
<HEAD>
<TITLE>Formatting Example></TITLE>
</HEAD>
<BODY>
<TABLE BORDER=10 CELLPADDING=10 CELLSPACING=10 WIDTH=100%>
  <TR>
    <TD>Width 100%</TD>
    <TD>Border<BR>CellPadding = 10<BR>CellSpacing</TD>
  </TR>
  <TR>
    <TD>
      <TABLE BORDER=5 CELLPADDING=5 CELLSPACING=5 WIDTH=75%>
        <TR>
          <TD>Width 75%</TD>
          <TD>Border<BR>CellPadding = 5<BR>CellSpacing</TD>
        </TR>
      </TABLE>
    </TD>
    <TD>Have a nice day!</TD>
  </TR>
</TABLE>
<BODY>
</HTML>
```

FIG. 9.9
HTML 3.2 gives you complete control over the appearance of HTML tables.

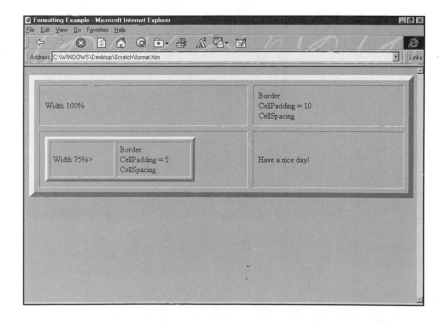

The attributes are as follows:

- **WIDTH attribute**—This enables you to specify the width of the table, either in pixels or as a percentage of the width of the browser window. You can also use this attribute with individual cells.

- **HEIGHT attribute**—This enables you to specify the height of the table, either in pixels or as a percentage of the height of the browser window. You can also use this attribute with individual cells.

- **BORDER attribute**—This attribute puts a border around the table. You specify the width of the border in pixels, like this: BORDER=2.

- **CELLPADDING and CELLSPACING**—These numerical attributes include extra space within each cell in the table and/or within the borders of the table. If the border is not being displayed, they are equivalent.

Using color in tables

HTML 3.2 makes no provision for setting a table's or cell's color. However, both Netscape and Internet Explorer 3.0 provide extensions that let you change the color of cells and borders. You use the BGCOLOR attribute to change the color of a cell's background, before any text or images are placed into the cell. You use the BORDERCOLOR attribute to change the color of the border around the cell. Both Netscape and Internet Explorer support these attributes.

The <TABLE>, <TD>, <TH>, and <TR> tags all support BGCOLOR and BORDERCOLOR attributes. Thus, you can apply colors to the entire table, an individual cell, or an individual row of the table. The example in Listing 9.9 shows you the HTML for three tables, which shows you an example of each case. Figure 9.10 shows you how these tables are rendered in Internet Explorer.

Listing 9.9

Formatting example

```
<HTML>
<HEAD>
<TITLE>Formatting Example</TITLE>
<HEAD>
<BODY>
```

```
<TABLE BORDER BORDERCOLOR=BLACK BGCOLOR=WHITE>
  <TR><TD>1-one</TD><TD>2-two</TD><TD>3-three</TD></TR>
  <TR><TD>4-four</TD><TD>5-five</TD><TD>6-six</TD></TR>
  <TR><TD>7-seven</TD><TD>8-eight</TD><TD>9-nine</TD></TR>
</TABLE>
Changing the entire tables color
<HR>
<TABLE BORDER>
  <TR BORDERCOLOR=BLACK BGCOLOR=WHITE><TD>1-one</TD>
           <TD>2-two</TD><TD>3-three</TD></TR>
  <TR><TD>4-four</TD><TD>5-five</TD><TD>6-six</TD></TR>
  <TR><TD>7-seven</TD><TD>8-eight</TD><TD>9-nine</TD></TR>
</TABLE>
Changing a single row's color
<HR>
<TABLE BORDER>
  <TR><TD BORDERCOLOR=BLACK BGCOLOR=WHITE>1-one</TD><TD>2-two
</TD>
           <TD>3-three</TD></TR>
  <TR><TD>4-four</TD><TD>5-five</TD><TD>6-six</TD></TR>
  <TR><TD>7-seven</TD><TD>8-eight</TD><TD>9-nine</TD></TR>
</TABLE>
Changing a single cell's color
</BODY>
</HTML>
```

FIG. 9.10

Changing the color of a cell without changing the color of the surrounding border looks very odd.

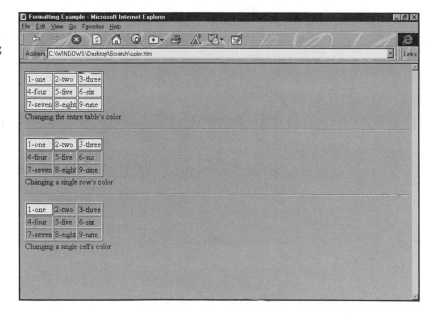

HTML 3.2 defines the following color names. For your convenience, you'll also find the equivalent hexadecimal RGB values next to each color.

BLACK	#000000
SILVER	#C0C0C0
GRAY	#808080
WHITE	#FFFFFF
MAROON	#800000
RED	#FF0000
PURPLE	#800080
FUCHSIA	#FF00FF
GREEN	#008000
LIME	#00FF00
OLIVE	#808000
YELLOW	#FFFF00
NAVY	#000080
BLUE	#0000FF
TEAL	#008080
AQUA	#00FFFF

Using a table alternative

Table support has become very widespread with most of the popular Web browsers, so there is less reason to avoid using them. Still, there are folks out on the Web, either because of their Internet service provider or because of the type of connection to the Internet they have, who are forced to use Web browsers that do not have table support. If you are worried about missing such people, there are some alternatives that you can use, either instead of or in addition to using tables themselves.

Listing 9.10 shows an HTML document for a fairly simple table shown in Figure 9.11.

Listing 9.10

Row and column spanning

```
<HTML>
<HEAD>
<TITLE>Row and Column Spanning</TITLE>
</HEAD>
<BODY>
<TABLE BORDER>
  <TR><TH COLSPAN=3>DC nationals</TH><TR>
  <TR><TH>Offense</TH><TH>Defense</TH><TH>Goalie</TH></TR>
  <TR>
    <TD>Husmann</TD><TD>O'Donnell</TD>
    <TD VALIGN=TOP ROWSPAN=5>Weinberg</TD>
  </TR>
  <TR>
    <TD COLSPAN=2>Popplewell</TD>
  </TR>
  <TR>
    <TD>McGilly</TD><TD>Longo</TD>
  </TR>
  <TR>
    <TD>Donahue</TD><TD>Seymour</TD>
  </TR>
  <TR>
    <TD>Camillo</TD><TD>Walsh</TD>
  </TR>
</TABLE>
</BODY>
<HTML>
```

Some other ways of displaying this information, not using tables, are as follows:

- Use a list. Information that is relatively straightforward can be displayed instead as a list, as coded in Listing 9.11 and rendered by Internet Explorer in Figure 9.12.

FIG. 9.11

A sample table showing a fairly straightforward organization of information.

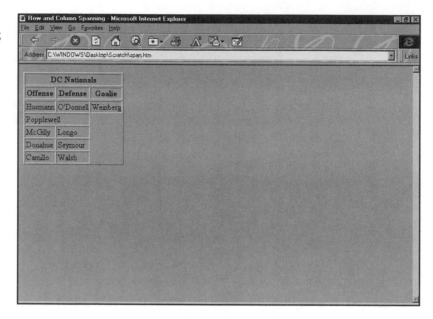

Listing 9.11

Row and column spanning

```
<HTML>
<HEAD>
<TITLE>Row and Column Spanning</TITLE>
</HEAD>
<BODY>
  <STRONG>DC Nationals</STRONG>
  <UL>
    <LI><EM>Offense</EM>
      <UL>
        <LI>Husmann
        <LI>Popplewell
        <LI>McGilly
        <LI>Donahue
        <LI>Camillo
      </UL>
    <LI><EM>Defense</EM>
      <UL>
        <LI>O'Donnell
        <LI>Popplewell
        <LI>Longo
        <LI>Seymour
        <LI>Walsh
      </UL>
    <LI><EM>Goalie</EM>
      <UL>
```

```
            <LI>Weinberg
              </UL>
       <UL>
    <BODY>
    </HTML>
```

FIG. 9.12
Because support for
lists is more widespread
than that for tables,
they can sometimes be
a good alternative.

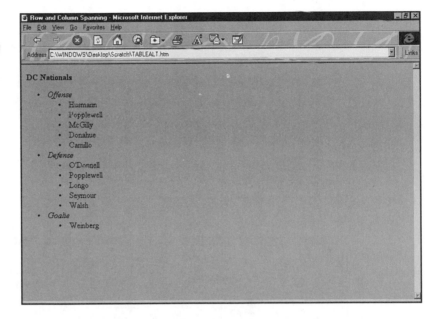

- Use an image instead. By creating the table in a word processor, or even in your own copy of a Web browser, such as Netscape Navigator, and then taking a screen shot and cropping it down to the size of the displayed table, you can include the table in your HTML document as an image. This may not be the best alternative, however, as Web browsers that do not support tables may not support images, either.

- Use preformatted text. This will give you a table that is pretty aesthetically unappealing, but it has the advantage of being displayed correctly in just about every Web browser, including text-only browsers such as Lynx. An example of this is shown in Listing 9.12 and Figure 9.13.

Listing 9.12

Row and column spanning

```
<HTML>
<HEAD>
```

Listing 9.12 Continued

Row and column spanning

```
<TITLE>row and Column Spanning</TITLE>
</HEAD>
<BODY>
<PRE>
+--------------------+--------------------+--------------------+
¦ Offense            ¦ Defense            ¦ Goalie             ¦
+--------------------+--------------------+--------------------+
¦ Husmann            ¦ O'Donnell          ¦                    ¦
¦ Popplewell         ¦                    ¦                    ¦
¦ McGilly            ¦ Longo              ¦ Weinberg           ¦
¦ Donahue            ¦ Seymour            ¦                    ¦
¦ Camillo            ¦ Walsh              ¦                    ¦
+--------------------+--------------------+--------------------+
</PRE>
</BODY>
</HTML>
```

FIG. 9.13

A preformatted table isn't very pretty, but it will be displayed correctly in just about any Web browser.

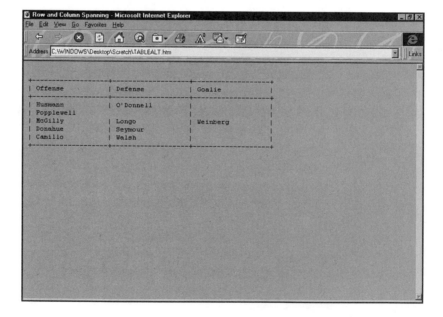

Table examples

The use of tables to display tabular information is, by definition, pretty obvious. Tables can also come in handy when using HTML forms, as they give you the capability to create a very well-organized form for entering information. Tables can be used in other ways as well, as mentioned briefly earlier. Because they give you the ability to group text and graphics with one another in many different ways, they can be used to enhance the way a page is displayed.

Using tables as a layout tool

Consider the HTML document shown in Listing 9.13. This document includes graphics and text information, and is meant to display it in a business card style. This document is shown, as rendered by Internet Explorer, in Figure 9.14.

Listing 9.13

Using tables to display information

```
<HTML>
<HEAD>
<TITLE>Using Tables to Display Information</TITLE>
</HEAD>
<BODY>
<TABLE>
  <TR>
    <TD ROWSPAN=4 VALIGN=BOTTOM><IMG SRC="init.gif"><TD>
    <TH VALIGN=TOP>Jerry Honeycutt</TH>
  </TR>
  <TR>
    <TD VALIGN=TOP><EM><Books:</EM><BR>
      Using the Internet with Windows 95<BR>
      Windows 95 Registry and Customization Handbook<BR>
      Special Edition Using the Windows 95 Registry<BR>
      VBScript by Example<BR>
      Using the Internet 2E<BR>
      Special Edition Using the Internet 3E<BR>
    </TD>
  </TR>
```

Listing 9.13

Continued

```
<TR><HR></TR>
<TR>
  <TD ALIGN=CENTER VALIGN=BOTTOM>Send e-mail to <EM>
            jerry@honeycutt.com</EM></TD>
</TR>
</TABLE>
<BODY>
</HTML>
```

Combining text and lists

To refine this Web page further, some of the information presented within it can be displayed differently—in this case, by using an HTML list (an unordered list, but any other kind of list could be used just as easily). The HTML code for this is shown in Listing 9.14—it makes sense to group lists of data by using HTML list elements, and the ability to include these within a table allows the information to be conveyed more clearly. The revised Web page is shown in Figure 9.15.

FIG. 9.14
Though at first glance this does not look like a "table," the use of an HTML table to organize the information has made the display more effective.

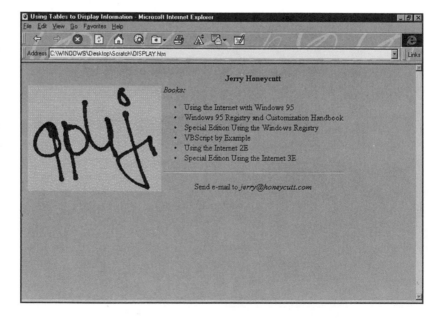

Listing 9.14

Using tables to display information

```
<HTML>
<HEAD>
<TITLE>Using Tables to Display Information</TITLE>
</HEAD>
<BODY>
<TABLE>
  <TR>
    <TD ROWSPAN=4 VALIGN=BOTTOM><IMG SRC="init.gif"><TD>
    <TH VALIGN=TOP>Jerry Honeycutt</TH>
  </TR>
  <TR>
    <TD VALIGN=TOP><EM><Books:</EM><BR>
      <UL>
        <LI>Using the Internet with Windows 95
        <LI>Windows 95 Registry and Customization Handbook
        <LI>Special Edition Using the Windows 95 Registry
        <LI>VBScript by Example
        <LI>Using the Internet 2E
        <LI>Special Edition Using the Internet 3E
      </UL>
    </TD>
  </TR>
  <TR><HR></TR>
  <TR>
    <TD ALIGN=CENTER VALIGN=BOTTOM>Send e-mail to <EM>
            jerry@honeycutt.com</EM></TD>
  </TR>
</TABLE>
<BODY>
</HTML>
```

Nesting HTML tables

Another way to display this information is to use tables within a larger table. Listing 9.15 shows the HTML code for the business-card Web page using "nested tables." It is displayed in Figure 9.16. Notice the nested tables are displayed with borders (and with cell spacing and padding reduced to make them more compact), while the outer table used to structure the whole page is not.

FIG. 9.15

Combining lists and tables gives you powerful means for organizing and displaying information within your Web pages.

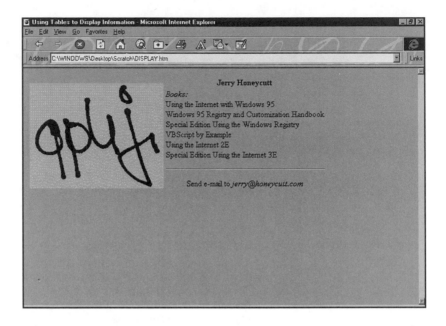

Listing 9.15

Using tables to display information

```
<HTML>
<HEAD>
<TITLE>Using Tables to Display Information</TITLE>
</HEAD>
<BODY>
<TABLE>
  <TR>
    <TD ROWSPAN=4 VALIGN=BOTTOM><IMG SRC="init.gif"><TD>
    <TH VALIGN=TOP>Jerry Honeycutt</TH>
  </TR>
  <TR>
    <TD VALIGN=TOP><EM><Books:</EM><BR>
      <TABLE BORDER CELLSPACING=1 CELLPADDING=1>
        <TR><TH>Book</TH><TH>Year</TH><TR>
        <TR><TD>Using the Internet with Windows 95</TD>
              <TD>1995</TD></TR>
        <TR><TD>Windows 95 Registry and Customization Handbook
              </TD><TD>1996</TD></TR>
        <TR><TD>Special Edition Using the Windows 95 Registry
              </TD><TD>1996</TD></TR>
        <TR><TD>VBScript by Example</TD><TD>1996</TD></TR>
        <TR><TD>Using the Internet 2E</TD><TD>1996</TD></TR>
        <TR><TD>Special Edition Using the Internet 3E</TD>
              <TD>1996</TD></TR>
```

```
        </TABLE>
      </TD>
    </TR>
    <TR><HR></TR>
    <TR>
      <TD ALIGN=CENTER VALIGN=BOTTOM>Send e-mail to
<EM>jerry@honeycutt.com</EM></TD>
    </TR>
  </TABLE>
  <BODY>
</HTML>
```

FIG. 9.16
Nested tables are another way to organize information effectively within a Web page.

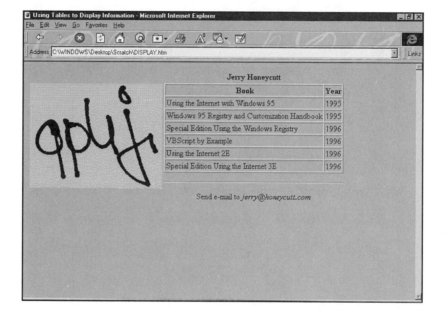

Using an image as a table header

You can easily spruce up a table by using an image as the table's header. That is, instead of displaying a plain-text heading for the table, create a snazzy image and use that instead. Listing 9.16 shows you the HTML for such a table, and Figure 9.17 shows you this table rendered in Internet Explorer. There are a couple of things you should note about this example:

- The width of the table is specified to be exactly the width of the image by using the WIDTH attribute, like this: <TABLE WIDTH=500>.

- In the <TABLE> tag, CELLSPACING is set to 0 in order to make sure the image lines up with the table correctly.

- The table heading is spanned across all columns in order to accommodate the image. In this case, the tag <TH COLSPAN=2> spans across the top two columns of the table.

- The <IMG> tag is used to insert the image into the spanned columns. Note the border is disabled by using BORDER=0; and the height and width is set to the exact dimensions of the image by using the HEIGHT and WIDTH attributes.

Listing 9.16

Pictures in headings

```
<HTML>
<HEAD>
<TITLE>Pictures in Headings</TITLE>
</HEAD>
<BODY BGCOLOR=WHITE>
<TABLE WIDTH=500 CELLSPACING=0 CELLPADDING=2 BORDER=0>
  <TR>
    <TH COLSPAN=2>
      <IMG SRC="head.gif" BORDER=0 HEIGHT=25 WIDTH=500>
    </TH>
  </TR>
  <TR>
    <TD VALIGN=TOP>
      <IMG SRC="internet.gif">
    </TD>
    <TD VALIGN=TOP>
      This book will show you how to get the most out of the
      Internet. You won't find intimidating, technical language
      here. You'll find no-nonsense instructions for using
      e-mail,UseNet, FTP, and the World Wide Web. You'll also
      learn how to find your way around the World Wide Web,
      read the UseNet newsgroups, and more.
    </TD>
  </TR>
</TABLE>
</BODY>
</HTML>
```

FIG. 9.17
When using an image for a table heading, use your favorite paint program to fade the image before adding headings.

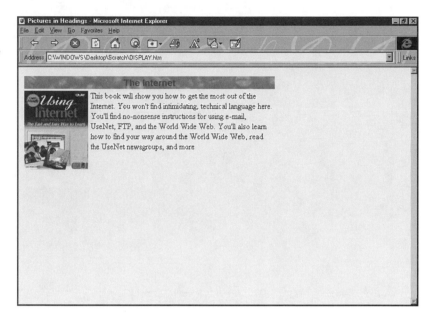

Using a table to lay out a homepage

Figure 9.18 shows you an example of a homepage that uses tables extensively for layout purposes. This happens to be Microsoft's homepage. Note that the toolbar at the top of the page is actually defined as a table. As well, each layout region on this page is actually a cell within the table.

FIG. 9.18
Use tables to split an HTML document into individual regions in which you put your elements.

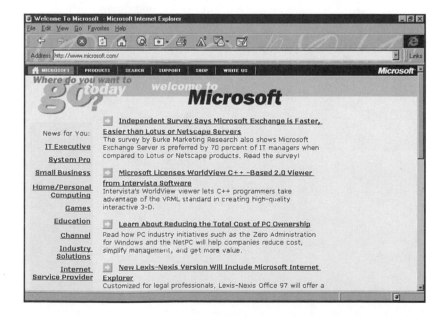

Part III: Advanced HTML

Frames

In this chapter:

- **Create navigational menus with frames**

- **How do you associate a link with a frame?**

- **Learn how to create complex frames**

Sometimes, just the right frame can make a painting look perfect—and the wrong frame can ruin it. Likewise, prudent use of frames can help make your HTML documents better organized, more easily navigable, and more impressive-looking. But used incorrectly or to excess, frames can ruin your site by making information inaccessible, fragmented, and just plain ugly.

You might wonder if you should even use frames on your pages at all, since they aren't supported by all browsers and are not a part of the current HTML standard. While it's true that not all browsers support frames, the top two—Netscape Navigator and Microsoft Internet Explorer—certainly do. That's well over 90 percent of your audience on the Web. If you can live with potentially alienating the other 10 percent who use nonframes-capable browsers (like the all-text UNIX browser, Lynx), frames can add a touch of class to your Web site. You'll find later in this chapter that this isn't necessarily an "either/or" decision, anyway—the HTML syntax for creating frames lets you provide alternate content for those who cannot display them. And if you're working on a corporate intranet that has standardized on Navigator or Explorer as the browser for all your users, of course compatibility isn't an issue at all.

The frames concept

First introduced in Netscape Navigator 2.0, HTML frames create independently changeable and (sometimes) scrollable windows that tile together to break up and organize a display so that it's not only more visually appealing, but easier to work with.

Frames are similar in many ways to HTML tables. If you understand how tables work, you'll have a jump start on how to work with frames.

However, unlike tables, frames not only organize data, they organize your browser's display window, too. In fact, they break up the window into individual, independent panes or frames. Each frame holds its own HTML file as content, and the content of each frame can be scrolled or changed independently of the others. In a way, it's almost as though each frame becomes its own "mini-browser."

Perhaps the best way to get a feel for what you can do with frames is to look at a few real-world examples.

Netscape's DevEdge site

As you might expect, Netscape—the inventor of frames—has some excellent examples of frames on their Web sites. Figure 10.1 is taken from their DevEdge developer's site, and shows a window that is broken into four separate frames.

FIG. 10.1

Netscape's DevEdge site at **http:// developer.netscape. com** showcases some excellent examples of using frames to separate information from navigation.

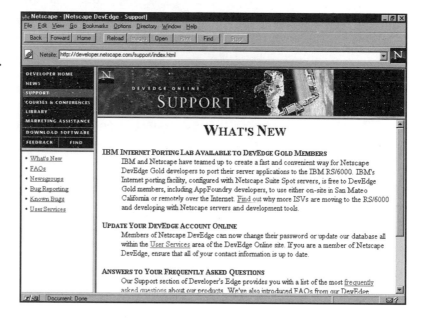

The frames on this page show how Netscape has split information display into the two frames on the right, while reserving navigation functions for the two frames on the left.

The top-right frame—which occupies about 80 percent of the width of the screen, but only about 20 percent of its height—holds a title graphic, which serves as a "landmark" to help you remember where you are. This is an important function, as HTML documents created using frames can get very complex very quickly. "Road signs" like this header graphic can help you get your bearings.

The top-left frame—which takes up about 20 percent of the horizontal real estate, and approximately 30 percent of the screen height—contains a top-level navigation menu, which stays in place wherever you go on the DevEdge site. Making a selection from this menu moves you to a new information category such as the support area or the library. This graphic menu also serves as a placeholder, since it shows the currently selected area as high-lighted.

The bottom-left frame—about 20 percent of the screen width and 70 percent of its height—is a list of text-based hyperlinks which makes up the informa-tion menu for the currently selected category. A new text menu is displayed in this frame whenever the user selects a new category from the graphic category menu in the frame above it.

 TIP **Note how Netscape has saved themselves a great deal of time and** development work by making only the category-level menus graphic, while using much easier-to-create, text-only lists of links for the more numerous subcategory menus.

Finally, the bottom-right frame—which occupies the majority of the screen area, about 80 percent of its width and 70 percent of its height—contains all of the actual information displayed on this site. The information in this window is selected from the category-specific text link menu in the frame to its left.

This site can definitely serve as a template for good frames-based HTML document design for any information that is hierarchically organized by category.

The CyberDungeon

But frames aren't just for business documents. Take a look at Figure 10.2, which depicts the online CyberDungeon adventure game.

FIG. 10.2
The CyberDungeon game lives at **http://www.cyberdungeon.com** on the Web. It uses a set of 10 frames to create a familiar and friendly adventure game interface.

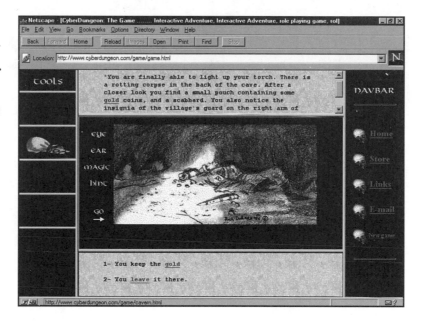

I doubt that you will ever find 10 frames used as gracefully as they are on this site. (Usually it's bad practice to use more than 4-6 frames at a time.) This artfully done Web site anticipates the recent mantra of both Microsoft and Netscape, who are now encouraging developers to use HTML to create graphical user interfaces (or GUIs) for application programming.

The CyberDungeon site uses a set of frames down the left side of the screen to hold graphical icons of objects you (the resident adventurer) pick up in your explorations. The top frame of the center set of three displays the text description of your current location, while the larger frame below it shows a picture of the same scene. The bottom frame gives you choices to make along the way.

Finally, the tall right frame keeps the navigational menu for the CyberDungeon site handy as you play.

This site provides a wonderful example of how a well-designed HTML document using frames can replicate applications that previously had to be written in high-level languages like C or C++.

Frame creation basics

Diving in head first, take a look at an entire block of HTML code that creates a frame document of medium complexity:

```
<HTML>
<HEAD>
</HEAD>
<FRAMESET ROWS="25%,50%,25%">
        <FRAME SRC="header.htm">
        <FRAMESET COLS="25%,75%">
                <FRAME SRC="label.htm">
                <FRAME SRC="info.htm">
        </FRAMESET>
        <FRAME SRC="footer.htm">
</FRAMESET>
<NOFRAMES>
Your browser cannot display frames.
</NOFRAMES>
</HTML>
```

This example ("Frames1.htm") produces the frames page shown in Figure 10.3. As you can see, this HTML code produces four frames. The top frame spans the page and includes a header. There are two central frames, one for a label on the left, which takes up 25 percent of the screen width, and one for information on the right, which takes up the remaining space. Another frame fills the entire width of the bottom of the screen and contains a footer.

FIG. 10.3
This is the frame document produced by the preceding HTML code, as displayed by Netscape.

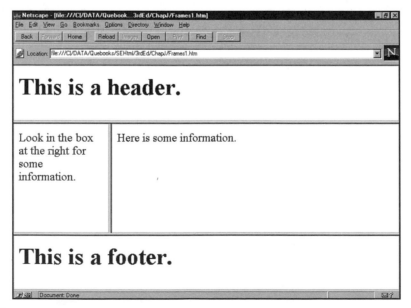

Though you won't get into the details for a couple more pages, it's important to note that this document calls four other HTML documents—header.htm, label.htm, info.htm, and footer.htm— containing the actual information that is displayed in each of the individual frames.

The *FRAMESET* container

Frames are contained in a structure called a FRAMESET which takes the place of the BODY container on a frames-formatted page. An HTML document which contains a FRAMESET definition has no BODY section in its HTML code, and a page with a BODY section cannot use the FRAMESET tag.

CAUTION

If you define a BODY section for a page that you compose with FRAMESET and FRAME commands, the frame structure will be completely ignored by browser programs, and none of the content contained in the frames will be displayed. Instead, you will only see the content contained in the BODY section.

Because there is no BODY container, FRAMESET pages can't have background images and background colors associated with them. (Remember, these are defined by the BACKGROUND and BGCOLOR attributes of the BODY tag, respectively.) However, the HTML files which contain the content for the individual frames can use background colors and images, since they do use the BODY tag.

Make sure you don't accidentally use BODY and FRAMESET within the same HTML document.

The <FRAMESET></FRAMESET> container surrounds each block of frame definitions. Within the FRAMESET container you can only have FRAME tags or nested FRAMESET containers.

Defining *ROWS* and *COLS*

The FRAMESET tag has two major attributes: ROWS and COLS (columns). Here's a fully decked-out (but empty) generic FRAMESET container:

```
<FRAMESET ROWS="value_list" COLS="value_list">
</FRAMESET>
```

You can define any reasonable number of ROWS or COLS, or both, but you have to define something for at least one of them.

CAUTION **If you don't define more than one row or column, browser** programs will ignore your FRAMES completely. Your screen will be left totally blank. In other words, you can't have a FRAMESET of just one row and one column—which would just be a single window, anyway. If you've defined at least two of either ROWS or COLS, however, you can safely omit the other attribute, and a value of 100 percent will be assumed for it.

The "value_list" in your generic FRAMESET line is a comma-separated list of values which can be expressed as pixels, percentages, or relative scale values. The number of rows or columns is set by the number of values in their respective value lists. For example:

```
<FRAMESET ROWS="100,240,140">
```

defines a frame set with three rows. These values are in absolute number of pixels. In other words, the first row is 100 pixels high, the second 240 pixels high, and the last 140 pixels high.

Setting row and column height by absolute number of pixels is bad practice, however. It doesn't allow for the fact that browsers run on all kinds of systems on all sizes of screens. While you might want to define absolute pixel values for a few limited uses—such as displaying a small image of known dimensions—it is usually better practice to define your rows and columns using percentage or relative values like this:

```
<FRAMESET ROWS="25%,50%,25%">
```

This example would create three frames arranged as rows, the top row taking up 25 percent of the available screen height, the middle row 50 percent, and the bottom row 25 percent.

TIP **Don't worry about having to do the math just right—if the** percentages you give for the ROWS or COLS attributes don't add up to 100 percent, they will be scaled up or down proportionally to equal 100 percent.

Proportional values look like this:

```
<FRAMESET COLS="*, 2*, 3*">
```

The asterisk (*) is used to define a proportional division of space. Each asterisk represents one piece of the overall pie. You get the denominator of the fraction by adding up all the asterisk values (if there is no number specified, "1" is assumed). In this example, with an overall pie that has six slices, the first column would get 1/6 of the total width of the window, the second column would get 2/6 (or 1/3), and the final column would get 3/6 (or 1/2).

Remember that bare numeric values assign an absolute number of pixels to a row or column, values with a % sign assign a percentage of the total width (for COLS) or height (for ROWS) of the display window, and values with an * assign a proportional amount of the remaining space.

Here's an example using all three in a single definition:

```
<FRAMESET COLS="100, 25%, *, 2*">
```

This example assigns the first column an absolute width of 100 pixels. The second column gets 25 percent of the width of the entire display window, whatever that is. The third column gets 1/3 of what's left, and the final column gets the other 2/3.

So what are the space-allocation priorities? Absolute pixel values are always assigned space first, in order from left to right. These are followed by percentage values of the total space. Finally, proportional values are divided up based on what space is left.

CAUTION Remember, if you do use absolute pixel values in a COLS or ROWS definition, keep them small so you are sure they'll fit in any browser window, and balance them with at least one percentage or relative definition to fill the remainder of the space gracefully.

If you use a FRAMESET with both COLS and ROWS attributes, it will create a grid of frames. Here's an example:

```
<FRAMESET ROWS="*, 2*, *" COLS="2*, *">
```

This line of HTML creates a frame grid with three rows and two columns. The first and last rows each take up 1/4 of the screen height, and the middle row takes up half. The first column is 2/3 as wide as the screen, and the second is 1/3 the width.

<FRAMESET></FRAMESET> sections can be nested inside one another, as shown in your initial example. But don't get ahead of yourself. You need to look at the FRAME tag first.

The *FRAME* tag

The FRAME tag defines a single frame. It must sit inside a FRAMESET container, like this:

```
<FRAMESET ROWS="*, 2*">
<FRAME>
<FRAME>
</FRAMESET>
```

Note that the FRAME tag is not a container so, unlike FRAMESET, it has no matching end tag. An entire FRAME definition takes place within a single line of HTML code.

You should have as many FRAME tags as there are spaces defined for them in the FRAMESET definition. In this example, the FRAMESET established two rows, so you needed two FRAME tags. However, this example is very, very boring, since neither of your frames has anything in it! (Frames like these are displayed as blank space.)

The FRAME tag has six associated attributes: SRC, NAME, MARGINWIDTH, MARGINHEIGHT, SCROLLING, and NORESIZE. Here's a complete generic FRAME:

```
<FRAME SRC="url" NAME="window_name" SCROLLING=YES¦NO¦AUTO
MARGINWIDTH="value" MARGINHEIGHT="value" NORESIZE>
```

Fortunately, frames hardly ever actually use all of these options.

Going to the source

The most important FRAME attribute is SRC (source). You can (and quite often, do) have a complete FRAME definition using nothing but the SRC attribute, like this:

```
<FRAME SRC="url">
```

SRC defines the URL of the content of your frame. This is usually an HTML format file on the same system (paths are relative to the page containing the FRAMESET), so it usually looks something like this:

```
<FRAME SRC="sample.htm">
```

Note that any HTML file called by the SRC attribute in a FRAME definition must be a complete HTML document, not a fragment. This means it must have HTML, HEAD, and BODY containers, and so on. For example, the file called by the SRC attribute in this example, "sample.htm", might look like this:

```
<HTML>
<HEAD>
<TITLE>
</TITLE>
</HEAD>
<BODY>
This is some Sample Text.
</BODY>
</HTML>
```

Of course, SRC can point to any valid URL. If, for example, you wanted your frame to display a GIF image that was located somewhere in Timbuktu, your FRAME might look like this:

```
<FRAME SRC="http://www.timbuktu.com/budda.gif">
```

If you specify an URL the browser can't find, space will be allocated for the frame, but it won't be displayed, and you will get a nasty error message from your browser. Note the effect is quite different than simply specifying a FRAME with no SRC at all. <FRAME> will always be created, but left blank; <FRAME SRC="unknown URL"> will not be created at all—the space will be allocated and left completely empty. The former will fill with background color, while the latter will remain the browser's border color.

 **CAUTION** **Plain text, headers, graphics, and other elements cannot be used** directly in a FRAME document. All of the content must come from the URL defined by the SRC attribute of the FRAME tags. If any other content appears on a FRAMESET page, it will be displayed and the entire set of frames will be ignored.

Providing alternate content

"All of this is well and good," you say, "and I really, really want to use frames in my HTML documents. But I can't help feeling guilty about all those users who don't have frames-capable browsers. They won't be able to see my beautiful pages!"

Don't worry. Here's where you can provide for them, too.

The <NOFRAMES></NOFRAMES> container is what saves your donkey. By defining a NOFRAME section and marking it up with normal HTML tags, you can provide alternate information for those without forms-capable browsers. This is how it works:

```
<NOFRAMES>
All your alternate HTML goes here.
</NOFRAMES>
```

You can safely think of this as an alternative to the BODY structure of a normal HTML page. Whatever you place between the <NOFRAMES> and </NOFRAMES> tags will appear on browsers without frames capability. Browsers with frames will throw away everything between these two tags.

 If you want to include background graphics or images, you can add the BODY tag to your alternate content like this:

```
<NOFRAMES>
<BODY BGCOLOR="red" BACKGROUND="bgimage.gif">
content...
</BODY>
</NOFRAMES
```

As long as the BODY container is kept within the bounds of the NOFRAMES container, your document will work just fine. But there's no need to use the BODY tag within the NOFRAMES container unless you want to take advantage of its special attributes.

A few simple frame examples

Frames are very flexible, which means they can get complicated quickly. Now that you understand the basics, take a look at a few frame examples so you can get our bearings.

A simple page with two frames

The simplest possible frame setup is one with two frames, like this:

```
<HTML>
<HEAD>
</HEAD>
<FRAMESET COLS="*, 2*">
```

```
            <FRAME SRC="label.htm">
            <FRAME SRC="info.htm">
        </FRAMESET>
        </HTML>
```

This HTML code ("2Frames.htm") defines a page with two frames, organized as two columns. The first column takes up 1/3 of the width of the screen and contains the HTML document "label.htm", and the second takes up the other 2/3 and contains the document "info.htm". Figure 10.4 shows how Netscape Navigator displays this page.

FIG. 10.4

Netscape displays the simple two-column FRAMESET defined by the preceding HTML code.

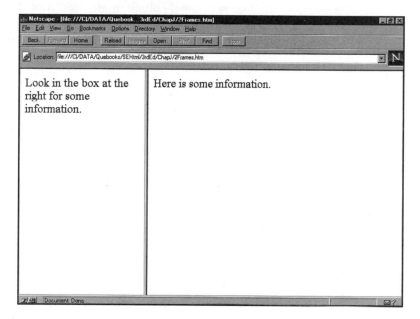

You could just as easily create 10 or more columns, or use the same syntax, substituting the ROWS attribute to create two (or 10) rows. However, 10 columns or rows is way too many for any browser to handle gracefully. Your pages should probably never have more than three or four rows or columns.

A simple rectangular grid of frames

A regular rectangular grid of rows and columns is just about as easy to implement as a rows-only or columns-only arrangement:

```
<HTML>
<HEAD>
</HEAD>
<FRAMESET ROWS="*, 2*" COLS="20%, 30%, 40%">
        <FRAME SRC="labela.htm">
```

```
                    <FRAME SRC="labelb.htm">
                    <FRAME SRC="labelc.htm">
                    <FRAME SRC="infoa.htm">
                    <FRAME SRC="infob.htm">
                    <FRAME SRC="infoc.htm">
        </FRAMESET>
        </HTML>
```

This example ("2by3Grid.htm") creates a grid with two rows and three columns (see Figure 10.5). Since you defined a set of six frames, you've provided six FRAME definitions. Note that they fill in by rows. That is, the first FRAME goes in the first defined column in the first row, the second frame follows across in the second column, and the third finishes out the last column in the first row. The last three frames then fill in the columns of the second row going across.

Also, note that the math didn't work out very well, since the percentage values in the COLS definition only add up to 90 percent. No problem, because the browser has adjusted all the columns proportionally to make up the difference.

FIG. 10.5

This two-by-three grid of frames was created by the preceding HTML example.

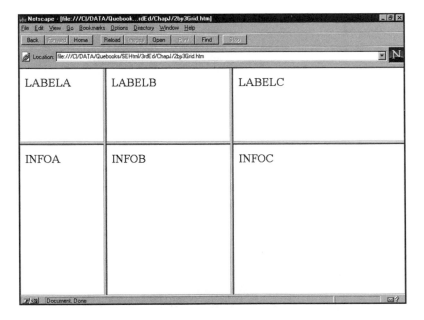

Creating a complex grid of frames

A bit tougher is the problem of creating a more complex grid of frames. For that, return to the example that opened this discussion.

```
<HTML>
<HEAD>
</HEAD>
<FRAMESET ROWS="25%,50%,25%">
        <FRAME SRC="header.htm">
        <FRAMESET COLS="25%,75%">
                <FRAME SRC="label.htm">
                <FRAME SRC="info.htm">
        </FRAMESET>
        <FRAME SRC="footer.htm">
</FRAMESET>
<NOFRAMES>
Your browser cannot display frames.
</NOFRAMES>
</HTML>
```

This example ("Frames1.htm") makes use of nested FRAMESET containers. The outside set creates three ROWS, with 25 percent, 50 percent, and 25 percent of the window height, respectively:

```
<FRAMESET ROWS="25%,50%,25%">
```

Within this definition, the first and last rows are simple frames:

```
<FRAME SRC="header.htm">
<FRAME SRC="footer.htm">
```

Each of these rows runs the entire width of the screen. The first row at the top of the screen takes up 25 percent of the screen height, and the third row at the bottom of the screen also takes up 25 percent of the screen height.

In between however, is this nested FRAMESET container:

```
<FRAMESET COLS="25%,75%">
        <FRAME SRC="label.htm">
        <FRAME SRC="info.htm">
</FRAMESET>
```

This FRAMESET defines two columns that split the middle row of the screen. The row these two columns reside in takes up 50 percent of the total screen height, as defined in the middle row value for the outside FRAMESET container. The left column uses 25 percent of the screen width, while the right column occupies the other 75 percent of the screen width.

The FRAMEs for the columns are defined within the set of FRAMESET tags, which include the column definitions, while the FRAME definitions for the first and last rows are outside the nested FRAMESET command, but within the exterior FRAMESET, in their proper order.

This is not as confusing if you think of an entire nested FRAMESET block as a single FRAME tag. In this example, the outside FRAMESET block sets up a situation in which you have three rows. Each must be filled. In this case, they are filled by a FRAME, then a nested FRAMESET two columns wide, and then another FRAME.

By now (if you are a perverse programming-type person) you may be asking yourself, "I wonder if it is possible for a FRAME to use as its SRC a document that is, itself, a FRAMESET?" The answer is "Yes." In this case, you simply use the FRAME tag to point to an HTML document which is the FRAMESET you would have otherwise used in place of the FRAME.

Redefine the previous example (which used nested FRAMESETs) in terms of referenced FRAME documents instead. All you're doing is moving the nested FRAMESET to its own document. Here's the first (outside) file ("Frames2.htm"):

```
<HTML>
<HEAD>
</HEAD>
<FRAMESET ROWS="25%,50%,25%">
        <FRAME SRC="header.htm">
        <FRAME SRC="nested.htm">
        <FRAME SRC="footer.htm">
</FRAMESET>
<NOFRAMES>
Your browser cannot display frames.
</NOFRAMES>
</HTML>
```

And here's the second (inside) file ("Nested.htm").

```
<HTML>
<HEAD>
</HEAD>
<FRAMESET COLS="25%,75%">
        <FRAME SRC="label.htm">
        <FRAME SRC="info.htm">
</FRAMESET>
</HTML>
```

In this case, the top and bottom rows behave as before. But the second row in the "outside" file is now just a simple FRAME definition like the others. However, the "inside" file that its SRC points to is "frameset.htm," which you created with a FRAMESET all its own. When inserted into the original FRAMESET, it will behave just as if it appeared there verbatim. The resulting screen is identical to the original example (see Figure 10.6).

FIG. 10.6
FRAMESET containers can be nested, or can call other documents containing their own FRAMESETs. The end result is the same.

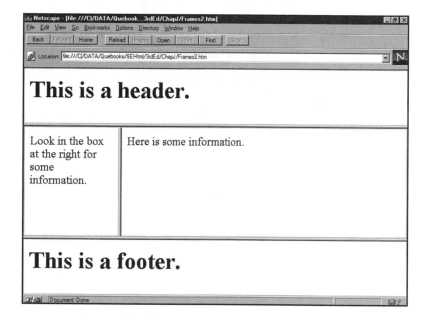

 CAUTION **Though it's possible to create nested FRAMESETs by using FRAME** tags which call the same URL, it certainly isn't a good idea. This is called *infinite recursion*, which creates an infinite loop in a computer that consumes all memory and crashes the machine. Fortunately, frames-aware browsers check for this—if a SRC URL is the same as any of its ancestors it's ignored, just as if there were no SRC attribute at all.

By using nested FRAMESET containers in clever combinations, it is possible to create just about any grid of frames you can dream up. But remember that you're trying to create a friendly, useful interface, not show off how clever you can be with frames.

Modifying a frame's look and feel

Now that you understand how framesets are used to create various grids of frames, take a look at some of the attributes that modify how frames look and feel.

Frame margins

The FRAME attributes MARGINWIDTH and MARGINHEIGHT give you control over the width of the frame's interior margins. They both look like this:

```
MARGINWIDTH="value"
```

The value is always a number, and always represents an absolute value in pixels. For example:

```
<FRAME MARGINHEIGHT="5" MARGINWIDTH="7">
```

would create a frame with top and bottom interior margins five pixels wide, and left and right margins seven pixels wide. Remember, you're talking interior margins here, not borders. MARGINWIDTH and MARGINHEIGHT define a space within the frame within which content will not appear. Border widths are set automatically by the browser, or by the BORDER attribute, which will be discussed later in this chapter.

Frame scrollbars

Your frames will automatically have scrollbars if the content you've specified for them is too big to fit the frame. Sometimes this ruins the aesthetics of your page, so you need a way to control them. That's what the SCROLLING attribute of the FRAME tag is for. Here's the format:

```
<FRAME SCROLLING="yes|no|auto">
```

There are three valid values for SCROLLING: "Yes," "No," and "Auto." "Auto" is assumed if there is no SCROLLING attribute in your FRAME definition. "Yes" forces the appearance of a scrollbar. "No" keeps them away at all costs. For example, this FRAME definition turns on scrollbars:

```
<FRAME SCROLLING=YES>
```

Frame resizing

Frames are normally resizable by the user. But if you let the user drag your frames around, it can quickly muck up the look and feel of your beautifully designed frames. You will therefore almost always want to use the NORESIZE attribute of the FRAME tag to keep users from resizing your frames. Here's how:

```
<FRAME NORESIZE>
```

That's it. No values. Of course, when you set NORESIZE for one frame, none of the adjacent frames can be resized, either. Depending on your layout, using NORESIZE in a single frame will often be enough to keep users from resizing all the frames on the screen.

When you move over a resizable frame border with the mouse cursor, it will change to a double-arrow, indicating that the frame can be resized. If you don't get the double-arrow, it means that resizing has been turned off with the NORESIZE attribute. To resize a resizable frame, grab the frame border by clicking and dragging it with your mouse to a new position.

Q&A *I've created a frame using the* NORESIZE *attribute. What do I do about users who are using small screens on which the entire contents of the frame may not fit?*

Your best bet is to make sure the frame will hold all of its content at lower screen resolutions. That is, redesign the frame. Otherwise, consider reenabling, resizing or adding scrollbars to the frame.

Figure 10.7 shows an example of a frames page where the lower left frame has had its MARGINHEIGHT set to 50, MARGINWIDTH set to 100, and SCROLLING set to "Yes." The NORESIZE attribute has not been used, so you can see what the resizing cursor looks like.

Frame borders

You use the BORDER, FRAMEBORDER, and BORDERCOLOR attributes to set the look and feel of the borders for your frameset.

The BORDER attribute is used only with the FRAMESET tag, and sets the width of all the borders in the frameset. It is assigned a value in pixels, like this:

```
<FRAMESET BORDER="5">
```

This example would set the width of the frame borders to 5 pixels. BORDER can be assigned a value of "0", in which case all the frames in your frameset will be borderless.

FIG. 10.7
The HTML source for this FRAMESET is shown in the upper frame.

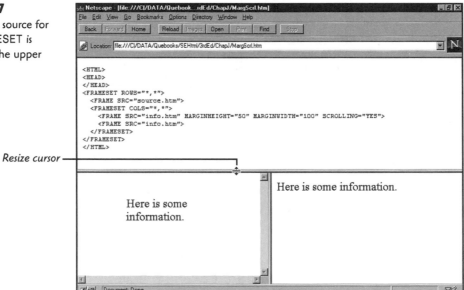

Resize cursor

TIP **The default value of BORDER (that is, the value it assumes if there** is no BORDER="n" attribute specified for a given FRAMESET) is "5".

The FRAMEBORDER attribute can be used with either the FRAMESET or FRAME tag. It has two legitimate values, "YES" and "NO". If FRAMEBORDER="YES", then frame borders are drawn with a 3-D look. If FRAMEBORDER="NO", frame borders are "invisible", which really means that they are drawn in the default background color of the browser.

The default value of FRAMEBORDER is "YES", which means that browser programs generally display 3-D frame borders.

The border for a frame will be invisible (not 3-D) only if FRAMEBORDER="NO" is set for all surrounding frames.

To create a page with entirely borderless frames, set
FRAMEBORDER="NO" and BORDER="0" in the top FRAMESET definition.

The BORDERCOLOR attribute can be used with the FRAMESET tag or with the
FRAME tag. BORDERCOLOR can be assigned a named color value, or a hexadecimal RGB color value. Here's an example:

```
<FRAMESET BORDERCOLOR="red" ROWS="*,*">
        <FRAME SRC="info.htm" BORDERCOLOR="#FF00FF">
        <FRAME SRC="info.htm">
</FRAMESET>
```

In this example, the outer FRAMESET tag sets the BORDERCOLOR to "red", one of
the named colors for most browsers. But the following FRAME tag sets
BORDERCOLOR to the hexadecimal value "#FF00FF" (which happens to be
purple). The lowest level definition takes precedence. Though the FRAMESET
BORDERCOLOR is defined as "red", the border color of the first frame will
instead be set to the hexadecimal RGB value "#FF00FF" The adjacent frame,
which has no BORDERCOLOR definition, will have a border of "#FF00FF" on the
edge it shares with the other frame, but a color of "red" on borders it does
not share with that frame.

 If two adjacent frames of the same priority attempt to define their
own BORDERCOLOR, neither will take effect. They will revert to the
BORDERCOLOR defined at the next higher FRAMESET level.

Figure 10.8 shows an example of using the BORDER, FRAMEBORDER, and
BORDERCOLOR attributes to control the look and feel of your frame borders.
Note that the only frame to maintain the BORDERCOLOR defined in the outside
FRAMESET definition is the one in the upper right, the only frame which
doesn't share a border with the leftmost center frame, which redefines the
BORDERCOLOR. Actually, the right-most center frame would have also had a red
border on the left, but it has had its left border turned off by the
FRAMEBORDER="NO" attribute it shares with the central frame. Note this
complex interplay of attributes carefully. If you use them often, their interre-
lationships are sure to throw you for a loop more often than they make sense.

FIG. 10.8
The HTML source for this border-manipulating example is shown in the top frame.

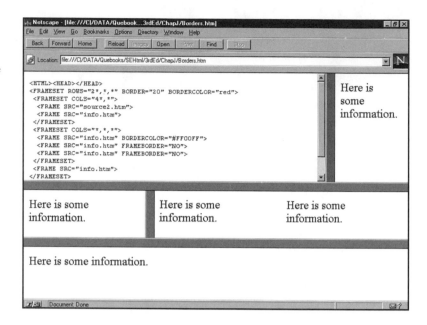

```
Netscape - [file:///C|/DATA/Quebook...3rdEd/ChapJ/Borders.htm]
File  Edit  View  Go  Bookmarks  Options  Directory  Window  Help
 Back  Forward  Home     Reload  Images  Open   Print   Find    Stop

 Location: file:///C|/DATA/Quebooks/SEHtml/3rdEd/ChapJ/Borders.htm

<HTML><HEAD></HEAD>                                      Here is
<FRAMESET ROWS="2*,*,*" BORDER="20" BORDERCOLOR="red">   some
 <FRAMESET COLS="4*,*">                                  information.
  <FRAME SRC="source2.htm">
  <FRAME SRC="info.htm">
 </FRAMESET>
 <FRAMESET COLS="*,*,*">
  <FRAME SRC="info.htm" BORDERCOLOR="#FF00FF">
  <FRAME SRC="info.htm" FRAMEBORDER="NO">
  <FRAME SRC="info.htm" FRAMEBORDER="NO">
 </FRAMESET>
 <FRAME SRC="info.htm">
</FRAMESET>
```

| Here is some information. | Here is some information. | Here is some information. |

Here is some information.

`Document: Done`

CAUTION   **Microsoft Internet Explorer supports one more attribute for**
FRAMESET, called FRAMESPACING. It is intended to define the space between frames, and can assume pixel values. However, since Netscape Navigator and other browser programs don't support the FRAMESPACING attribute, it is strongly advised that you not use it unless you are creating content for an audience that uses Internet Explorer exclusively, and you have a good reason for having to specify the spacing between frames.

Targeted hyperlinks

Though you've examined in depth how to create and nest framesets, and how to control the look and feel of frames, you have yet to understand how to use frames to control navigation, which is their major application. To use frames to their full advantage, you need to know how to name and target frames.

Naming and targeting frames

The NAME attribute assigns a name to a frame that can be used to link to the frame, usually from other frames in the same display. This example:

```
<FRAME SRC="info.htm" NAME="Joe">
```

creates a frame named "Joe", which can be referenced via a hyperlink like this:

```
<A HREF="moreinfo.htm" TARGET="Joe">Click Here to Jump to
Joe</A>
```

Note the TARGET attribute in the hypertext link that references the name of your frame. When selected, this hyperlink will replace the content of the named frame "Joe"—which was given the content file "info.htm" when it was created—with the content in the file "moreinfo.htm". Note that, while a hyperlink without a named TARGET replaces the content in its own window or frame with the content named in the HREF attribute, a hyperlink with a named TARGET instead replaces the content in the targeted frame or window with the content named in the HREF attribute. This is the only trick you need to know for creating killer frames-based navigational systems. Of course, there are some fine points.

Legitimate names

If you don't create an explicit name for a frame, it will simply have no name, and you won't be able to use links in one frame to open documents or images in another. You'll want to name all frames whose content will be changed by clicking a link in a different frame.

All frame names must begin with an alphanumeric character. Don't use an underscore "_" as the first character in a frame name. Other than that, you're pretty much on your own.

However, there are four reserved *implicit* names built into HTML, and all of them *do* start with an underscore. These are listed in Table 10.1 below. All other names starting with an underscore will be ignored.

Table 10.1 Reserved implicit frame names

Name	Purpose
_blank	Load content directed to this name into a new, unnamed window. This name is used to completely wipe out the current frameset and start with a new, blank window.
_self	Load content directed to this name into the calling frame.

continues

Table 10.1 Continued

Name	Purpose
_parent	Load content directed to this link to the calling frame's parent frameset window. If it has no parent frameset, this is the same as using the name _self.
_top	Load content directed to this link to the top level frameset related to the calling frame. If the calling frame is already the top level, this is the same as using the name _self.

Here are a few examples to help clarify how these reserved names work.

If a frame contains the following link:

```
<A HREF="stuff.htm" TARGET="_blank">
```

then clicking the link will launch a new, unnamed browser display window which will contain the content defined in "stuff.htm". This can be a simple HTML document, or an entirely new FRAMESET definition. Whichever, this call wipes the slate clean and starts completely over.

If a frame contains this link:

```
<A HREF="stuff.htm" TARGET="_self">
```

then clicking the link will simply cause the frame which contains the link to clear, and its content will be replaced with whatever is in "stuff.htm".

If a frame contains this link:

```
<A HREF="stuff.htm" TARGET="_parent">
```

then the frameset which contains the frame which contains this link will be replaced by "stuff.htm".

Finally, if a frame contains the link:

```
<A HREF="stuff.htm" TARGET="_top">
```

then clicking the link replaces the entire browser window with the contents of "stuff.htm".

NOTE **Hyperlinks using the <A> or anchor tag aren't the only tags that** can make use of the TARGET attribute. The AREA, FORM, and BASE tags also use the TARGET attribute, and can be used effectively to extend and expand the utility of named frames.

Remember, too, that windows can also be named by using the TARGET attribute within the <A> tag; using named windows in conjunction with named frames adds a whole new dimension to HTML document navigation.

Updating more than one frame at a time

You've seen that you can click a link in one frame to change the content in another by naming the target frame using the NAME attribute of the FRAME tag when creating the target frame, and then using the TARGET attribute of the <A> hyperlink tag when defining the link, as in this example:

```
<FRAME SRC="info.htm" NAME="Joe">
<A HREF="moreinfo.htm" TARGET="Joe">Click Here to Jump to
Joe</A>
```

The first line of HTML above is used in the frame definition document, and the second line is used in the document which links to the first.

You've also seen that you can use special implicit names to target some frames and framesets, depending on their relationship to the frame which contains the calling link.

But what if you want to update more than one frame by clicking a single link? This is possible if you set up your document correctly. The key is to update a frameset, not a single frame.

To do this, you need to create a subframeset that is contained in its own file, as was done in an earlier example. If you recall, you began with an HTML document that included one frameset nested inside another:

```
<HTML>
<HEAD>
</HEAD>
<FRAMESET ROWS="25%,50%,25%">
        <FRAME SRC="header.htm">
        <FRAMESET COLS="25%,75%">
                <FRAME SRC="label.htm">
                <FRAME SRC="info.htm">
        </FRAMESET>
        <FRAME SRC="footer.htm">
</FRAMESET>
</HTML>
```

Then you took the nested frameset out, and put it into its own file.

Here's the original file, with the nested frameset replaced by the FRAME definition pointing to the second file, "nested.htm". Note that you'll named this frame this time using the NAME attribute, calling it "Inner":

```
<HTML>
<HEAD>
</HEAD>
<FRAMESET ROWS="25%,50%,25%">
        <FRAME SRC="header.htm">
        <FRAME SRC="nested.htm" NAME="Inner">
        <FRAME SRC="TestLink.htm">
</FRAMESET>
</HTML>
```

Also note the last FRAME SRC file has been renamed "TestLink.htm"—this file will contain the targeted link we want to test. Call this modified file "NameTest.htm". Now here's the file ("nested.htm") that the frame named "Inner" calls:

```
<HTML>
<HEAD>
</HEAD>
<FRAMESET COLS="25%,75%">
        <FRAME SRC="label.htm">
        <FRAME SRC="info.htm">
</FRAMESET>
</HTML>
```

The file which occupies the bottom frame contains the file "TestLink.htm", which is listed below:

```
<HTML>
<HEAD>
<TITLE>
</TITLE>
</HEAD>
<BODY>
<A HREF="NewStuff.htm" TARGET="Inner">Click me</A>
to put new stuff into the upper center frameset.
</BODY>
</HTML>
```

The frameset created by these two files (and their associated content files) is shown in Figure 10.9.

FIG. 10.9
Here's your test page, all set to change two frames with one mouse click.

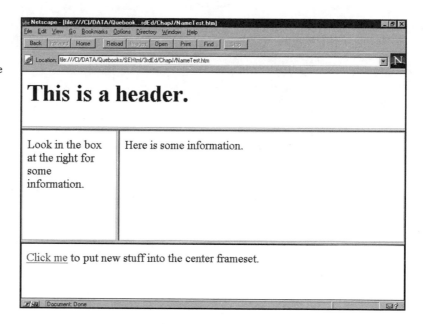

When the link "Click me" in the bottom window is clicked, it will replace the two frames in the center frameset (which was defined in the file "nested.htm") with new information from the document "NewStuff.htm". Say that this is the content of "NewStuff.htm":

```
<HTML>
<HEAD>
<TITLE>
</TITLE>
</HEAD>
<BODY>
Here is some NEW STUFF!
</BODY>
</HTML>
```

When you click the link in the bottom window, you now get the result shown in Figure 10.10.

With one click, you've replaced the two frames of the central frameset with a single frame containing new content. You could just as easily have replaced the two frames with two new frames—the same size, or different sizes—or with three frames, or with a whole new frameset. All you would have to do is define the new frameset in your new content file, "NewStuff.htm".

FIG. 10.10

Clicking the hyperlink in the bottom window has replaced the two-frame central frameset with the single frame of content from a different file.

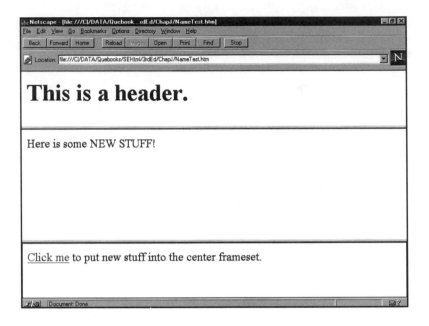

If you're careful and think ahead when defining your framesets, you can easily create hyperlinks that can update almost any combination of frames with a single mouse click.

Forms

● **In this chapter:**

● **What are HTML forms? What are they useful for?**

● **Add forms to your own Web pages**

● **Design and lay out your HTML forms**

F orms are one of the most popular, interactive features on the World Wide Web. They enable users to interact with the text and graphics that are displayed on your machine. You can make forms with simple yes or no questions, you can make highly complex order forms, or you can make forms for people to send you comments.

You create forms by providing a number of fields in which a user can enter information or choose an option. Then, when the user submits the form, the information is returned to a server-side script. A *script* is a short program that is written specifically for each form. You can create scripts to do any number of things. You can also handle the contents of a form by using a client-side script.

Introducing HTML forms

HTML forms give you the opportunity to gather input from people reading your Web page. Just as HTML provides many mechanisms for outputting information, the use of HTML forms enables input. These forms can be used to solicit free-form text information, get answers to yes or no questions, and get answers from a set of options.

You can add forms to your Web page with many different results in mind. You can do something simple, like asking visitors to sign a guest book or comment about your Web site. You can also use forms to gather input for a discussion group or, when combined with a secure method of transmission, take online orders for your $10 widgets. These and many other uses can be achieved with HTML forms.

Working with HTML forms tags

The HTML tags you use to display forms are straightforward. There are three types of tags for creating fields: `<TEXTAREA>`, `<SELECT>`, and `<INPUT>`. You can put any number of these tags between the `<FORM>` and `</FORM>` container tags.

The following is a brief description of each tag (you'll learn more about each a bit later in this chapter):

    <TEXTAREA>   This tag defines a field in which the end user can type multiple lines of text.

    <SELECT>   This tag enables the end user to choose among a number of options in either a scroll box or pop-up menu.

    <INPUT>   This tag provides all of the other types of input: single lines of text, option buttons, check boxes, and the buttons to submit or clear the form.

<FORM>

The <FORM> tag comes at the beginning of any form. When you create a <FORM> tag, you also define the script it uses and how it sends data using the ACTION and METHOD attributes:

    ACTION   This attribute points the form to an URL that will accept the form's information and do something with it. If you don't specify an ACTION, it sends the information back to the same URL the page came from.

    METHOD   This attribute tells the form how to send its information back to the script. The most common method is POST, which sends all the information from the form separately from the URL. The other option for METHOD is GET, which attaches the information from the form to the end of the URL.

The following is an example of a <FORM> tag:

```
<FORM METHOD="POST" ACTION="/cgi-bin/comment_script">
...
</FORM>
```

This example says that you want the browser to send the completed form to the script comment_script in the cgi-bin directory on your server and to use the POST method to send it.

CAUTION **You can put any number of forms on the same HTML page, but** be careful not to nest one form inside another. If you put in a <FORM> tag before finishing the last one, that line is ignored, and all the inputs for your second form are assumed to go with the first one.

<TEXTAREA>

With <TEXTAREA>, you can provide a field for someone to enter multiple lines of information. By default, a <TEXTAREA> form shows a blank field four rows long and 40 characters wide. You can make it any size you want by using the ROWS and COLS attributes in the tag. You can also specify some default text by simply entering it between the <TEXTAREA> and </TEXTAREA> tags.

TIP <TEXTAREA> **fields are ideal for having users enter comments or** lengthy information because they can type as much as they want in the field.

The options for the <TEXTAREA> tag are as follows:

NAME	This is required. It defines the name for the data.
ROWS	This sets the number of rows in the field.
COLS	This sets the width of the field in characters.
Default text	Any text between the <TEXTAREA> and </TEXTAREA> tags is used as default text and shows up inside the field.

While the ROWS and COLS attributes are not required, there is no default value for these that you are guaranteed to get on every Web browser, so it's always a good idea to set them. Listing 11.1 shows you an example using the <TEXTAREA> tag. Figure 11.1 shows you what this example looks like.

TIP **All input fields in a form—**<TEXTAREA>**,** <SELECT>**, and** <INPUT>**—** must each have a NAME defined for its information.

Listing 11.1

TEXTAREA.HTM   **<TEXTAREA> default text**

```
<HTML>
<HEAD>
<TITLE>TEXTAREA.HTM</TITLE>
```

```
</HEAD>
<BODY>
<FORM>
<TEXTAREA NAME="comments" ROWS=4 COLS=40>Default text
1 2 3 ...
</TEXTAREA>
</FORM>
</BODY>
</HTML>
```

FIG. 11.1
The default text is shown as preformatted text in the *<TEXTAREA>* element.

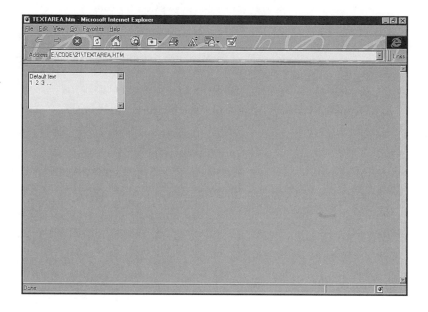

<SELECT>

The <SELECT> element shows a list of choices in either a pop-up menu or a scrolling list. It's set up as an opening and closing tag with a number of choices listed in between. Just like the <TEXTAREA> element, the <SELECT> tag requires you to define a name. You can specify how many choices to show at once by using the SIZE attribute.

The options for the <SELECT> element are as follows:

NAME	This is required. It defines the name for the data.
SIZE	This attribute determines how many choices to show. If you omit SIZE or set it to 1, the choices are shown as a drop-down list. If you set it to 2 or higher, it shows the choices in a

scroll box. If you set SIZE larger than the number of choices you have within <SELECT>, a NOTHING choice is added. When the end user chooses this, it's returned as an empty field.

MULTIPLE   This allows multiple selections. If you specify multiple, a scrolling list appears—regardless of the number of choices or the setting of SIZE.

TIP **Some WWW browsers don't properly display a scrolling list if the** SIZE *is 2 or 3. In that case, leave it as a drop-down list box or think about using the* <INPUT> *tag's option buttons.*

You present the choices the end user can make within the <SELECT> and </SELECT> tags. The choices are listed inside the <OPTION> tag and don't allow any other HTML.

The options for the <OPTION> tag are the following:

VALUE   This is the value to be assigned for the choice, which is what is sent back to the script and doesn't have to be the same as what is presented to the end user.

SELECTED   If you want one of the choices to be a default, use the SELECTED option in the <OPTION> tag.

Consider Listing 11.2, the results of which are shown in Figures 11.2 and 11.3. This HTML adds a list called network to the document that contains four options: ethernet, token16, token5, and localtalk.

Listing 11.2

SELECT1.HTM   **Selection via drop-down list box**

```
<HTML>
<HEAD>
<TITLE>SELECT1.HTM</TITLE>
</HEAD>
<BODY>
What type of connection:
<FORM>
<SELECT NAME="network">
        <OPTION SELECTED VALUE="ethernet"> Ethernet
        <OPTION VALUE="token16"> Token Ring - 16MB
        <OPTION VALUE="token4"> Token Ring - 4MB
```

```
                  <OPTION VALUE="localtalk"> LocalTalk
          </SELECT>
          </FORM>
          </BODY>
          </HTML>
```

FIG. 11.2
The <SELECT> tag uses the default of a drop-down list (size=1).

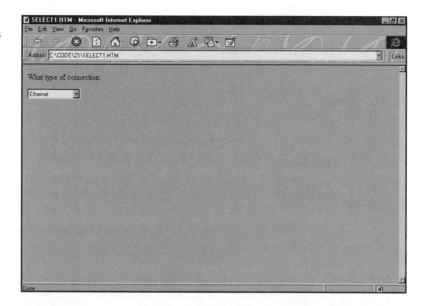

FIG. 11.3
The width of the dropdown list box is determined by the size of the entries listed with the <OPTION> tags.

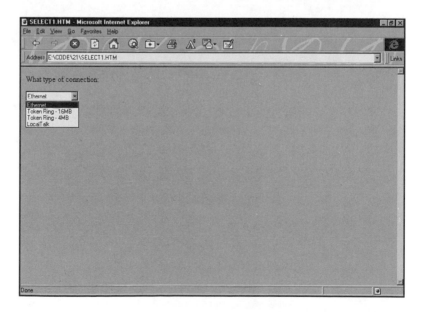

Suppose you set the tag as shown in Listing 11.3, the result of which is shown in Figure 11.4.

Listing 11.3

SELECT2.HTM *Selection via scrolling list*

```
<HTML>
<HEAD>
<TITLE>SELECT2.HTM</TITLE>
</HEAD>
<BODY>
<FORM>
What type of Connection:
<SELECT MULTIPLE NAME="network">
        <OPTION SELECTED VALUE="ethernet"> Ethernet
        <OPTION VALUE="token16"> Token Ring - 16MB
        <OPTION VALUE="token4"> Token Ring - 4MB
        <OPTION VALUE="localtalk"> LocalTalk
</SELECT>
</FORM>
</BODY>
</HTML>
```

FIG. 11.4

If you use MULTIPLE within the <SELECT> tag, then the field becomes a list of choices.

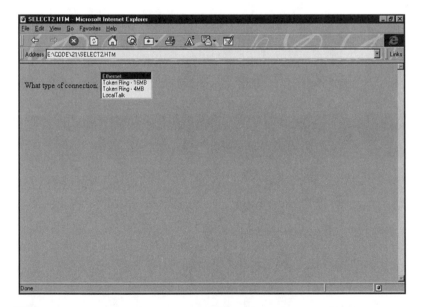

Q&A *I know the most common choices I want to present, but I want to allow people to enter their own value if they want to. How can I do that?*

Your best bet is to display the common choices in a <SELECT> box or pop-up menu, with one of the options set to Other. Then include an <INPUT> text field or a <TEXTAREA> field right after the list of choices (see Listing 11.4).

Listing 11.4

SELECT3.HTM   Selection with other option

```
<HTML>
<HEAD>
<TITLE>SELECT3.HTM</TITLE>
</HEAD>
<BODY>
<FORM>
What type of Connection:
<SELECT MULTIPLE NAME="network">
        <OPTION SELECTED VALUE="ethernet"> Ethernet
        <OPTION VALUE="token16"> Token Ring - 16MB
        <OPTION VALUE="token4"> Token Ring - 4MB
        <OPTION VALUE="localtalk"> LocalTalk
        <OPTION VALUE="other"> Other...
</SELECT>
<BR>
If other, please specify:<INPUT TYPE="text"NAME="network_other">
</FORM>
</BODY>
</HTML>
```

The result of Listing 11.4 is shown in Figure 11.5.

FIG. 11.5

This type of form layout provides both a common list and a place for exceptions.

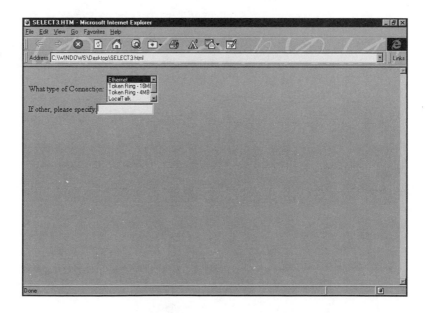

TIP **You can use the** <SELECT> **tag as a navigational aid in your Web** pages. You can provide a number of URLs in a list. The user then can choose one and click a SUBMIT button. Then you can have the server-side or client-side script jump to the URL indicated by that choice. Microsoft uses this method to direct users to different international Web sites (see **http://www.microsoft.com**).

<INPUT>

<INPUT>, unlike <TEXTAREA> and <SELECT>, is a single tag option for gathering information. <INPUT> contains all of the other options for acquiring information, including simple text boxes, password text boxes, option buttons, check boxes, and the buttons to submit and reset the form.

The attributes for the <INPUT> tag are the following:

NAME	This defines the name for the data. This field is required for all the types of input except SUBMIT and CLEAR.
SIZE	This is the size of the <INPUT> field in number of characters for text or password.
MAXLENGTH	This specifies the maximum number of characters to be allowed for a text box or password text box.
VALUE	For a text box or password text box, it defines the default text displayed. For a check box or option button, it specifies the value that is returned to the server if the check box or option button is selected. For the SUBMIT and RESET buttons, it defines the text inside the button.
CHECKED	This sets a check box or option button to on. It has no meaning for any other type of <INPUT> tag.
TYPE	This sets the type of <INPUT> field you want to display (see the types in the following section).

Setting the *<INPUT>* tag's *TYPE*

This section describes the possible values for the <INPUT> tag's TYPE attribute.

TEXT

TEXT, the default input type, gathers a simple line of text. You can use the attributes NAME (this is required), SIZE, MAXLENGTH, and VALUE with TEXT. For example, consider Listing 11.5, the result of which is shown in Figure 11.6

Listing 11.5

INPUT1.HTM   Text input box

```
<HTML>
<HEAD>
<TITLE>INPUT1.HTM</TITLE>
</HEAD>
<BODY>
<FORM>
A Phone Number: <INPUT TYPE="text" NAME="Phone" SIZE="15"
➥MAXLENGTH="12">
</FORM>
</BODY>
</HTML>
```

FIG. 11.6
The TEXT input type provides a very flexible input field.

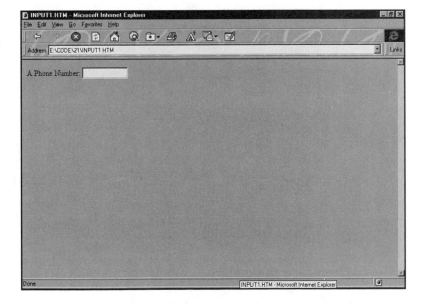

PASSWORD

PASSWORD, a modified TEXT field, displays typed characters as bullets instead of the characters actually typed. Possible attributes to include with the

PASSWORD type include NAME (required), SIZE, MAXLENGTH, and VALUE. Consider Listing 11.6, the result of which is shown in Figure 11.7.

Listing 11.6

> **INPUT2.HTM** **Text input box with no echo**

```
<HTML>
<HEAD>
<TITLE>INPUT2.HTM</TITLE>
</HEAD>
<BODY>
<FORM>
Enter the secret word: <INPUT TYPE="password"
➥NAME="secret_word" Size="30" MAXLENGTH="30">
</FORM>
</BODY>
</HTML>
```

FIG. 11.7
Although it will look different in different browsers, the PASSWORD element hides the text that is typed.

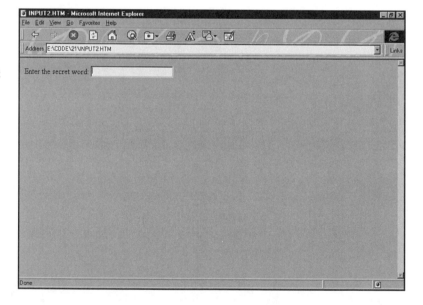

CHECKBOX

CHECKBOX displays a simple check box that can be checked or left empty; use a check box when the choice is yes or no and doesn't depend on anything else. Possible attributes to include with the TYPE text include NAME (required), VALUE, and CHECKED (which defaults the check box as checked). Consider

Listing 11.7, the result of which is shown in Figure 11.8. Check boxes are useful when you have a list of options, more than one of which can be selected at a time.

Listing 11.7

CHECKBOX.HTM **Checkbox form input**

```
<HTML>
<HEAD>
<TITLE>CHECKBOX.HTM</TITLE>
</HEAD>
<BODY>
<FORM>
<INPUT TYPE="checkbox" NAME="checkbox1" VALUE="checkbox_value1">
A checkbox
<INPUT TYPE="checkbox" NAME="checkbox2" VALUE="checkbox_value2"
CHECKED>A pre-selected checkbox
</FORM>
</BODY>
</HTML>
```

FIG. 11.8
Select the check boxes that are commonly checked to make the form easier to use.

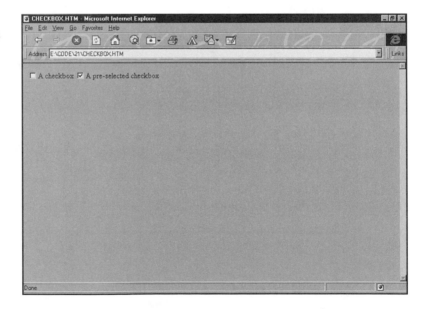

CAUTION **You want to be especially careful when using check boxes and** option buttons in HTML documents with custom backgrounds or background colors. Depending on the Web browser used, check boxes and option buttons sometimes do not show up with dark backgrounds.

RADIO

RADIO is a more complex version of a check box, allowing only one of a related set to be chosen. You can group option buttons together by using the NAME attribute; this keeps all buttons in the same group under one NAME. Possible attributes to include with the TYPE text include NAME (required), VALUE, and CHECKED. Consider Listing 11.8, the result of which is shown in Figure 11.9.

Listing 11.8

RADIO1.HTM   Option button form input

```
<HTML>
<HEAD>
<TITLE>RADIO1.HTM</TITLE>
</HEAD>
<BODY>
Form #1:
<FORM>
        <INPUT TYPE="radio" NAME="choice" VALUE="choice1"> Yes.
        <INPUT TYPE="radio" NAME="choice" VALUE="choice2"> No.
</FORM>
<HR>
Form #2:
<FORM>
        <INPUT TYPE="radio" NAME="choice" VALUE="choice1"
        ➥CHECKED> Yes.
        <INPUT TYPE="radio" NAME="choice" VALUE="choice2"> No.
</FORM>
</BODY>
</HTML>
```

FIG. 11.9
In the top form, without selecting yes or no, the end user can send back a "blank" value for this selection because none of the boxes were preselected with the CHECKED attribute.

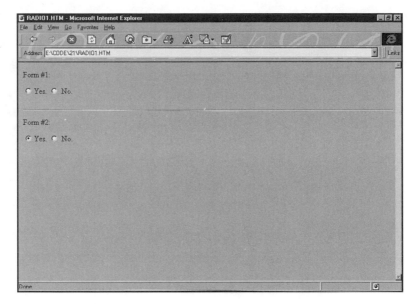

Listing 11.9 is a variation on Listing 11.8. The result is shown in Figure 11.10.

Listing 11.9

RADIO2.HTM   Radio button form input with more choices

```
<HTML>
<HEAD>
<TITLE>RADIO2.HTM</TITLE>
</HEAD>
<BODY>
<FORM>
One Choice:<BR>
        <INPUT TYPE="radio" NAME="choice1" VALUE="choice1"
        ➡CHECKED>(1)
        <INPUT TYPE="radio" NAME="choice1" VALUE="choice2">(2)
        <INPUT TYPE="radio" NAME="choice1" VALUE="choice3">(3)
<BR>
One Choice:<BR>
        <INPUT TYPE="radio" NAME="choice2" VALUE="choice1"
        ➡CHECKED>(1)
        <INPUT TYPE="radio" NAME="choice2" VALUE="choice2">(2)
        <INPUT TYPE="radio" NAME="choice2" VALUE="choice3">(3)
        <INPUT TYPE="radio" NAME="choice2" VALUE="choice4">(4)
        <INPUT TYPE="radio" NAME="choice2" VALUE="choice5">(5)
</FORM>
</BODY>
</HTML>
```

FIG. 11.10
The end user has more choices in this variation. The first choice was the default in each list; this choice has been overridden in the second list.

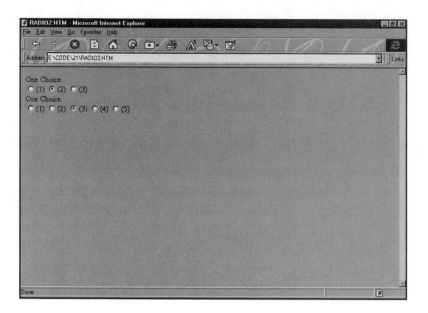

 **TIP** If you want to provide a long list of choices, use the `<SELECT>` tag so the choice doesn't take up as much space on the page.

 CAUTION If you don't specify a set of option buttons or check boxes with **one** of the values as CHECKED, you could receive an empty field for that `<INPUT>` name.

RESET

RESET displays a button with the preset function of clearing all the data in the form to its original value. You can use the VALUE attribute with the RESET tag to provide text other than Reset (the default) for the button. For example, consider Listing 11.10. The result is shown in Figure 11.11.

Listing 11.10

RESET.HTM **Form Reset button**

```
<HTML>
<HEAD>
<TITLE>RESET.HTM</TITLE>
</HEAD>
<BODY>
<FORM>
        <INPUT TYPE="reset">
```

```
            <BR>
            <INPUT TYPE="reset" VALUE="Clear that form!">
    </FORM>
    </BODY>
    </HTML>
```

FIG. 11.11
The top button shows
the default text for the
RESET element.

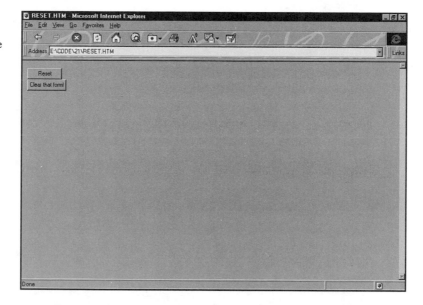

SUBMIT

SUBMIT displays a button with the preset function of sending the data in the form to the server to be processed by a server-side script. You can use the VALUE attribute with SUBMIT to provide text other than Submit Query (the default) for the button. Consider, for example, Listing 11.11. The result is shown in Figure 11.12.

Listing 11.11

SUBMIT.HTM   Form Submit button

```
<HTML>
<HEAD>
<TITLE>SUBMIT.HTM</TITLE>
</HEAD>
<BODY>
<FORM>
        <INPUT TYPE="submit">
```

continues

Listing 11.11

Continued

```
        <BR>
        <INPUT TYPE="submit" VALUE="Send in the data!">
</FORM>
</BODY>
</HTML>
```

FIG. 11.12

The top button shows the default text for the SUBMIT element.

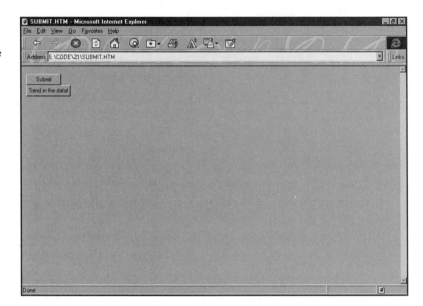

Formatting and designing forms

Forms can be easy to read, simple one- or two-entry affairs with little to display; they can also be terrifically complex devices. As your forms get more complex, you need to carefully consider their layout. Think about how to make it obvious that certain titles are connected to certain fields, and think about how to make your forms easy for anyone to use. People are often put off by complex forms that are hard to understand, so it's in your best interest to make them easy and fun to use—regardless of their complexity.

Using line break tags

When you mark up HTML documents, you usually just let the words wrap across the screen. Although this flexibility is wonderful to have for segments of text, it can make reading a form incredibly difficult to read. A quick and simple solution is to include the line break tag, <BR>, to move something to the next line.

Forcing fields onto separate lines

If you want to have two fields, Name and E-Mail Address, for example, you can simply mark them up as shown in Listing 11.12.

Listing 11.12

LB1.HTM   Forms without line breaks

```
<HTML>
<HEAD>
<TITLE>Form Layout and Design</TITLE>
</HEAD>
<BODY>
<H1>Line Break Tags</H1>
<FORM>
        Name: <INPUT NAME="name" SIZE="30">
        E-Mail Address: <INPUT NAME="email" SIZE="40">
</FORM>
</BODY>
</HTML>
```

Although this might look great now, it can wrap strangely on some WWW browsers and look shabby when displayed (see Figure 11.13).

FIG. 11.13
Without some type of organization, your forms can be very hard to read.

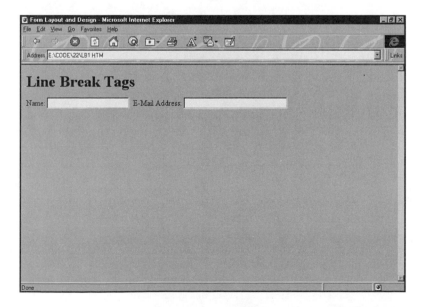

To split these lines and make them more readable, you need to include the line break tag <BR> between them, as shown in Listing 11.13.

Listing 11.13

LB2.HTM   Line breaks within forms

```
<HTML>
<HEAD>
<TITLE>Form Layout and Design</TITLE>
</HEAD>
<BODY>
<H1>Line Break Tags</H1>
<FORM>
        Name: <INPUT NAME="name" SIZE="30">
        <BR>
        E-Mail Address: <INPUT NAME="email" SIZE="40">
</FORM>
</BODY>
</HTML>
```

Adding the <BR> tag between the two fields forces the browser to wrap the field to the next line, regardless of the width of the screen. The result of Listing 11.13 is shown in Figure 11.14.

FIG. 11.14
The <BR> tag enables you to control the placement of form text.

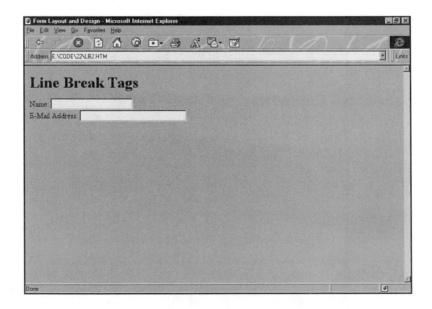

The wrapping feature of HTML can work for you to help keep a form small in size. If you have several multiple-choice items that could take up huge amounts of space on your form, you can try to keep them small and let them wrap closely together on the page.

If you're using the <SELECT> tag, the width of the pop-up menu on the screen is directly related to the words in the options to be selected. If you keep all the words small, you can provide a relatively large number of choices in a small area.

 ## Working with large-entry fields

If you're working with long text-entry fields or perhaps with a <TEXTAREA> field, it's often easier to put the text just above the field and then separate the different areas with paragraph breaks.

For example, if you have a text input line that is very long or a long field description, it doesn't work well to put them side by side. Also, if you want to leave a space for comments, it's easier—and looks nicer—to have the field description just above the comment area. This makes it appear that there's more space to write in. Listing 11.14 is an example of this sort of design. The result of this code is shown in Figure 11.15.

Listing 11.14

LARGE.HTM **Large fields for text input**

```
<HTML>
<HEAD>
<TITLE>Form Layout and Design</TITLE>
</HEAD>
<BODY>
<H1>Line Break Tags</H1>
<FORM>
      Please enter the new title for the message:<BR>
      <INPUT NAME="name" SIZE="40">
      <HR>
      Your comments:<BR>
      <TEXTAREA ROWS="6" COLS="70"></TEXTAREA>
</FORM>
</BODY>
</HTML>
```

FIG. 11.15
Using the line break tags enables you to put a label just above the field.

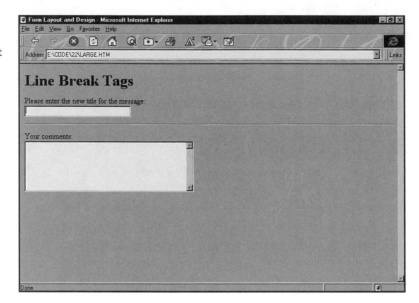

 NOTE **Most browsers automatically wrap a large field to the next line,** treating it like an image. Because you don't know how wide (or narrow!) the client screen is, take steps to ensure the form will look as you want. If, for example, you want the field to be on the next line, put in a <BR> tag to make sure it will be!

Using the preformatted text tag to line up forms

A very common sight on many forms are simple text entry fields aligned haphazardly. A great trick for aligning text fields is to use the <PRE> tag. This ensures that some spaces appear before the field.

 **CAUTION** **If you're using the <PRE> tags to line up fields, don't use any other** HTML tags inside that area. Although the tags won't show up, they'll ruin the effect of lining everything up perfectly.

Listing 11.15 is an example of an entry form that only uses line breaks. The result of this code is displayed in Figure 11.16.

Listing 11.15

PRE1.HTM **Form fields not aligned by default**

```
<HTML>
<HEAD>
<TITLE>Form Layout and Design</TITLE>
</HEAD>
<BODY>
<H1>Using PRE tags</H1>
<FORM>
        Name: <INPUT TYPE="text" NAME="name" SIZE="50"><BR>
        E-Mail: <INPUT TYPE="text" NAME="email" SIZE="50"><BR>
        Street Address: <INPUT TYPE="text" NAME="street1"
    ➡SIZE="30"><BR>
        <INPUT TYPE="text" NAME="street2" SIZE="30"><BR>
        City: <INPUT TYPE="text" NAME="city" SIZE="50"><BR>
        State: <INPUT TYPE="text" NAME="state" SIZE="2"><BR>
        Zip: <INPUT TYPE="text" NAME="zip" SIZE="10">
</FORM>
</BODY>
</HTML>
```

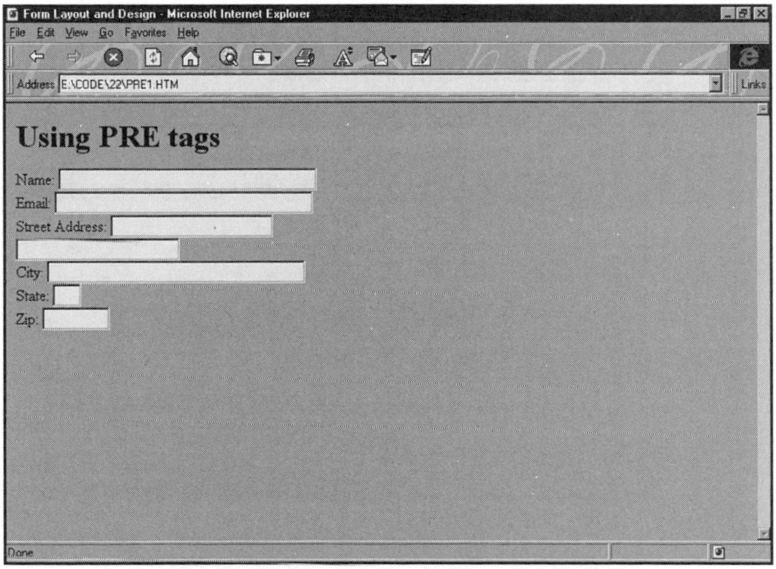

FIG. 11.16

These fields were organized only with line breaks, so they align haphazardly.

If you space things out and use the tags for preformatted text, you can create a very nice looking form. Listing 11.16 is an example of aligning fields by using the <PRE> tag, which produces the layout shown in Figure 11.17.

Listing 11.16

PRE2.HTM   Aligning forms fields with preformatted text

```
<HTML>
<HEAD>
<TITLE>Form Layout and Design</TITLE>
</HEAD>
<BODY>
<H1>Using PRE tags</H1>
<FORM>
      <PRE>
      Name:           <INPUT TYPE="text" NAME="name" SIZE="50">
      E-Mail:         <INPUT TYPE="text" NAME="email"SIZE="50">
      Street Address: <INPUT TYPE="text" NAME="street1" SIZE="30">
                      <INPUT TYPE="text" NAME="street2"SIZE="30">
      City:           <INPUT TYPE="text" NAME="city" SIZE="50">
      State:          <INPUT TYPE="text" NAME="state" SIZE="2">
      Zip:            <INPUT TYPE="text" NAME="zip" SIZE="10">
      </PRE>
</FORM>
</BODY>
</HTML>
```

CAUTION **Make sure you keep the size of the fields smaller than the general** browser, or your lines will wrap off the screen. If the input fields have to be large, you can use a line break to put it on its own line.

FIG. 11.17
The layout of the preformatted text is organized and easy to follow.

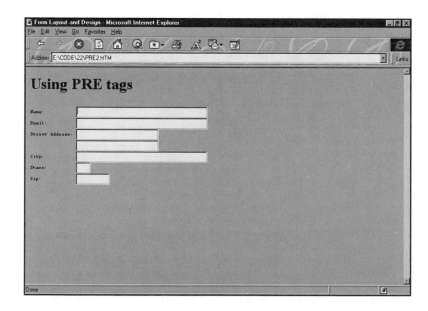

Q&A *When I set up the preformatted text, it doesn't come out aligned in my HTML document! Why doesn't it match up?*

In some text editors, the width of each letter on the screen isn't the same. If you're creating HTML documents with a text editor or word processor, make sure you use a monospaced font such as Courier New (each character, including spaces, takes up exactly the same amount of space). That should solve the problem.

Using HTML tables to line up forms

Another way to line up form fields is to place them in an HTML table. This can produce an effect similar to using preformatted text but, because you are using regular HTML rather than preformatted text, you can also include other HTML constructs within the form. So, by using a table rather than preformatted text to align your form, you're also able to include images, hypertext links, or other HTML elements as part of the form.

Listing 11.17 is an example of the entry form shown in Figures 11.16 and 11.17, formatted using an HTML table. The result of this code is displayed in Figure 11.18.

Listing 11.17

TABLE.HTM   Aligning forms fields with tables

```
<HTML>
<HEAD>
<TITLE>Form Layout and Design</TITLE>
</HEAD>
<BODY>
<H1>Using HTML Tables</H1>
<FORM>
      <TABLE>
            <TR><TD>Name:</TD><TD><INPUT TYPE="text"
            NAME="name" SIZE="50"></TD></TR>
            <TR><TD>E-Mail:</TD><TD><INPUT TYPE="text"
            NAME="email" SIZE="50"></TD></TR>
            <TR><TD>Street Address:</TD><TD><INPUT TYPE="text"
            NAME="street1" SIZE="30"></TD></TR>
            <TR><TD></TD><TD><INPUT TYPE="text" NAME="street2"
            SIZE="30"></TD></TR>
            <TR><TD>City:</TD><TD><INPUT TYPE="text"
            ➥NAME="city"
```

continues

Listing 11.17

Continued

```
                    SIZE="50"></TD></TR>
                    <TR><TD>State:</TD><TD><INPUT TYPE="text" NAME="state"
                    SIZE="2"></TD></TR>
                    <TR><TD>Zip:</TD><TD><INPUT TYPE="text" NAME="zip"
                    SIZE="10"></TD></TR>
            </TABLE>
        </FORM>
        </BODY>
        </HTML>
```

FIG. 11.18
HTML tables text can
be combined with
forms to enable the
aligning of different
form fields.

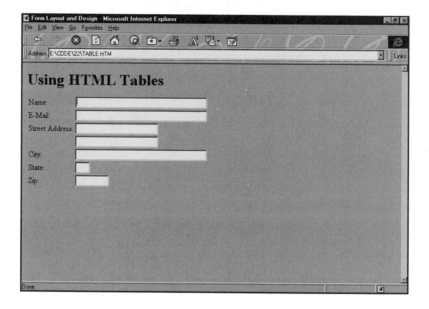

Using paragraph marks to separate form sections

If you have a large form with different sections, it's handy to separate those
sections. The paragraph container tag, `<P>...</P>`, provides a way of adding
some space without making the delineation so hard that it appears to be
another form. Note that Web browsers also allow you to use the `<P>` opening
tag without the `</P>` closing tag to give identical results.

For example, a simple comment form might have places for a name and an e-
mail address, but these might not be a required part of the form. In this case,
separate the comment part of the form from the area that's optional. It's also
possible to make it more obvious by simply making some comments in the

form, such as a small heading titled Optional. A simple comment form with optional Name and E-Mail fields can have the code shown in Listing 11.18.

Listing 11.18

P.HTM **Using paragraphs to improve spacing**

```
<HTML>
<HEAD>
<TITLE>Form Layout and Design</TITLE>
</HEAD>
<BODY>
<H1>Using &lt;P&gt; tags</H1>
<FORM>
        <PRE>
        <I><B>Optional:</B></I>
        Name:   <INPUT TYPE="text" NAME="name" SIZE="50">
        E-Mail: <INPUT TYPE="text" NAME="email" SIZE="50">
        </PRE>
        <P>
        Your comments:<BR>
        <TEXTAREA ROWS="6" COLS="70"></TEXTAREA>
</FORM>
</BODY>
</HTML>
```

Listing 11.18, using both <PRE> tags and line break tags, produces the layout shown in Figure 11.19. A similar effect can be achieved by using a table instead of preformatted text.

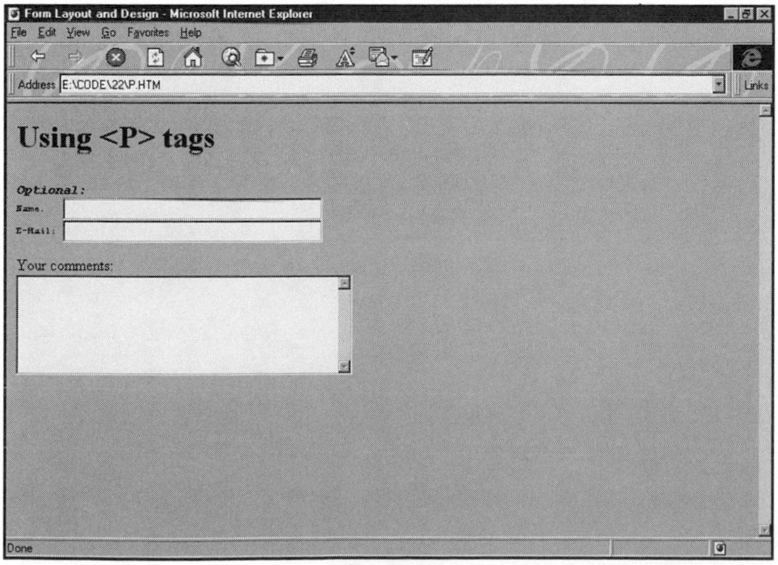

FIG. 11.19
Combining preformatted and wrapped areas can make your form very easy to use.

Using list tags

There are a few occasions when line breaks and paragraph tags can't set up the form exactly as you'd like. At these times, list tags can provide just the right look! The best use of list tags is for the indenting and numbering of text.

Indenting form entries with descriptive lists

On the WWW, it's common to see order forms for merchandise. Finding out the method of payment is a perfect use for descriptive list tags to lay out the choices. Indenting some items more than others makes the options obvious and easy to read.

 NOTE **When you lay out lists, consider indenting the areas in your HTML** documents that will be indented on-screen. This makes it easier to remember to finish with the descriptive list tag, </DL>.

For example, Listing 11.19 shows how to separate a section of credit cards from the rest of the payment methods. The result of this code is shown in Figure 11.20.

Listing 11.19

LIST1.HTM **Organizing forms by using a descriptive list**

```
<HTML>
<HEAD>
<TITLE>Form Layout and Design</TITLE>
</HEAD>
<BODY>
<H1>Descriptive List Tags</H1>
<FORM>
        <DL>
        <DT>How would you like to pay for this?
        <DD><INPUT NAME="pay" TYPE="radio" VALUE="cash"
        ➥CHECKED>Cash
        <DD><INPUT NAME="pay" TYPE="radio" VALUE="check">Check
        <DD><INPUT NAME="pay" TYPE="radio" VALUE="debit">Debit
        ➥Card
            <DL>
            <DT>Credit Card
            <DD><INPUT NAME="pay" TYPE="radio"
            ➥VALUE="mc">Mastercard
```

```
                       <DD><INPUT NAME="pay" TYPE="radio"
                       ➥VALUE="visa">Visa
                       <DD><INPUT NAME="pay" TYPE="radio"
                       ➥VALUE="disc">Discover
                       <DD><INPUT NAME="pay" TYPE="radio"
                       ➥VALUE="ae">American Express
                       </DL>
                  </DL>
          </FORM>
          </BODY>
          </HTML>
```

FIG. 11.20
Descriptive lists make
the breakdown of
choices obvious.

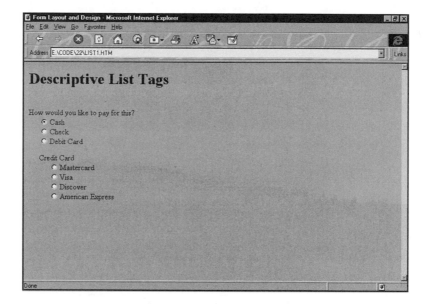

Using ordered lists to number fields

It's easy to display a numbered list if you use the ordered list tag, <OL>. Listing
11.20 uses the <OL> tag to automatically number the fields. The result of this
code is shown in Figure 11.21.

Listing 11.20

LIST2.HTM   **Organizing forms by using an ordered list**

```
<HTML>
<HEAD>
<TITLE>Form Layout and Design</TITLE>
```

continues

Listing 11.20

Continued

```
</HEAD>
<BODY>
<H1>Ordered List Tags</H1>
<FORM>
        What are your three favorite books?
        <OL>
        <LI><INPUT NAME="1st" SIZE="20">
        <LI><INPUT NAME="2nd" SIZE="20">
        <LI><INPUT NAME="3nd" SIZE="20">
        </OL>
</FORM>
</BODY>
</HTML>
```

FIG. 11.21

Using ordered lists, you can reorder fields without retyping all those numbers!

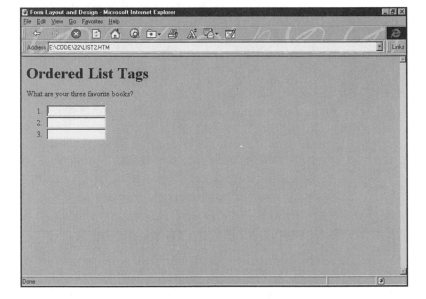

12

Imagemaps

● **In this chapter:**

● **What makes a good graphic for an imagemap?**

● **Create an image and map definition and insert the HTML**

● **Learn about programs you can use to create imagemaps**

A large number of advanced Web pages use *imagemaps* as a sort of graphical menu from which the user chooses a Web page to open. Imagemaps are just pictures on which well-defined areas of the image are linked to other Web pages (or any other Internet resource). Virtually every corporate home page uses an imagemap. Some use an imagemap on the home page as the home page's primary content; others use an imagemap as a toolbar or navigational aid. For example, take a look at Hewlett Packard's Web site: **http://www.hp.com**.

You may think that adding an imagemap to your Web site is a lot of work. Once upon a time, it was a lot of work. Not anymore. Considering the difficulty of everything else you do as a Web master, imagemaps are child's play. They also add a good bit of class to your Web site and so are worth careful consideration. On the other hand, there are a few drawbacks to using imagemaps, so you should carefully consider the issues described in this chapter before doing so.

Introducing imagemaps

Because imagemaps make use of pictures, they let users navigate content-related links in a friendly fashion. The Web uses the first Internet standard (HTML) that allows for the easy display of graphics. This is in sharp contrast to past standards, which were all text-based, such as Gopher, WAIS, and FTP. Although these older standards could transport images; this capability was never designed into them (see Figure 12.1).

 TIP   **In the wide world of HTML, you'll also see imagemaps** referred to as *area maps* or *clickable maps*.

Different parts of an imagemap's graphic point to different URLs. Because the user has to know where these clickable regions are in the imagemap, you'll often find borders around each region, as shown in Figure 12.2. Note these borders are part of the graphic itself, and are not created by the Web server.

You can use two different types of imagemaps: server-side and client-side. Here's how each type of imagemap works:

Server side   The browser sends the coordinates of the mouse pointer to the Web server when the user clicks somewhere on the imagemap. Then, the server looks up the coordinates and determines the region on which the user clicked. Armed with this information, the server looks up the corresponding URL and returns it to the browser. As a result, the browser opens the URL.

FIG. 12.1
Using imagemaps is easier than text links because most folks relate to pictures better than the written word.

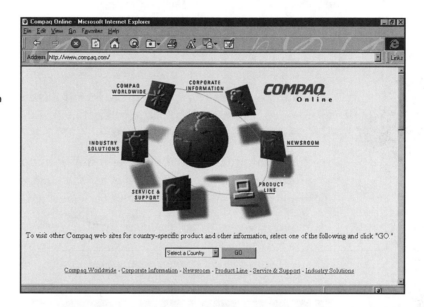

FIG. 12.2
For imagemaps to be useful, the user must be able to easily distinguish each region in the imagemap.

Regions ────

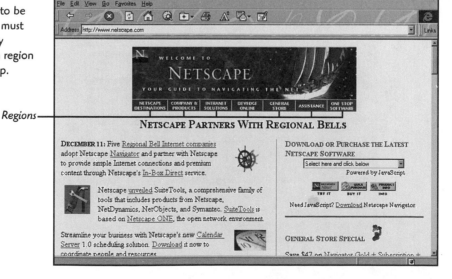

Client side   You define an imagemap's region within the Web page. When the user clicks somewhere on the imagemap, the browser looks up the region in the HTML file, determines the associated URL, and opens that URL. The browser doesn't communicate with the Web server at all.

When to use imagemaps

In many situations, you should consider using imagemaps instead of hypertext links. Here's a short list of some times when using imagemaps is appropriate:

- **When you want to represent links that have a physical relation to each other.** For example, clicking a map of the world is easier than picking from a list of countries.

- **When you want to enable users to go to important points on your site at any time.** You can even make imagemaps a constant staple in every page on your Web site—like a toolbar.

- **When you want to give your Web site a sense of consistency.** Whenever you add new pages to your Web site, you'll probably want to add the navigation imagemap graphic to them (see Figure 12.3).

FIG. 12.3
By using imagemaps as a navigational tool for the user, you make getting around your home page easier.

Imagemap used as a Toolbar —

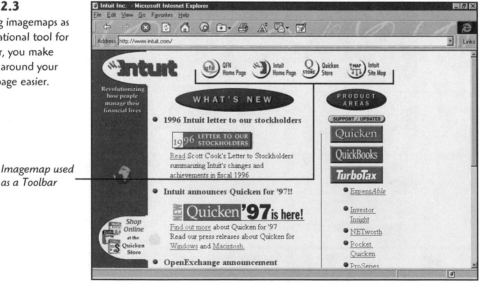

When not to use imagemaps

Although imagemaps might be useful in most situations, sometimes you shouldn't use them. For example:

- **Server-side imagemaps require a Web server capable of handling them properly.** You can get a free copy of Microsoft's Personal Web Server at Microsoft's Web site: **http://www.microsoft.com**.

- **Server-side imagemaps can't be tested without a Web server.** This means that while you're designing your imagemaps, you can't test them easily. You either have to get Web server software loaded on your own computer, or put the imagemap files on your server.

- **You should consider nongraphical browsers when designing your Web pages.** Many people still use text-based browsers when surfing the Web. Still more folks disable images in their browser so they can open Web pages faster. You should provide a textual alternative to your imagemaps as shown in Figure 12.4.

FIG. 12.4
Making textual alternatives for your imagemaps is essential for users with text-based browsers or users who have disabled graphics in their graphical browser.

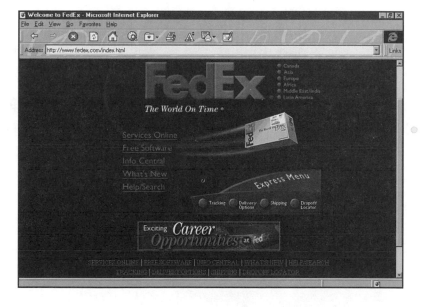

- **If you're concerned about your Web site's performance, you should avoid using imagemaps (or consider using text alternatives).** Because imagemaps can be rather large, they can take awhile to download (particularly if the user has a 14.4K modem). Also, network traffic can sometimes make large graphics take longer than normal to download.

Building client-side imagemaps

Until HTML 3.2, the client-side imagemap was an extension limited to Netscape and Internet Explorer. Now, client-side imagemaps are no longer an extension; they are part of the standard.

Client-side imagemaps are very similar to server-side imagemaps. The only difference is that instead of using an imagemap file and CGI script on the server, you use an imagemap that you store right there in the HTML file. The greatest benefit is in the reduced network traffic. That is, instead of hitting the Web server to look up an URL, the browser handles the imagemap itself.

Defining a client-side imagemap

The HTML format for an imagemap definition contains the same types of information as in NCSA and CERN imagemap definition files, but it uses HTML tags. Here's what the syntax of an imagemap definition in HTML looks like:

```
<MAP NAME="mapname">
<AREA [SHAPE="shape"] COORDS="x,y,..." [HREF="URL"][NOHREF]>
</MAP>
```

 NOTE **Originally, CERN (Conseil Europeen pour la Recherche Nucleaire)** was founded as a research group of European physicists. The group slowly expanded their research into the field of computers. Because they were the ones who first thought of the idea, they rightfully claim the honor of being "the birthplace of the Web." When imagemaps were deemed necessary, CERN developed their format for the image-map definition file. On Web servers that follow the CERN format, you can find files that look like this:

region_type (x1,y1) (x2,y2) ... URL

The horizontal (*x1* and *x2*) and vertical (*y1* and *y2*) coordinates must be in parentheses and separated by a comma. Each pair of coordinates means something different for each region type. The ... specifies additional coordinates, such as for the *poly* region type. Here's an example of a CERN imagemap definition:

```
rect (60,40) (340,280) http://www.rectangle.com/
```

The first wildly popular browser, Mosaic, came from the University of Illinois' National Center for Supercomputing Applications (NCSA). When this group heard about the demand for imagemaps, they came up with their own imagemap definition file format. A typical entry in one of their files would look like this:

```
region_type URL x1,y1 x2,y2 ...
```

Subtle (but significant) differences distinguish the CERN and NCSA formats. The URL for the region type comes before the coordinates with NCSA, not after, like CERN. The coordinates defining the region need to be separated by commas, but they don't need the parentheses around them. Here's an example of an NCSA imagemap definition:

```
rect http://www.rectangle.com/ 60,40 340,280
```

The imagemap definition starts with the <MAP> tag and ends with the </MAP> tag. It's a container. So that you can refer to the imagemap definition later in the IMG, you give it a name by using the NAME attribute.

You define each region, or hot spot, by using the AREA tag. The coordinate system starts from the upper-left corner of the imagemap. Table 12.1 describes each of the AREA tag's attributes:

Table 12.1   The *AREA* tag's attributes

Attribute	Description
SHAPE	Defines the shape of the region. Just like the server-side, image map definition files, you can use rect, poly, circle, or default. If this attribute is missing, the browser assumes rect. When two regions overlap, the browser uses the first one in the list.
COORDS	Defines a comma-separated list of coordinates. Note that there is a comma between each set of coordinates.
HREF	Defines the URL of the Internet resource to which the region is linked. All relative links are relative to the document containing the MAP tag, not the one containing the USEMAP attribute, if different. If you use a BASE tag in the HTML file containing the MAP tag, that URL is used.
NOHREF	Specifies the region is a dead area within the imagemap. That is, that area is not linked to any Internet resource. Note that HREF and NOHREF are mutually exclusive.

Listing 12.1 shows you a complete example of an imagemap definition in HTML. Figure 12.5 shows the Web page created by this HTML code.

Listing 12.1

A client-side imagemap

```
<MAP NAME=mymap>
<AREA SHAPE=RECT COORDS="0,0,100,100" HREF=item1.html>
<AREA SHAPE=RECT COORDS="101,0,200,100" HREF=item2.html>
<AREA SHAPE=RECT COORDS="201,0,300,100" HREF=item3.html>
</MAP>
<IMG SRC=mymap.gif USEMAP=#mymap>
```

FIG. 12.5
The client-side imagemap produced by the example HTML code.

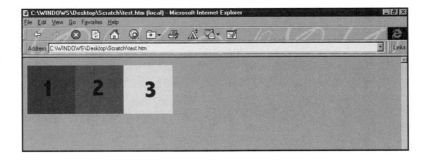

Referencing the client-side imagemap definition

The final line of the previous example shows how to reference an imagemap after it's built:

```
<IMG SRC=mymap.gif USEMAP=#mymap>
```

This IMG tag loads the image called MYMAP.GIF. USEMAP is a new HTML 3.2 attribute that specifies the name of the imagemap definition that you define elsewhere in the HTML file using the MAP tag.

Working with mapping programs

The easy way to create imagemap definition files is to use one of the many programs that will create the file for you. These programs are called *mapping tools*, and they let you draw various imagemap region types on top of a specified image.

Many map-editing programs are available for both Windows and the Macintosh. Generally speaking, most map-editing programs have the same basic features. They all support the three basic geometric region types: rect, poly, and circle. Some of the more advanced map-editing programs support the point- and default-region types. The only thing you should look for in imagemap-editing programs is how the user interface feels. Because such a wide variety is available, if one doesn't feel right to you, you don't have to use it.

 TIP **Even though a map-editing program might not support every** region type, you can still add other region types by editing the imagemap definition file after you have saved it.

Working with Mapedit

Mapedit is a shareware, no-frills, map-editing program for Windows 95 and UNIX. You can get Mapedit from **http://www.boutell.com/mapedit**. It was written by Thomas Boutell, maintainer of the FAQ (frequently asked questions) for the World Wide Web. This program allows you to create imagemap definition files in either CERN or NCSA format. Mapedit provides support for the basic geometric shapes, although the point-region type isn't supported.

Navigating Mapedit is pretty straightforward. To create a new imagemap definition file for your imagemap graphic, simply choose File and then choose Open/Create. Mapedit's Open dialog box then appears. You must have an existing imagemap graphic, which you can find by using the Browse button under the Image Filename heading. Mapedit supports GIF, JPEG, and the little-used PNG (Portable Network Graphics) image format for imagemap graphics.

 NOTE **PNG (Portable Network Graphics) is a new graphics file format** that's similar to GIF. It's lossless, so you don't lose colors when it's compressed, and portable across multiple platforms. The biggest advantage of PNG over GIF is that you're not stepping on anyone's patents when you use it. As well, PNG provides many technological benefits, such as interlaced images that appear on the screen quicker than GIF's interlaced images. Many browsers, including Internet Explorer, don't yet support PNG.

To edit an existing imagemap definition file, you can use the Browse button under the Map or HTML File heading (see Figure 12.6). To create a new imagemap definition file, simply type in the file name you want to use. Be sure to also specify whether you want a CERN or NCSA imagemap definition file, using the appropriate radio buttons. Mapedit then asks you to confirm that you want to create a new imagemap.

FIG. 12.6

When you want to create or edit an imagemap file with Mapedit, you have to fill in the information for this dialog box.

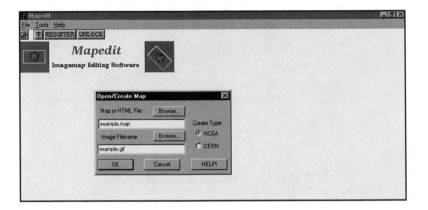

After you click the OK button, the shareware notification appears. After the graphic is loaded, the shareware dialog box is dismissed, and the whole image is loaded into Mapedit. If the image is bigger than the current screen resolution, you can use the scroll bars to see different parts of the picture.

 NOTE **If the colors on the imagemap graphic you specified look a little** weird, don't worry. Mapedit isn't concerned with the way the picture looks; it's more concerned with the imagemap region types.

You can create any number of imagemap region types by choosing options from the Tools menu. You can create circle-, polygon-, or rectangle-region types. For people accustomed to many paint programs, or other imagemap creation programs, the region-creation interface is counterintuitive (see Table 12.2). Generally speaking, you can create shapes in other programs by clicking and holding the right mouse button, dragging the shape, and then releasing the mouse button. Unfortunately, in Mapedit, it's a matter of clicking and releasing the mouse button, dragging the shape, then reclicking and rereleasing the mouse button. After you have created a region type on the imagemap graphic, you can't delete it by using Mapedit.

Table 12.2 Creating region types by using Mapedit

Region type	How to create it
Circle	Click the left mouse button to specify the center of the desired circle. Use the mouse to specify the size of the circle. Click the right mouse button when the circle is the desired size.
Rectangle	Click the left mouse button to specify one corner of the rectangle. Use the mouse to specify the size of the rectangle. Click the right mouse button to specify the diagonally opposite corner of the first corner.
Polygon	Click the left mouse button to specify a corner of the polygon. Move the mouse to the next corner you want to specify. Repeat these steps for each corner of the polygon. When you're back to the first corner, click the right mouse button.

CAUTION   **Mapedit works in very distinct "modes." That is, whatever option** you last selected from the <u>T</u>ools menu is still active. If, for example, you just specified an URL for a rectangle–region type, the next region type you'll create is a rectangle. If you just selected the Test+Edit menu item, you remain in Test+Edit mode until you specify a region type.

After you create a region type, the Object URL window opens (see Figure 12.7). Simply type in the URL to associate with the newly created region. You can define the default URL for the entire image-map graphic by choosing <u>F</u>ile and then <u>E</u>dit Default URL.

FIG. 12.7
After you create a region type, Mapedit asks for the URL to which that region should refer.

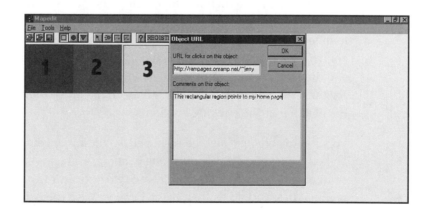

If you can't see the outline of the region type as you're creating it, don't worry. Mapedit doesn't care about the appearance of the image in its window. To change the color of the outlines for each region type, choose File and then Edit Hotspot Color.

TIP **If you make a mistake in the location of the region type, you can** cancel its creation in two ways. You can either press Escape while you're specifying the size of the region, or you can click the Cancel button in the Object URL dialog box.

Using Mapedit, you can test the regions you've created. You choose Tools and then Test+Edit. When you press the left mouse button while moving the mouse over an imagemap, the URL for the corresponding region shows up. This testing capability is a function of Mapedit, and doesn't require a Web browser or server to use.

You can save your current imagemap definition file by choosing File and then either Save or Save As.

NOTE **Mapedit doesn't force any file-name extensions on you. As a** result, when you're creating a new image-map definition file, you need to specify the extension yourself. Most imagemap servers look for a file with the MAP extension.

Mapedit also allows you to easily change the position of hotspot regions. To move any clickable region, simply select the Tools menu heading, followed by the Move menu item. Next click the region you want to move, and a number of "control points" will show up. By clicking and dragging any of the control points that bound the region, you can reshape or resize it. If you click and drag the control point in the middle of the region, you'll move the entire region itself. Since Mapedit will still be in the Move mode, you can fine tune the position of the clickable region.

Polygon regions can also be reshaped by adding or removing points in Mapedit. Just click the Tools menu heading, and choose either the Add Points or Remove Points menu items. These two options only work on polygon region types, and do as their name implies. With the Add Points option, click the polygon you want to add a point to, then put your mouse on roughly where you want the new point to appear. Similarly, for Remove Points, you click the polygon from which you want to remove a point, then select the point to remove.

Mapedit can also be used to create client-side imagemaps. Instead of loading in a MAP file, you specify an HTML file. Mapedit will look for any HTML that includes a graphic. Whatever images are found, it'll present a dialog box with the pictures that were found (see Figure 12.8). Select the picture you want to create a client-side imagemap for, and click the OK button. The file name for the image is automatically filled in Mapedit's Select Inline Image dialog box. Once you click the OK button, you'll be taken into Mapedit as usual. After you've created all the shapes you want, saving the changes will cause the HTML file to be updated.

FIG. 12.8
To create client-side imagemaps, just select the picture you want to make an imagemap for.

Using WebMap

WebMap, a capable Macintosh map-editing program, is currently free, until it's released commercially. You can get WebMap from **http://www.city.net/cnx/software/webmap.html**. It lets you create all the geometric region types from rectangles to circles and ellipses to polygons to points. It can create imagemap definition files for CERN, NCSA, or MacHTTP Web servers. It also enables you to easily move and change regions that have already been defined.

With this user-friendly program, you can easily create imagemap definition files. Simply choose File and then New. Then, using the Mac file selector, find the location of your imagemap graphic. This picture can be in either GIF or PICT graphics formats.

You can create as many imagemap region types as you want by using the floating toolbox next to the WebMap window. The interface is similar to drawing programs (see Table 12.3). The only difference between the circle- and ellipse-region type is the circle has a constant radius. If you make a mistake in either the placement, size, or mere existence of a region type, you can fix it.

Table 12.3 Creating region types by using WebMap

Region type	How to create it
Circle	Click and hold the mouse button to specify a corner of the square to contain the circle. Hold down the mouse button and move the mouse to specify the size of the circle. Release the mouse button when the circle is the desired size.
Ellipse	Click and hold the mouse button to indicate a corner of the square in which the ellipse will reside. While holding down the mouse button, move the mouse to size the ellipse. Let go of the mouse button when the ellipse is the size and shape you want.
Rectangle	Click and hold the mouse button to indicate a corner of the rectangle. Release the mouse button when the rectangle is the size you want.
Polygon	Click the mouse button to specify a corner of the polygon. Release the mouse button. Move the mouse pointer to the next corner you want to indicate. Repeat these steps for each corner of the polygon. After you specify the last corner, move the mouse pointer close to the first vertex and then click the mouse button.

CAUTION **With WebMap, you can't create a smaller region on top of a larger** one. However, you can easily place larger region types on top of smaller ones. As a result, you have to plan carefully which regions you place where. You should place the smaller region types first and then work your way up to the largest regions.

After you've created all the regions you want, you can save the image-map definition file by choosing File and then Save. This saves the image-map definition file with an .m extension, which is the default extension that MacHTTP looks for in an imagemap definition file. WebMap also automatically saves the file in MacHTTP's custom format, making it unusable for the prevalent Web servers around. To create an imagemap definition file that other Web servers can use, choose File, Export As Text. You can specify to create either a CERN- or NCSA-compatible file.

CAUTION **WebMap assumes your imagemap definition file has the same** name as the graphic. When you're editing an existing imagemap definition file, WebMap looks for an .m file based on the imagemap graphic's name. You therefore can't simply rename one of the files; you have to rename both of them. Otherwise, WebMap cannot see the other and will assume you're creating a new imagemap definition file.

TIP **Sometimes the Undo feature doesn't work with WebMap. If** you've accidentally created a region and Undo doesn't work, just clear the region. Go to the toolbox and select the Arrow icon. Then use the mouse to select the region you created by accident. Next, choose Edit and then Clear.

Netscape/Microsoft Extensions

● In this chapter:

● **The Browser Wars**

● **The W3C and the HTML "standard"**

● **HTML tags that work exclusively with Netscape Navigator and Microsoft Internet Explorer**

Have you heard about the war? It's going on right now. It's not in Germany, or Korea, or Vietnam this time. It's not about land, or dictators, or personal freedoms. This is a marketing war over who has the best Web browser. It's taking place in cyberspace, and the victor will gain control of your desktop and the way the Internet looks to you for years to come—or until something else better comes along.

The participants are fighting tooth and nail yet shedding little blood. Netscape claims theirs is faster. Microsoft denies that. Microsoft is planning to integrate theirs into their operating system. Netscape screams "anti-trust!"

Both want you on their side. Who will you choose? Do you have to choose?

The Browser Wars

Currently, Microsoft and Netscape are battling, release after release, for control of the Internet. Neither company really is selling very many browsers (Internet Explorer is free and Navigator is shareware, which relatively few people are actually registering and paying for). Nevertheless, the company that commands the browser market will be able to enjoy a corresponding increase in sales of their server product. And that's just a bonus. Many people believe that the winner of the browser wars will be able to dictate how the Internet will evolve.

The real prize is the support of the Webmasters. Webmasters, like many technical people, continually try to be on the cutting edge. It's a source of pride to them to have the latest and greatest hardware and software. Since the Web is the most progressive technology available to the most people, it's reasonable to believe that Webmasters will want to have the most current configurations (hardware and software both) available.

Some Webmasters express their loyalty to the companies that supply their hardware and software by publicly aligning themselves and their site with their favorite product by putting a logo on their own page. You may have seen pages declaring that a Web site is powered by a Digital Alpha server, or more commonly, that a Web site is "Designed for Netscape" or "Designed for Internet Explorer" (see Figures 13.1 and 13.2).

FIG. 13.1
Some Webmasters design for Netscape Navigator.

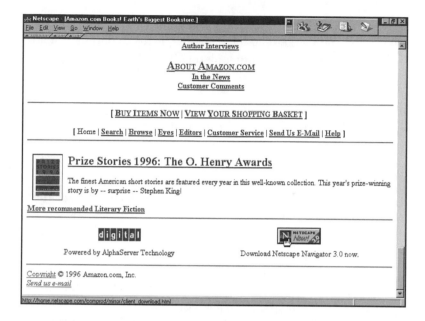

FIG. 13.2
Some Webmasters design for Internet Explorer.

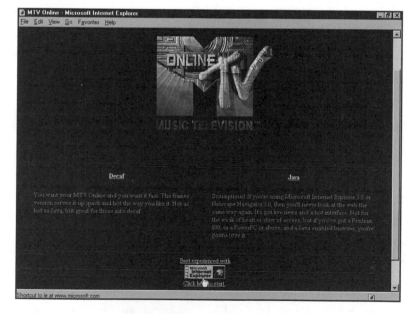

Are differences good?

I hear you asking, "So what is the difference between Microsoft Internet Explorer and Netscape Navigator?"

Well, Internet Explorer has a snazzier interface and is free. Navigator has a much larger market share and, in my experience, loads pages slightly faster. All in all, they both look relatively the same. They are both pretty user-friendly.

Both browsers support the HTML 3.2 standard, but above and beyond that, both Microsoft and Netscape have enabled their browsers to recognize tags that are not recognized by that standard—and not recognized by the other browser.

 NOTE **The significant differences that will determine who ultimately wins** the Browser Wars are not found in how you interact with the browser but in how the browser interacts with your favorite Web pages. All in all, people will use the browser that the Webmasters of their favorite sites recommend, not the browser that may be most user-friendly or has the most bells and whistles. After all, if you can't see the Web page correctly with a certain browser, who'll want to use it?

Both Microsoft and Netscape add features to their browser that other browsers don't recognize. So, when you don't use Navigator to look at a site that is "Designed for Netscape," it may not look the way the Webmaster intends it to look. It may not, for example, have newspaper-style columns displayed correctly. And when you fail to use Internet Explorer to look at a site that is "Designed for Internet Explorer," it may not show you a marquee scrolling across your page.

Both companies are recruiting your favorite Web sites to fight the battle on their side. Table 13.1 shows where some sites have enlisted there support.

Table 13.1 Where the sites are

Microsoft Internet Explorer	Netscape Navigator
ESPN Sportszone (**www.sportszone.com**)	Amazon Booksellers (**www.amazon.com**)
Mr. Showbiz (**www.mrshowbiz.com**)	The Pointcast Network (**www.pointcast.com**)
MTV (**www.mtv.com**)	Clinique Cosmetics (**www.clinque.com**)
Dell Computers (**www.dell.com**)	Express—Women's Clothing (**express.style.com**)
Mirsky's Worst of the Web (**www.mirsky.com**)	Warner Brothers (**www.warnerbrothers.com**)

Microsoft Internet Explorer	Netscape Navigator
Gateway 2000 Computers (**www.gw2k.com**)	Babylon 5 (**www.babylon5.com**)
Webcrawler WWW Search Engine (**webcrawler.com**)	Merrill Lynch Financial Services (**www.ml.com**)

All this may lead you to believe there are only two browsers to be had. This is not completely true, although Internet Explorer and Navigator are by far the two most well known and prevalently used browsers on the market.

Others are out there, waiting, nay, *begging* to be downloaded. Table 13.2 is a sampling of other, less popular Web browsers.

Table 13.2 A few other sites

Browser Name	URL	Notes
Lynx	**http://lynx.browser.org/**	Text-only, telnet-based browser
NCSA Mosaic	**http://www. ncsa.uiuc.edu/SDG/ Software/Mosaic/**	The forerunner of all advanced Web browsers
Arena	**http://www.w3.org/pub/WWW/Arena/**	Developed by W3C (the same organization that approves the HTML standards)
Opera	**http://traviata.nta.no/opera.htm**	It's the fastest graphical browser around

But let me stress that although these browsers are useful to some people, in hard marketing percentages, they are hardly significant. And not all of them even keep up with the current HTML standard. For example, NCSA Mosaic doesn't support nested tables. Horrors!

Joining the fracas

There was a time when office workers would literally get into fistfights over which was the "perfect" word-processor. Should the company standardize on WordPerfect or WordStar? And when mice were uncommonly used on IBM-compatible PCs, my father would tell me: "You'll take my Mac away from me when you pry my cold, dead fingers off my mouse." Although important at the time, their significance pales when put next to the importance of the Browser Wars.

So should you join the Browser Wars? Should you once again take that plunge? Are you afraid? Did you go to all the trouble to learn and love WordStar just to see the IS department switch you to WordPerfect the next year? What if you choose wrong?

As a Web surfer, you really don't have to make that choice. You can run both browsers on your Windows 3.x or Windows 95 machine very comfortably. Each will occasionally try to persuade you to make it the default browser, but most times, it really doesn't matter which one you award that title.

However, if you are a Webmaster, your choice is critical. If you choose to design especially for Netscape or especially for Internet Explorer, you are enlisting as a foot soldier in their battalion. When people who like your site see the choice that you have made, they will be more likely to agree with you and take your side by using that browser. The more popular your site becomes, the more people you will be recruiting. Of course, some people promote both (see Figure 13.3).

FIG. 13.3
Some Webmasters, like those of the Illini Student Union at the University of Illinois, like to straddle the fence.

As a Webmaster, your mission should be to serve as many Web surfers as possible. Does that mean you have to write your pages for the lowest common denominator? Make your graphics so small that your pages can be loaded quickly even by the last person on Earth actively using a 9600 baud modem? Eschew tables and imagemaps because someone might be trying to load your page with a browser that can't handle them? Limit your background choices to 16 colors because more than a few folks can't afford a SuperVGA video card?

Well, maybe everyone doesn't have to go that far. You should first profile your customer. Are you an inner-city library that serves a largely poor clientele mostly from the text-only, donated PCs in your reading room? Then maybe you should limit your graphics and shy away from the cutting edge. On the other hand, are you a corporate intranet running on high-speed ethernet and you control the choice of browser? Then, by all means, choose your army, install your browsers, and write especially for it.

However, there is a path that leads away from the battle. And this may be the wisest choice of all. You can stick to the letter of the current HTML standard. You will be bypassing some of the "cooler" capabilities of the advanced browsers, but in the end, you will be able to reach many more people, take no chances at alienating any of them, and still be able to design pages that are creative, informative, and pleasing to the eye.

The HTML "standard" and the W3C

Standard. You've heard that mentioned a couple of times already. On the battlefield, a standard is an army's flag, and it is raised to inspire that army on to victory. In peacetime, it is a set of rules to which others are compelled to conform. When talking about HTML, do either of these definitions apply?

Well, to tell you the truth, they both apply to the HTML situation. There really are three "standards," and they are very similar. There is the W3C standard, the Microsoft standard, and the Netscape standard.

The W3C (The World Wide Web Consortium) has approved HTML standard 3.2. This is equivalent to saying that they have met to rewrite the rules of how to write a Web page. They may add tags, and they may recommend changes to the way current tags are used. They may also recommend that Webmasters not use certain older tags anymore. So far, they have been very careful about not dropping tags from the standard, remaining backwards compatible.

The W3C defines itself as "an international industry consortium, jointly hosted by the Massachusetts Institute of Technology Laboratory for Computer Science [MIT/LCS] in the United States; the Institut National de Recherche en Informatique et en Automatique [INRIA] in Europe; and the Keio University Shonan Fujisawa Campus in Asia.

All of the major Internet players are members. The membership includes Adobe, Microsoft, Netscape, Apple, IBM, Pointcast, Spyglass, CompuServe, and The Hong Kong Jockey Club.

TIP   **You can find out exactly what the W3C is currently considering by** looking at **www.w3.org**. Also, the full list of member organizations is at **www.w3.org/pub/WWW/Consortium/Member/List.html**.

You can imagine the politics of these standards meetings. Microsoft and Netscape both want certain tags to be included in the standard because they both have visions for the future of the Internet. These visions certainly include their browser at the center of the Internet. However, as in most committees, everyone must compromise a little. Microsoft doesn't always get what it wants and neither does Netscape.

A standard is "a set of rules to which others are compelled to conform." Well, by that you would think that Microsoft and Netscape would then go back to the drawing board and write their new browsers not for their proposed standards but for the standards that the W3C has approved, right? Wrong.

Microsoft and Netscape, due to sheer dominance of the market, have successfully been able to take that W3C standard, implement it fully, but then add on their own tags. They've come up with the Microsoft standard and the Netscape standard that they are actively trying to convince the W3C to include in future HTML standards. These are the flags that these respective armies rally around and are commonly referred to as "extensions to the HTML standard." Critics of this practice have derisively called the extra tags "Microsoftisms" and "Netscapisms."

Netscape extensions

Nevertheless, if you make a choice to implement some or all of these tags, you will need to know what they are and what they do. Let's start with Netscape.

Blink

Blinking text on a page is probably the most annoying thing that I've ever come across on the Web. First it's there; then it isn't. Then it is; then it isn't.

Stylistically, it's not pleasing to any design, either. And it's a Netscape invention. Yuck.

```
<H1><CENTER><ALIGN="CENTER"><BLINK>This </BLINK>is the
➥Headline of My Page!</CENTER></H1>
```

Newspaper-style columns

Netscape has added a nice tag that allows you to show newspaper-style columns on a Web page. To use it, you should use the following HTML:

```
<MULTICOLS COLS=2 GUTTER=20 WIDTH=800>
This would be where you would put your text and graphics.
</MULTICOLS>
```

There are three attributes that you can use with the MULTICOLS tag. Those are COLS, GUTTER, and WIDTH.

COLS is the number of columns you want to have (see Figure 13.4).

GUTTER defines the amount of white space in pixels that you want between your columns.

WIDTH defines the total width in pixels of your browser screen.

FIG. 13.4
Columns can be used to give a newspaper-style feel to your Web page.

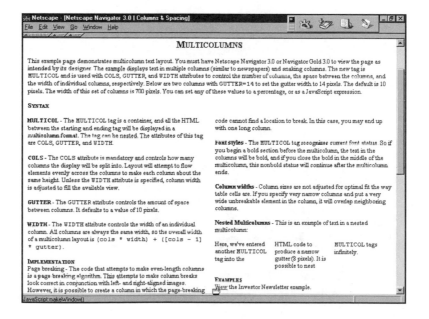

Whitespace

I just hate when I can't control how much space goes between words and lines. Since HTML ignores extra spaces, tab characters, carriage returns, and multiple </P> tags put in a row, it's practically impossible to really control whitespace on a Web page. Sure, to control vertical spacing you could use multiple <BR> tags, but what if I wanted a half line, instead of a full one? For horizontal spacing, I could use a <PRE> tag, but that makes my font take that horrible typewriter quality.

Now Netscape has introduced the <SPACER> container tag to help control both horizontal and vertical spacing. For example,

```
The spacer tag can put whitespace in the
<SPACER TYPE-"HORIZONTAL" SIZE="75">middle of a line.<P>
It can also control how much space until
<SPACER TYPE="VERTICAL" SIZE="100">the next line starts.<P>
```

It also has a more powerful value for the TYPE attribute. You can use TYPE="BLOCK" to create a rectangle or square of whitespace, such as the following:

```
<SPACER TYPE="BLOCK" HEIGHT="50" WIDTH="30" ALIGN="LEFT">
```

Embedding technologies

With Netscape, you can use plug-in technologies to turn Navigator into a hotbed of multimedia. Built right in to the browser is support for LiveAudio (which can play WAV, AU, AIFF, and MIDI sound formats), Live3D (VRML), LiveVideo (AVI movies), and QuickTime (MOV files that include text and MIDI sound).

All you need to do to incorporate any of these into your Web pages is to use the <EMBED> tag.

 NOTE Although *<EMBED>* is a Netscape extension, Internet Explorer supports it for most of these technologies through ActiveX controls.

Microsoft extensions

Let's face it. Internet Explorer 2.0 was a sad excuse for a browser. It had support for practically nothing. But when looking at IE 3, you realize that it's incredible what Microsoft can do when it really puts its money and resources behind the cause. Not only did IE 3 propel Microsoft into the forefront of the Internet browser competition, but it made the company into a major player in the HTML standards decisions. Yet, they still didn't get everything they wanted. So these are some of the tags that Internet Explorer supports that aren't in the current HTML standards.

TIP **A great place to learn about HTML is the Microsoft Site Builder** Workshop at **www.microsoft.com/workshop**. Make sure you visit the section especially for Web authors—**www.microsoft.com/workshop/ author/**.

Background music

Microsoft allows you to embed background music right into your pages with a simple tag <BGSOUND>. <BGSOUND> takes the attribute LOOP to determine how many times your sound file will play. Your sound file can be a WAV, AU, or MIDI file. An example of this is the following:

honkyTonk. MID

```
<BGSOUND SRC="chimes.wav" LOOP=5>My, aren't those
pretty chimes playing five times in a row?
```

CAUTION **Sound files can be rather large, so make sure you don't use files** that will slow down your users dialing in from modem connections.

TIP **MIDI files can be used as background sounds, which is advanta-** geous because they can be much smaller than other sound files.

Fixed backgrounds

This is the same as a normal background, except when your viewers scroll down the screen, it doesn't move with them. This has been called the "watermark" background because of its similarity to the watermark that some companies have on their letterhead.

Just add the attribute BGPROPERTIES=FIXED to your BODY tag:

```
<BODY BACKGROUND="mypattern.gif" BGPROPERTIES=FIXED>
```

Marquees

Microsoft has also included a container tag called MARQUEE that allows you to animate a line of text. The text in the MARQUEE tag will scroll in the direction of your choice. It takes the attributes BEHAVIOR, DIRECTION, SCROLLDELAY, and SCROLLAMOUNT to determine specifically how you will see the marquee. For example,

```
<MARQUEE BEHAVIOR=SCROLL DIRECTION=LEFT SCROLLDELAY=100
SCROLLAMOUNT=40>Now we all want to use Microsoft
Internet Explorer because of this cool scrolling
marquee, right?</MARQUEE>
```

When you use this tag, text will be scrolling from the right to the left, as specified by BEHAVIOR and DIRECTION. SCROLLAMOUNT and SCROLLDELAY specify that the text moves 40 pixels after a delay of 100 milliseconds.

AVI video

Microsoft has made embedding AVI video into your Web pages rather easy by adding an attribute to the <IMG> tag, as follows:

```
<IMG DYNSRC="VIDEO.AVI">
```

If you want the user to get play, pause, forward, and other buttons so that they can watch the video over and over again, modify your tag as follows:

```
<IMG DYNSRC="VIDEO.AVI" CONTROLS>
```

And if you want to provide a still image for those viewers that still aren't using Internet Explorer to view your site:

```
<IMG DYNSRC="VIDEO.AVI" SRC="STILLPHOTO.JPG CONTROLS">
```

CAUTION **If you thought I was being overly careful when warning you about** using large sound files in your Web pages, you should really pay attention now. Video files are almost always huge and may take forever and a day to download. Unless you expect everyone to be logging on to your site from a fast ethernet connection, I'd be real careful about alienating my viewers coming in from modem connections.

Style Sheets

Microsoft has taken the lead in bringing a resolution to the W3C Standards committee for Cascading Style Sheets (CSS1). Style Sheets will allow the author to contol properties such as margins, fonts, and colors from within a Web page or from an external document. Internet Explorer currently supports Cascading Style Sheets.

The *<OBJECT>* tag

The <OBJECT> tag is a container tag used by authors to implement ActiveX Controls into a Web page. It merely gives the ActiveX Control a name and points to URLs where the actual ActiveX code resides.

14

Graphics

Without graphics, the World Wide Web would simply be just a souped up version of Gopher. But thanks to its support for graphics as part of documents, the Web quickly grew to become one of the top sources of Internet traffic.

The same could be said about any document, whether in print or published electronically. Without graphics, the document is flat, stagnant, and less interesting. Thus, a properly placed graphic in a document does two things: it makes the document more visually appealing and, more importantly, it conveys one of the document's critical ideas.

However, it's possible to reduce a document's impact by using graphics inappropriately. You've probably seen your share of Web pages with distracting animated GIFs, cluttered background images, and graphics that are just plain overused. As you plan your documents, make sure you have a proper reason for using each graphic. Whatever you do, don't throw in graphics just for their own sake!

This chapter examines some of the specifics behind Internet graphics. After a review of the different storage formats available, you'll also learn how to make your images bandwidth-friendly, how to use scanned images in your documents, and how to use several popular graphics software tools.

How graphic information is stored

When you see a graphic on your computer screen, what you're really seeing is a collection of colored screen pixels that, taken together, produce a meaningful image. An image file, therefore, has to contain information on how to reproduce that collection of pixels on-screen. This is accomplished by describing the pixels' properties mathematically and storing these descriptions in the file.

The catch in this situation is that there's not a unique way to mathematically describe image data. Given time, you can come up with your own way and, thus, your own storage format. Because you can express image data many ways, there are correspondingly many image file formats—on the order of several dozen!

Fortunately, each of these formats can be classified as one type or another: a bitmapped graphic or a vector graphic. The next two sections examine the specifics of each type.

Bitmapped graphics

With a bitmapped graphic, information about each pixel is stored as sequence of bits in the file. Depending on the storage formats, these bits could represent colors, saturation levels, brightness, or some other visual characteristic of the pixel. What's important is that each sequence of bits tells the computer how to paint the pixel on the screen.

Bitmaps are something of a natural format because they store information in exactly the same way the computer displays it on a monitor. This means the program that renders the image has to do very little processing. It just reads in the data and passes that information along to the screen drivers which, in turn, display the pixels.

 NOTE   **The above is not entirely true if the bitmapped image is compressed.** Compression reduces the size of an image file by reducing the amount of information needed to replicate the image. A compressed file will download more quickly, owing to its smaller size, but it needs to be decompressed before the image can be displayed. This decompression step means additional processing effort.

Vector graphics

A vector graphic file contains mathematical information that is used to redraw the image on-screen. When a computer displays a vector image file, it reads in the redrawing instructions and follows them. This might sound like a lot of unnecessary processing, but there is an important advantage to this approach: You can rescale the image to new sizes without loss of resolution because there's no fixed relationship between how its defined in the file and the pixel-by-pixel image on the screen. When you try to resize a bitmapped file, you often get a loss of resolution that detracts from the image.

Vector graphic formats are typically used for images with distinct geometric shapes. Computer Aided Design (CAD) drawings are examples of this type of image.

NOTE **Some file formats combine the best of both bitmapped and vector** graphics into what's called a metafile format. Windows metafiles (.WMF) are frequently used to store clip-art images that need to be resized often.

Web graphic formats

When you focus your attention on Web graphics, the vast field of usable graphic storage formats quickly reduces to two. The Graphics Interchange Format, or GIF, was developed by CompuServe in 1987 to store graphics used over its network. The other format came about more recently and is named for the group that developed it: the Joint Picture Experts Group or JPEG. Both formats are bitmapped formats. Currently, there is virtually no support for vector storage formats.

The specifics of each of these formats, and instances when you would want to use one over the other, are discussed in the following sections.

GIF

CompuServe released the GIF standard in 1987 and updated it in 1989 and again in 1990. The current standard is 89a and it supports 8-bit color. That is, a GIF image can contain up to 2^8 or 256 colors.

How GIF works

Image data in a GIF file is organized into related blocks and subblocks that provide information on how to paint screen pixels to reproduce the image. When transmitting a GIF, a program called an encoder is used to produce a GIF data stream of control and data blocks that are sent along to the destination machine. There, a program called a decoder parses the data stream and assembles the image.

GIF is a compressed format as well. GIF files employ the LZW compression scheme to reduce the amount of information needed to completely describe the image. The LZW scheme is best suited to simple images like line drawings or images with just a few unique colors. As the number of colors grows, LZW compression becomes less efficient, providing compression ratios of 2:1 or less.

NOTE **The LZW compression used with GIFs was actually conceived by** the Unisys Corporation and not by CompuServe. CompuServe and Unisys were entangled in patent disputes for awhile. The end result was CompuServe's licensing of the GIF format—a move that had Internet developers worried that they would have to pay for a license. Fortunately for them, the license agreement only pertained to software that was primarily used for accessing CompuServe. The downside was these developers still had to worry about licensing with Unisys as well. Unisys has yet to pursue this with any vigor though, and the GIF format continues to be one of the most popular formats on the Internet.

Transparent GIFs

GIF supports many effects that are desirable on Web pages. Chief among these is transparency. In a transparent GIF, you can designate one color to be the transparent color. Then, whenever the GIF is rendered on-screen, pixels painted with the transparent color will actually be painted with the color of the page background. This gives the illusion of the pixels being transparent, since they allow what's behind them to show through.

The advantage of transparent GIFs is that they make a graphic appear to float freely on a page. To see what this means, take a look at Figure 14.1. The image at the top is nontransparent. The words you see are sitting inside of a rectangular bounding box and both the words and the bounding box are visible. The bottom image is a transparent GIF in which the color of the bounding box was designated as the transparent color. The result is that the bounding box disappears and the words seem to sit on the background with no particular boundary around them.

Many graphics programs available today come with support for creating transparent GIFs. LView Pro, a graphic utility discussed later in this chapter, makes it very easy to designate a transparent color in a GIF.

FIG. 14.1
You can make images
float on a page by
using a transparent GIF.

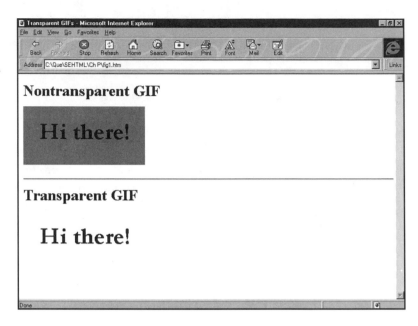

Interlaced GIFs

When you store a GIF in an interlaced format, nonadjacent parts of the image are stored together. As the GIF is decoded, pixels from all over the image are filled in rather than being filled in row by row. The result is that the image appears to "fade on" to the page, as if it were being revealed from behind a set of Venetian blinds. This permits the user to get a sense of the entire image right away instead of having to wait for the whole thing to be read in from top to bottom.

It usually takes several passes for the image to fade in completely. Figure 14.2 shows an interlaced GIF on the Discovery Channel site in the process of being read in. The complete image is shown in Figure 14.3.

Just as with transparency, most good graphics programs give you the option of saving a GIF as interlaced. All three programs discussed in this chapter support interlaced GIFs.

FIG. 14.2
An interlaced GIF appears fuzzy as it is read in.

Interlaced GIF (partially decoded)

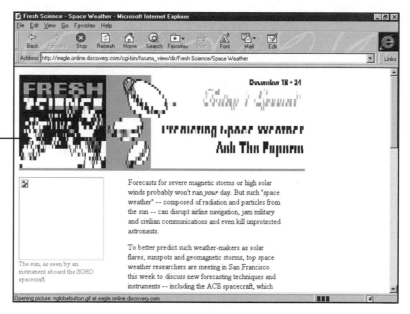

FIG. 14.3
As the last pieces of image data are read in, the interlaced GIF comes into sharper focus.

Interlaced GIF (fully decoded)

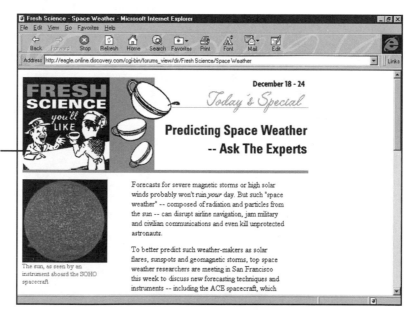

Animated GIFs

The first animations that appeared on the Web required a great deal of effort. Using an approach introduced by Netscape called server push, you could create an animation by having a server literally push several images down an open HTTP connection. When presented in sequence on the browser screen, these images created the illusion of animation. Setting this up required knowledge of the Common Gateway Interface (CGI) and some type of programming language. Since most digital media graphic artists don't have knowledge of CGI programming, producing a Web animation often required collaboration between the artists and the server administrator.

Then, about a year ago, it occurred to someone that the GIF 89a standard supports multiple images stored in the same file. Further, you could place instructions in the file header that describe how the images should be presented. In short, the 89a standard gives you everything you need to produce an animation! The individual frames that comprise the animation can all be stored in one file, and you can specify parameters like how much delay before starting the animation and how many times the animation should repeat in the file header. Figure 14.4 shows several animated GIFs on the 7-Up site.

FIG. 14.4
Animated GIFs let you place animations on a page without knowledge of programming.

Animated GIFs—

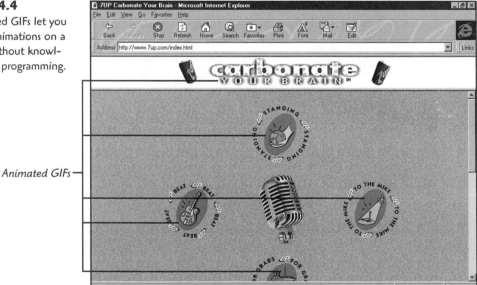

Creating animated GIFs has become fairly easy with the advent of software tools like the GIF Construction Set. In this program, you can specify the individual GIF files that make up the animation and presentation instructions in a set of dialog boxes. When you're finished with the setup, the program will create the animated GIF file by using the information you specified.

 **CAUTION** **Like many popular Web page components, a number of animated** GIFs have been made publicly available for download at many sites. The result is that these GIFs quickly become overused. Placing such a GIF on your pages does nothing to distinguish them. If you really need an animated GIF on your page, create your own unique animation. Don't put a trite animated GIF on a page just for the sake of having one there.

JPEG

JPEG actually refers to a set of formats that supports full-color and grayscale images and stores them in compressed form. JPEG stores color information at 24 bits per pixel, allowing an image to contain 224 or over 16.7 million colors! This makes it the format of choice for photographs, especially photographs of things in nature, where a continuum of colors is in play (see Figure 14.5).

FIG. 14.5
Photographs of naturally occurring objects are prime candidates for being stored as JPEGs.

JPEG Image

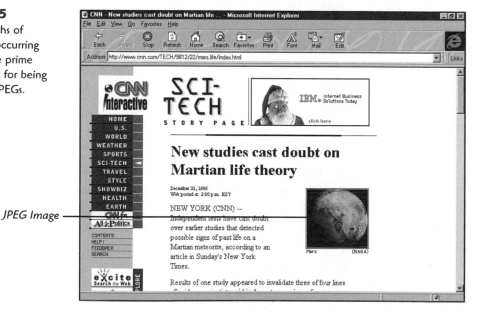

How JPEG works

JPEG can handle so many colors while still keeping file sizes reasonable because it compresses the image data. You even have some control over how big or small the file ultimately is. You can specify a high level of compression to get a very small file, but the quality of the image on-screen will be reduced.

When you decompress a JPEG image, there is always some amount of loss, meaning that the image will not look the way it did originally. Fortunately, JPEG's compression/decompression scheme is such that the lost image data tends to be in the higher color frequencies, where it is harder for the human eye to detect the differences. In spite of this loss, you can still use JPEG to achieve compression ratios between 10:1 and 20:1 without appreciable change in the image. This means you've essentially reduced the amount of storage space per pixel from 24 bits to 1 or 2 bits—quite a savings! You can take the compression ratios even higher but, as previously noted, the loss will become more detectable and image quality will suffer.

 TIP Always do your conversion to JPEG as your very last step in creating a Web image. Resaving as a JPEG after each change can increase the amount of loss since the image is recompressed each time.

Progressive JPEGs

JPEG isn't as versatile a format as GIF is when it comes to supporting desirable Web page effects. However, a new type of JPEG, called a progressive JPEG or p-JPEG, provides an analogy to the interlaced GIF. A p-JPEG is stored as a series of scans that together comprise the entire image. When the first scan is read in, users see an approximation of the whole image, so they can quickly get an idea of what they're ultimately going to see. As subsequent scans are read in, the image comes into sharper focus.

 NOTE People often ask if there will ever be transparent JPEGs. Unfortunately, the answer to this question is no. To understand why, recall that there is always some loss during JPEG compression/decompression. This means that some pixels are not colored with the same color as they originally were.

Now suppose you've specified a transparent color for the JPEG. If a pixel originally colored with the transparent color is assigned a new color due to the loss, then that pixel will no longer be transparent. Similarly, nontransparent pixels could be colored with the transparent color after compression/decompression, meaning that they will end up being transparent. Either way, you get the opposite of what you wanted and the on-screen results would be disastrous.

Unless JPEG is changed to become a lossless format, there is little hope of there ever being transparent JPEGs.

When to use GIF or JPEG

Given that you have the choice between two formats for Web graphics, you may find yourself wondering when to use one or the other. To help you answer that question, review some in the following guidelines.

You have to use a GIF if you want transparency or animation, since it's the only format that supports them. Beyond that, you should consider GIF for the following types of images:

- Black-and-white line art and text.
- Images with a limited number of distinct colors.
- Graphics with sharp or distinct edges (most menus, buttons, and graphs fit this category).
- Graphics that are overlaid with text.

JPEG is better suited for the following situations:

- Scanned photographs and ray-traced renderings.
- Images that contain a complex mixture of colors.
- Any image that requires a palette of more than 256 colors.

Because the compression computations work better with a continuum of color, the JPEG format is not well suited to images that have very sharp color changes.

Making good use of images

While it is true that a properly designed image can enhance a document, a poorly designed image can detract from it. Graphic images certainly have their place in Web documents and, in fact, they are expected in many places by users. The next few sections look at the types of graphics commonly found on the Web and give you some tips on how to maximize the effectiveness of each kind.

Main page graphics

If you've visited many Web sites, you've very likely noticed the tendency to put a large graphic on the main page of a site that lets a visitor navigate to all of the major sections of the site. Such a graphic is a good idea for many reasons. It lets the user know right away what major content sections are available. Additionally, it lets the site designer establish a visual look for each section which can be helpful to the user later as they navigate through the site. But there are pitfalls to this type of image. Some things to think about include:

- **Keep the file size small**—Forcing the user to wait a long time for a large image to load can prompt them to interrupt the loading and move on to another site. Make sure that your main-page graphics are of a reasonable size—somewhere between 50K and 100K, if possible.

- **Be consistent**—Use the graphics elements (colors, icons, headings) that you associate with each content section consistently throughout the site. This gives the visitor a better chance of figuring out where they are and how to get to where they want to go.

- **Provide a text-based alternative**—Users with text-only browsers or who have image loading turned off won't be able to see your main-page graphic at all. Be sure to include a set of hypertext links that these users can use to navigate to the major areas of your site.

Your main-page graphic is the first thing a user will see when visiting your site and sets the tone for the rest of their time there. The best rule of thumb for this kind of graphics is to make sure it is eye-catching and distinctive, without falling prey to one of the earlier issues.

Icons

Icons are small graphics that are meant to represent a certain content section or piece of information on your site. Commonly used icons include a question mark for Help and Frequently Asked Questions (FAQ) sections or a magnifying glass for a search engine.

Because icons are small, file size is usually not a problem. Icons download quickly and, once they are in a user's cache, can be reused again and again without further downloading. But an icon's smallness can also be a disadvantage because you have to pack a very specific concept into a fairly small part of the screen. For this reason, your chief concern when designing icons is *intuitiveness*. Users should be able to look at an icon and almost immediately discern what it means.

The best way to see if your icons are intuitive is to test them with a group of users as you're designing the site. A commonly used test involves presenting users with a set of potential icons and asking them to write down what they think each icon represents. If you find that most users interpret an icon the same way, you can feel pretty good about using that icon to represent the idea they say it does. If there's no clear interpretation of an icon, you should scrap it or send it back to the drawing board.

Once you have your icons chosen, be sure to use them consistently. This helps to reinforce their meaning with the user and makes navigating your site much less stressful.

 If you expect a global audience to visit your site, you also need to consider how your icons will be interpreted by users from cultures different from your own. This typically requires bouncing your icons off users from those cultures, if at all possible.

Navigation bars

Very large sites have to support the user with some kind of navigation aid. Navigation imagemaps are frequently found at the top or bottom (and sometimes both) of a document and give the user single click access to the major content areas of the site and other useful resources like a Table of Contents or a search engine. You may also include some navigation options that point to places within a given section of a site, particularly if the user has had to drill down several levels to get to a document.

Navigation graphics present some of the same design issues as main page graphics. These include:

- **Being consistent**—Consistency is much more important at this level, since the user may have forgotten what the main-page graphic looks like. Be sure to incorporate the visual cues you built into your main-page graphic when you design navigation graphics and also make use of your icons. If you have an iconographic representation of each section of your site, you can line them up in a row to produce a simple navigation bar that the user should be able to use easily.

Consistency also applies to where you place the navigation graphic in a document. If users see navigation options at the bottom of the first few pages, they'll come to expect it to be there on every page.

- **Providing a text-based alternative**—Again, you can't forget about users who can't see graphics or who have shut them off. Make sure there is always a set of hypertext links available that duplicate the links found in the navigation graphic.

Backgrounds

A well-chosen background image can make a page look very distinctive. Many corporate sites have a faded version of the company logo in the background. This approach reinforces the company's corporate identity, while not being so obtrusive that it obscures the primary content of the document.

Another popular approach to background images is to use a very small pattern that is tiled to fill the browser window. Typically these files are very small and load quickly. However, if the tiling isn't smooth, it can produce seams on the page that can distract a user. Fortunately, more and more graphics programs are including a tessellating function that allows you to produce seamless tiling in all directions when using a tiled background pattern. Both Paint Shop Pro and Adobe Photoshop come with this useful feature.

 TIP Whether you're using a large image or tiling a small image in your background, you can use the BGCOLOR attribute of the <BODY> tag to immediately paint the background with a color that approximates the dominant color of your background image. This smooths over the transition to the image and, if the image fails to load, the user can at least have a sense of what color your background was supposed to be.

The worst thing you can do is use a background image that is so busy that it detracts from content in the foreground. If you're not using a solid color or a pattern, make sure that the visual elements in your background image are sufficiently muted so that they don't interfere with the user's ability to read and understand the content of your document.

Finding graphics online

Not everyone is lucky enough to have a team of digital graphic artists on staff to support a Web site. If your role as a Webmaster is "jack-of-all-trades," that most likely means you're responsible for graphic content as well. Fortunately, there are many sites out on the Web that provide royalty-free graphics that you can download and use on your own site.

One particularly good public repository of graphics is Microsoft's Multimedia Gallery at **http://www.microsoft.com/workshop/design/mmgallry/**. Not only can you find icons, background patterns, and navigation graphics in the Gallery, but you can also download audio clips as well!

One caution about using graphics from a public-download site: other people might be using them, too. This robs your site of a truly distinctive look and, in cases where the graphics are overused, can make your pages seem trite. Do you remember the little colored balls people used to use as bullets in a bulleted list? This is a classic example of an overused graphic. The colored balls even made a comeback as animated GIFs where the color of the ball cycles through many different colors!

Don't let your pages be common—try to customize the graphics you download to set them apart. One easy way to do this is to repaint the graphics in the color scheme of your site. This makes them seem more like they were designed just for your site.

Bandwidth issues

As popular as graphics are with users, they can become immensely unpopular when they take forever to download. By keeping file sizes small, you minimize the time your users spend waiting to see your pages. A good rule of thumb is to keep each large image to between 30K and 50K. Icons should be even smaller—between 5K and 10K.

Think of your audience

Even with small file sizes, different users may have to wait different lengths of time for an image to download. A 50K image may transfer in just a few seconds over a T1 connection, but dial-up users who are limited to 14.4Kbps or 28.8Kbps may have to wait several minutes. Be sure to remember your users with slower connections when you design your graphics. You may even ask a few of them to test your image files to see if they require a long time to download.

 TIP **Don't forget to use the ALT attribute in your <IMG> tags so that** the user can see a description of your image in case it fails to load.

Corporate intranet designers tend to be a little more fortunate in this department. Most intranet users are on a high-speed connection over the company's Wide Area Network (WAN). With such a homogeneous group, it's usually possible to design higher-end graphics and still have reasonable download times. You should still have some coworkers test your images though, especially those who are located a great distance from your server.

Tips for reducing file size

If you think you have an image file that's too big, don't despair! There are plenty of techniques for bringing the size down. Depending on the makeup of the image and the format you saved it in, you may want to try one of the following:

- Resize the image—Larger images take up more disk space because there are more pixels and, hence, more color information that has to be stored. By shrinking the height and width of an image to the smallest they can be, you take a big step toward making the file as small as it can be.

 **CAUTION** **Always resize an image in a graphics program, keeping the aspect** ratio the same. If you try to use the WIDTH and HEIGHT attributes of the <IMG> tag to resize the image, you're relying on the browser to do the resizing and you're likely to be disappointed with the results. Additionally, resizing with the browser doesn't save you download time because the original image file still has to be downloaded.

- **Use thumbnails**—Thumbnails are very small versions of an image, usually a photograph. Because they're smaller, their file sizes are smaller, too.

TIP   **Thumbnails are typically set up so that a user can click them to see** the full image. If you do this, be sure to include the size of the full image file in parentheses next to the thumbnail so that users can make an informed decision about viewing it or not.

- **Store GIFs as JPEGs**—JPEG compression works best on images with lots of color gradation. If you have a GIF file that fits this description, try saving it as a JPEG to see if that makes the file any smaller.

- **Increase the compression ratio**—If you're working with a JPEG, you can resave it at a higher compression ratio to shrink the file size. But don't forget the trade-off: higher compression reduces the quality of the image.

- **Reduce the color depth**—Color depth is another way to express how many colors can be stored by a format. A GIF image has a color depth of eight bits (256 colors)—but what if there are fewer than 256 colors in the image? In this case, you can reduce the color depth to a smaller number of bits per pixel. With less information to store per pixel, the resulting file will be smaller.

- **Adjust contrast levels in the image**—Contrast refers to the brightness of objects in the image relative to one another. Most popular graphics programs offer retouching options like gamma correction and highlight/midtone/shadow that change contrast within an image. By tweaking these values, you can usually bring down your file size.

- **Suppress dithering**—Dithering refers to the use of colors in an existing color palette to approximate colors that are not in the palette. Dithering tends to increase file size in GIFs because the GIF compression scheme is less efficient when adjacent pixels are painted with different colors. Disabling dithering will make more adjacent pixels have the same color so the compression can better shrink the file.

Working with scanned images

It's not always necessary to create your own graphics. In fact, it's very often convenient to scan something in (if you have access to a scanner) or use an image that someone else has already scanned in. Either approach is perfectly valid. No one will ever expect you to create all of your own images. When you do use a scanned image though, you should make sure that it really contributes to the message you're trying to convey in your document, and that you're not just using it for the sake of using it.

CAUTION **Some people will let you use images that they scanned as long as** you give them credit in your document. Make sure you acknowledge the sources of your scanned images.

When to use them and where to get them

If you do have a flatbed scanner, making your own scanned images is a simple task. You can use the software that came with the scanner, or you can use a program like Photoshop or Paint Shop Pro.

If you're looking for existing scanned images, you can try any of the following sources:

- **Graphics service bureaus**—A graphics service house may have existing images you can use on a royalty basis. It can also probably scan images at a higher quality than you could on a desktop scanner.

- **Stock Photo and Clip Art CD-ROMs**—Many companies sell CD-ROMs with stock photos and simple line art you can use. You usually have to acknowledge the producer of the CD in your document as the source of the images.

Manipulating scanned images

Scanned images invariably need some kind of touch-up done on them so they are a truer representation of the original. By zooming in on the scanned image in an editor, you can usually see imperfections along the edges of objects and in the coloring of pixels. Be sure to give your scan a good "once over" in this way, so it can look its best in your document.

Useful graphics tools

Throughout this chapter, reference has been made to many different manipulations and edits you can make to an image. Now it's time to look at some of the programs you can use to make these modifications. The next five sections introduce you to the following image-editing programs:

- LView Pro

- Paint Shop Pro

- Adobe Photoshop

- Microsoft Image Composer

- GIF Construction Set

Each of these is a great graphics program in its own right. You should consider each one and then select the one the meets your needs and is within your means.

This section concludes with a look at the GIF Construction Set, a shareware program you can use to create animated GIFs.

LView Pro

LView Pro is a great shareware program you can use to edit existing graphics or to convert them to GIF or JPEG format. It offers many of the common manipulation features found in most paint programs plus several other options that give you very fine control over image appearance.

NOTE **The information on LView Pro presented here is based on the** evaluation copy of version 1.D2. You can download the latest version of LView Pro by pointing your browser to **http://www.lview.com/**. A license costs $30 U.S. plus $5 U.S. for shipping and handling.

Figure 14.6 shows the LView Pro window along with its extensive tool palette. Almost every tool in the palette corresponds directly to one of LView Pro's menu options.

The only LView Pro tool for creating anything is the Add Text tool. It stands to reason that you'll probably have to use a different program to create your graphics. But, what LView Pro lacks in ability to create, it makes up for with its ability to make very particular changes to an image. These program features are found under the Edit and Retouch menus.

FIG. 14.6
LView Pro's tool palette enables you to make modifications to most aspects of an image.

The Edit menu

LView Pro's Edit menu provides options for many of the basic manipulations that Paint can perform, including horizontal and vertical flips and rotations by 90 degrees to the right or left. The Add Text option, discussed previously, is also found under the Edit menu.

The Resize and Redimension options can create some confusion for the user who is unfamiliar with them. Resize changes the dimensions of an image, with the option to retain the image's aspect ratio (the ratio of the width and height). When you Resize, you can choose from a standard set of sizes or you can enter your own size. Redimension only lets you choose from the standard set of sizes and doesn't permit you to keep the same aspect ratio.

The Capture option under the Edit menu does a screen capture of either the Desktop, the Window, or the Client Area. When you invoke one of the screen capture options, LView Pro will minimize itself and capture the region that you requested on screen.

The Retouch menu

The options under LView Pro's Retouch menu really expand the program beyond a simple graphics manipulator. One option of note is Gamma Correction, a parameter that can impact the contrast in an image (and therefore, the size of the image file). Gamma correction is used to increase or decrease the brightness of pixels in the image. You can set gamma correction values for

Red, Green, and Blue color components separately by moving the scroll bar next to each color. A gamma correction value bigger than zero will brighten the color, and values less than zero will darken the color. If you want to adjust the gamma correction for all three colors simultaneously, check the Lock RGB Scrollbars check box. This moves all three scroll bars whenever you move any one of them. To reduce the size of an image file, you can reduce the contrast in the image. This means you want a negative value for gamma correction.

Another useful option under the Retouch menu is Palette Entry. Choosing this option calls up the Select Color Palette Entry dialog box, shown in Figure 14.7. From this dialog box, you can select one of the colors in the current image's palette and change its RGB color specification. You can also select the image's transparent color from this dialog box.

FIG. 14.7

Changing a particular palette color is easy with the Palette Entry option of the Retouch menu.

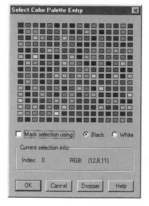

A final Retouch option of interest is Color Depth (see Figure 14.8). This option is used to select a True Color image (24 bits per pixel, 16.7 million colors) or a Palette image (up to eight bits per pixel and 256 colors). Palette images can be two colors (black and white), 16 colors (like the default Windows palette), 256 colors (as with a GIF image), or a custom number of colors. If you're decreasing your color depth, you may want to activate Floyd-Steinberg dithering, a process that uses combinations of colors in the palette to approximate colors that are not in the palette.

FIG. 14.8
If you need to reduce your color depth to make an image file smaller, you can do it in LView Pro from the Color Depth dialog box.

LView Pro Properties settings

The Properties dialog box (choose File, Properties) lets you do much more than set up retouch instructions. There are 11 different tabs on the panel that enable you to configure LView Pro to run according to your own image-editing preferences.

Two of the tabs deserve special attention because of their relevance to creating Web graphics. The GIF tab, shown in Figure 14.9, has two check boxes which can be used to instruct LView Pro to save a GIF file as either interlaced or transparent.

FIG. 14.9
LView Pro can make interlaced and transparent GIFs if you tell it to do so.

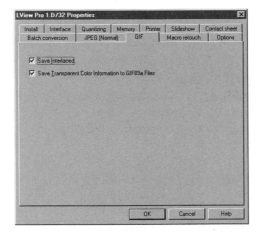

 NOTE To designate the transparent color in LView Pro, choose Retouch, Background Color and select the color you want to be the background color from the palette you see. When you save the image as a transparent GIF, the background color will become the transparent color.

The other noteworthy tab is the JPEG tab, shown in Normal mode in Figure 14.10. From this tab, you can choose compression and decompression options, including progressive decompression for making a progressive JPEG.

FIG. 14.10
LView Pro can also make a progressive JPEG once you activate progressive compression.

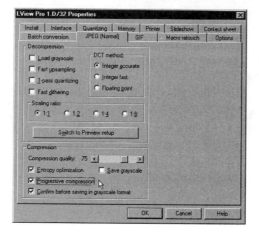

Paint Shop Pro

Another good shareware program for graphics work is Paint Shop Pro from JASC, Inc. Paint Shop Pro handles many types of image storage formats, enables you to do the most common image manipulations, and even comes with a screen capture facility.

Figure 14.11 shows an image loaded into Paint Shop Pro, along with the many available tool panels that give you single-click access to Paint Shop Pro's functions. The Zoom panel lets you zoom in to magnifications as high as 16:1, and out to magnifications as low as 1:16. Tools located on the Select panel allow you to sample colors, move the image around in the window, define a custom area of the image to clone or resize, and change the foreground and background colors.

The Paint panel is a welcome addition that was not available in earlier versions of Paint Shop Pro. It supports 22 different tools you can use to make your own graphics. These tools enable you to: create brush, pen, pencil, marker, and chalk effects; draw lines, rectangles, and circles; fill a closed region with color; add text; and sharpen or soften part of an image. The Histogram window displays a graphic representation of the luminance of all colors in the image, measured with respect to the brightest color.

FIG. 14.11
Paint Shop Pro's tool panels give you easy access to common painting and image manipulation.

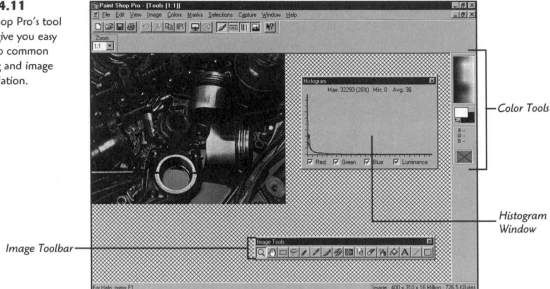

Color Tools

Histogram Window

Image Toolbar

TIP **You can toggle any of the tool panels on or off by using the** options found under the View menu.

Paint Shop Pro's versatility enables you to open images stored in 25 bitmapped formats, including GIF and JPEG, and 9 meta/vector formats (image components stored as geometric shapes that combine to produce the entire image), including CorelDRAW!, Micrografx, and Ventura. However, it can only save in one of the raster formats. Nevertheless, Paint Shop Pro is still handy for converting to bitmapped formats. The Batch Conversion option under the File menu lets you select any number of files to convert to a new storage format (see Figure 14.12).

TWAIN refers to a set of industry standards that allow graphics programs to work with image acquisition hardware like scanners. If you have a TWAIN-compliant scanner attached to your computer, you can use the File, Acquire option to scan in a new image. The Select Source option, also under the File menu, lets you choose which device you want to use for the acquisition.

FIG. 14.12
Have a bunch of files to convert? Paint Shop Pro can be set up to handle them all at once.

The Image menu includes the options used to do many of the standard manipulations like flipping the image upside down, creating a mirror image of an image, and rotating the images. The Image, Resample option is used to change the size of an image, without the jagged edges caused by standard resizing. You'll also find several effect filters under the Image menu that let you add or remove noise, enhance darker or lighter colors, and blur (sharpen or soften) the image. You can even define effect filters of your own.

The Colors menu is host to many of the advanced image manipulations you read about in the LView Pro section, including: adjustment of brightness, gamma correction, RGB values, and conversion to grayscale or photographic negative versions of an image. You can also load, modify, and save color palettes from the Colors menu. The Increase and Decrease Color Depth options allow you to change the number of colors being used to render the image.

Paint Shop Pro adds some color editing functionality that LView Pro doesn't have. The Highlight/Midtone/Shadow option under the Adjust pop-up list lets you skew an image's contrast to emphasize highlights, shadows, or mid-range colors. The posterizing effect (choose Colors, Posterize) makes the image look more like a poster by reducing the number of bits used per RGB color channel. You can also use the Colors, Solarize option to invert colors that are above a luminance level specified by you.

One very useful feature of Paint Shop Pro is its screen and window capture facility. Options in the Capture, Setup dialog box are used to capture the whole screen, a single window on the screen, the client area inside a window, or a user-defined area. You can also choose whether the mouse pointer should be included in the capture and which hotkey will activate the capture.

The current release of Paint Shop Pro comes bundled with many more special effects filters than in previous versions. These include:

- **Add Drop Shadow**—Drop shadows are a great way to make your graphics appear to float over the document. The Add Drop Shadow function makes it simple to add drop shadows to your images. Just make sure that you use a common light source for images that will be placed on the same page.

- **Create Seamless Pattern**—Earlier in the chapter, it was noted that background images are often small files that are read in and tiled to fill the browser window. To avoid seams between tiled copies of the same image, you need to tessellate the edges of the image so that they come together smoothly. Paint Shop Pro has automated this procedure with the Create Seamless Pattern function.

- **Cutout**—The Cutout function allows you to remove a section of an image, allowing you to see through it to what lies behind it.

- **Chisel**—Applying the Chisel function to a selected area of an image transforms it to make it appear as if it were chiseled out of stone.

- **Buttonize**—You can use the Buttonize function to apply a three-dimensional border to a selected portion of an image to make it appear raised. This is especially useful in creating clickable buttons that readers can use to select different navigation options.

- **Hot Wax Coating**—Rather than holding a burning candle over an image on your computer monitor, you can avail yourself of the Hot Wax Coating effect to make it look like you did.

Additionally, you can install Adobe Photoshop-compatible plug-ins and define your own effect filters.

When it comes to saving an image as a GIF or JPEG, Paint Shop Pro can handle the basic format, as well as most of the associated effects. About all that Paint Shop Pro won't do is allow you to save a progressive JPEG.

Paint Shop Pro is a very capable image editing program. You can also purchase it bundled with Kai's Power Tools SE for added functionality. To order this combination package, contact JASC sales at **1-800-622-2793**. For more information about Kai's Power Tools, consult **http://www.metatools.com/**. To learn more about Paint Shop Pro, direct your browser to **http://www.jasc.com/**.

Adobe Photoshop

Adobe promotes Photoshop as the "camera for your mind," but it's really much more—it's the premier software package for doing graphical manipulations. You can use Photoshop to create your own original artwork, scan in an image, or make edits to an existing image. Photoshop can read in files stored in over a dozen formats and save them in just as many formats, including GIF and JPEG.

Making your own artwork

Photoshop supports you in graphics creation with an extensive toolbar, located on the left side of the window (see Figure 14.13). You can choose tools for placing text, filling regions, drawing lines, airbrushing, painting, freehand drawing, smudging, blurring, and lightening.

FIG. 14.13
Many of the drawing options found in other image creation programs are available in Photoshop as well.

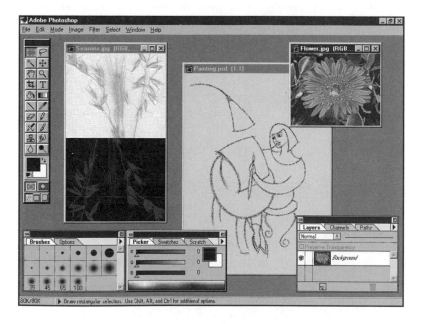

TIP **Many toolbar tools have special options available in the dialog box** at the bottom left of the Photoshop window.

Layers and channels

One of Photoshop's nicest features is image layers—different levels of the image you can overlay to produce the entire image. Figure 14.14 shows an image that uses layers. The sun is on a separate layer from the checkered background, but when the two are superimposed, they produce the desired image.

FIG. 14.14
Layers separate the different components of an image into their own separate entities, so you can work on them individually.

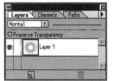

A graphic element in a given layer can be painted with RGB color and Photoshop will provide access to each component color through color channels. Figure 14.15 shows the channels for the sun layer from the graphic in Figure 14.14. The sun is painted yellow, which is formed by a combination of green and blue. Notice in Figure 14.15 that there is no contribution from the red channel—only from the green and blue channels.

FIG. 14.15
Color channels split a color into its individual red, green, and blue components.

Web graphics effects

Photoshop can help you apply a number of desirable effects to Web graphics. One important one is anti-aliasing, a process that softens the jagged edges that often occur at a boundary between two different colors. Anti-aliasing an edge is fairly easy to do. You just select the item with the edge to be anti-aliased by using the Lasso (freehand region selection) tool, and then check the Anti-aliased box on the Options tab in the dialog box at the bottom-left of the window.

 Anti-aliasing is available when using the magic wand, fill, and line tools as well.

Embossing is an effect that makes an image look "raised," just as lettering on an engraved invitation is raised. Photoshop has an embossing filter that is easy to apply to an image. You select the part of the image to emboss, then choose Filter, Stylize, and then select the Emboss option from the pop-up list that appears. An image and its embossed equivalent are shown in Figure 14.16.

FIG. 14.16
Embossing "raises up" parts of an image and gives your pages the illusion of depth.

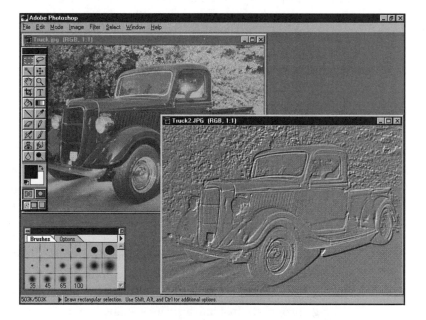

Photoshop also supports saving files in GIF, interlaced GIF, transparent GIF, JPEG, and progressive JPEG formats, although plug-in programs are required to accomplish this. Two of the most popular plug-ins are PhotoGIF and ProJPEG from BoxTop Software, Inc. You can download the latest versions from BoxTop's Web site at **http://www.boxtopsoft.com/**.

So much more!

Trite as it may sound, Photoshop is much more than what has been noted here. Some of the program's other handy features include:

- Numerous built-in effects filters, and many more available from plug-in programs; Kai's Power Tools is one set of utilities that is particularly well integrated into Photoshop.

- Options for dithering to lower color depths and different color palettes.

- Highly efficient memory management.

- A flawless interface with other Adobe products like Illustrator and PageMaker.

Photoshop is a powerful image creation and modification tool that makes a worthy addition to your software library. For many folks, the limiting factor is often price since Photoshop can cost between $500 and $1,000 per license, depending on which platform you're running it on. Students can obtain a "light" version of Photoshop at a substantial discount. If you're running a highly graphical Web site and you can afford Photoshop, you should seriously consider purchasing it as your graphics tool of choice.

Microsoft Image Composer

Microsoft continues to expand its software offerings that support Internet publishing by producing Microsoft Image Composer (see Figure 14.17), which is a full-featured, image-editing program that works with Microsoft FrontPage and the Microsoft GIF Animator.

Image Composer breaks new ground in developing graphics for Web documents by introducing *sprite technology*. Put simply, a sprite is an image whose shape is not necessarily rectangular (like it would be in any other image program). Instead, a sprite's shape is exactly the shape of the object in the image. Microsoft provides a good example on one of their Image Composer Web pages (see Figure 14.18). The image on the left is a sprite. It does have a rectangular bounding box, but the image's shape is that of the bunch of flowers. The image on the right would be done in a traditional image editor. You could make the black background transparent to achieve the same effect as you get in the sprite, but this would require extra steps that aren't needed with Image Composer.

FIG. 14.17
Microsoft Image Composer comes bundled with either Microsoft FrontPage or Microsoft's Visual InterDev.

FIG. 14.18
A sprite is an image that takes on the shape of the object in it, instead of just being rectangular.

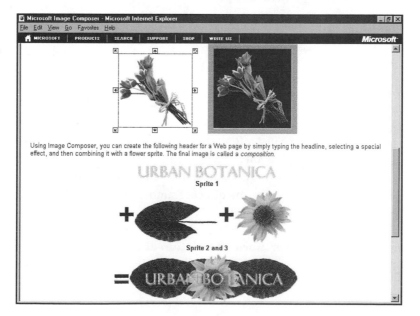

CAUTION   **Macromedia Director users should not confuse Image Composer** sprites with Director sprites. Although they share the same name, they are not the same thing.

Sprites are made possible by an Image Composer feature called the alpha channel. Every sprite has a built-in, 8-bit (256 color) alpha channel that stores transparency information. This means you can have up to 256 levels of transparency—much more flexible than the single transparent color you get in a transparent GIF! You can use the levels of transparency to seamlessly overlay sprites (refer to Figure 14.18) and create eye-catching effects. When you've finished your composition, you can export the whole thing as a GIF, and place it in any of your Web documents.

Beyond sprite technology, Image Composer offers many of the things you'd want in a graphics-editing program. It saves images in both the GIF (including transparent GIF) and JPEG formats. You get all of the standard image creation tools like paint, fill, text, and shapes. Further, you get over 500 different special effects filters that include:

- Angled Strokes
- Dry Brush
- Fresco
- Halftone Screen
- Neon Glow
- Pencil Sketch
- Stained Glass

Those are just a few. Image Composer can also work with Adobe-compatible plug-ins like Kai's Power Tools 3.0, KPT Convolver, and Andromeda Series 1 Photography. The Impressionist plug-in package is shipped with Image Composer, and the effects found in Adobe Gallery Effects 1.51 are resident in Image Composer already.

NOTE   **For more information about Microsoft Image Composer, point** your Web browser to **http://www.microsoft.com/imagecomposer/**.

GIF Construction Set

A program that will help you build animated GIFs is the GIF Construction Set from Alchemy Mindworks. The program is shown running in Figure 14.19. The text you see in the window denotes the different blocks that comprise the animated GIF. The animated GIF always begins with a header block and can be followed with images, text, comments, controls, and looping instructions. Each of these can be placed by pressing the Insert button you see in the figure.

FIG. 14.19
Assembling the building blocks of an animated GIF is easy with the GIF Construction Set.

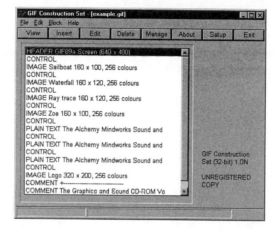

You don't even need to be familiar with the GIF Construction Set's GIF building "language" to use the program. By choosing File, Animation Wizard, you are taken through a series of dialog boxes (see Figure 14.20) that ask whether the animation is for the Web or not, whether it should loop once or indefinitely, whether the frames are line drawings or photorealistic, how much delay there should be between frames, and what files contain the images for the individual frames. The GIF Construction Set uses this information to author the animated GIF file for you automatically.

 **CAUTION**   **Think twice before letting an animation run indefinitely. An** animation that's going constantly can be a distraction from the rest of the content on your page.

FIG. 14.20
The Animation Wizard makes preparing an animated GIF as easy as answering a few questions.

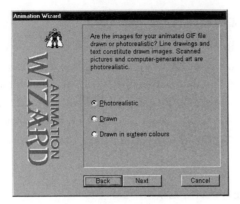

The GIF Construction Set is robust enough to support you in other Web graphics endeavors. It can:

- Create transparent GIFs.

- Convert AVI videos to animated GIFs.

- Add transition effects to still graphics.

- Create animated text banners.

- Add words to images as blocks of plain text.

You can download the GIF Construction Set from the Alchemy Mindworks Web site at **http://www.mindworkshop.com/alchemy/gifcon.html**. Registering your copy of the GIF Construction Set will set you back $20 U.S. plus $5 U.S. for shipping.

 TIP **Macintosh users should check out GifBuilder for creating** animated GIFs.

Part IV: Web Site Management and Tools

15

Putting Your Pages Online

● In this chapter:

- Publish your site

- Hosting your Web site

- Running your own server

Once your Web site is completed, it has to be published in a way that allows others to access it. There are presently two methods for publishing a Web site: uploading to your Web directory on an ISP or running your own Web server. This chapter will discuss both methods. After reading this chapter, you should be able to determine which method is best suited to your needs.

What are your options?

Before you publish your Web site to the Internet you should consider the options available; your choice will depend on your individual situation. Read this section to gain a better understanding of the two Web-site publishing options—your own server versus having your site hosted by an ISP—and select the one that best suits your needs.

The most common choice, considering the initial cash outlay required to set up and run your own server, is to let someone else worry about the equipment upkeep. Unless you're developing a complete Internet solution for a large company, one that will make use of other Internet features such as FTP, e-mail, and possibly a database, you probably do not require your own server. Make a few phone calls, do a price and service comparison, and have your site hosted by one of your local ISPs.

The focus of this chapter is getting your Web site published on someone else's system. Considering the differences between the policies of the various ISPs, you should look for certain features before signing on with any particular ISP. In addition to a standard dial-up account with e-mail, you will need a shell and an FTP account. It is only common sense that you have easy access to your Web files.

Uploading files to an ISP

This is the easiest method if you can find an ISP that offers shell accounts and FTP (not a requirement but makes it much easier). If you plan to make frequent modifications to the content of your site, having shell and FTP access means you can quickly add and remove files, add new subdirectories, and include server-side scripts (depending on the ISP) among other benefits like using the UNIX mail to sort your e-mail.

Run your own server

This option needs to be considered very carefully. The initial cash layout for the appropriate telephone line service and modem is in excess of $1,000, not a commitment to be taken lightly. In addition to purchasing the digital telephone line service and the digital modems, you will also need a computer to act as the server. You do not want your accounting files and sales strategy on the same machine the world is connected to.

Whether finding an ISP or running your own server, you will achieve the same goal of making the data on the Web site available to anyone on the Internet with a Web-client application (browser). The delivery methods are the same as well. The only difference is that, by running your own server, you are burdened with maintenance of the networked system—which can become an enormous task if any major problems arise.

Running your own server means you have total control over who sees your Web site and what kinds of content you include with your Web site. You can make sections of the site available to anyone with a browser and restrict other parts of your Web site so that only authorized users can access it. You own the Web site, and you own the space on the Internet that the Web site is occupying. This option is usually only available if you have a direct connection to the Internet.

 TIP **You can run a server off your hard drive through a dial-up** account, but the Web site would only be available when you are logged on. Also, you would have to make arrangements with your ISP to make sure you had the same IP address each time you log on.

Uploading to an ISP is actually like renting space to store your Web site files. Along with the many benefits, saving money being the biggest, there are a few drawbacks. For one, you have very little control over who can actually use, or even see, the site. You can't include server-side script files unless arrangements have been made with the administrator (often requiring no more than a call to the ISP).

 TIP **Talk to your ISP if you wish to use CGI scripts or server-side Java** and JavaScript.

The benefits to using someone else's system are that you don't have to put out the cash to upgrade to a server grade computer, you are not responsible for ensuring that the system is always operating, and you don't have the monthly bill for having dedicated Internet access.

Choosing an option

It is important to determine the resources available to you (see Table 15.1).

Table 15.1   Examine the requirements

Requirement	Own server	ISP
Dedicated access	✔	
Dial-up access		✔
System Monitoring	✔	
System Maintenance	✔	

It's not all that difficult to choose the appropriate publishing method once you have determined the resources available to you. Answer the following questions about your operation and Web site:

- Do you or your firm have dedicated Internet access or the resources to set it up?

- Do you or your firm have the resources/manpower to maintain a server?

- Is the site a large Web application type site, using Java applets, server-side scripts, movies, and audio files?

- Do you require a secure server?

If you answered "yes" to the above questions, you will probably want to run your own server. You are not required to, but it would be to your benefit. If you answered "no" to the first two questions and "yes" to the other questions, you may want to have a discussion with your ISP about your needs. She may have a reasonably priced solution for someone in your situation; if she can't help you, shop around. Many ISPs will try to accommodate your needs; be prepared to pay.

Do you already have the money, the equipment, and the dedicated access to the Internet? Your choice is obvious. You will look over the information about servers in another section of this chapter and go with the one that best matches your requirements. Not much of a decision if you're already set up for it.

Still think you need the power of running your own server, but you do not have the resources or the dedicated account? There is still a chance that you can run a server (like Microsoft's Personal Web Server) from your local computer.

Your Web site would only be accessible while you were online. The rest of the time the user would get a "file not found" error.

It is beyond the scope of this book to get into the particulars of this option. If you want to find out more, talk to your ISP.

Everyone else will be uploading to the ISP. This choice still offers a range of options for dynamic content inclusions. Many ISPs will put your CGI script on their systems to work with your order form, guestbook, or whatever else you may need a CGI script for.

There will most likely be a fee for putting your custom CGI script on the system. The ISP will have to test the script first, to make sure it isn't going to mess up the system by inadvertently allowing someone access to the system. If it passes the test it will be put on the system. If it poses a security threat, it isn't likely that it will be on the system until the threat is eliminated.

Obvious to all is the benefit that you don't have to worry about monitoring the system. If there are any problems, the administrator will fix it. You can concentrate on producing the Web site and let someone else worry about keeping the system alive.

Carefully consider the next two sections when deciding which option to go with. The first, "Uploading to an ISP," takes you through the steps to publish your Web site on someone else's server. "Running your own server" discusses running your own server and talks about the requirements of running it.

Uploading to an ISP

Uploading to the ISP is relatively easy. Follow the steps outlined in this section. This section is a generic set of instructions based on a UNIX account. Check with your ISP to see if there is any special procedure that must be followed on that system.

 TIP   **Some ISPs require you to e-mail the HTML files to them. They will** place the files in a directory area designated for your Web site.

These ISPs charge a fee for putting the files on, and they charge a fee for any updates to your Web site. If the ISP you are dealing with works like that, shop around. It could quickly become very expensive to keep your content fresh in a situation like that.

As you progress through this section, notice the following steps:

- Preparing your UNIX shell account for a Web site
- Setting the permissions in the Web site directory
- Making any subdirectories that your site requires
- Uploading the HTML files
- Uploading any other files that are related to your site
- Preparing the files for presentation on the Internet

Make yourself a checklist of all the required steps. When it's time to put your files online, refer to the checklist to ensure that you do not make any mistakes or forget any steps.

Preparing your site

The first thing you must do when putting a new Web site on the Internet is prepare the home on the networked computer in which the files will reside while they are on the Internet.

 TIP   **Check with your ISP before you attempt to put a Web Site on** their network. They may not allow UNIX telnet sessions, or they may complete the following steps for you.

As was stated at the beginning of this chapter, you should have an account with an ISP that offers shell account access. This section assumes you have the shell account.

You have to be online first. Once you are online, initiate a telnet session. The telnet client will communicate with the remote system requesting telnet access. The telnet session will go like this:

1 Enter the host address in the telnet client. Telnet will establish a connection.

2 Enter your logon ID and password when prompted.

3 Type **pwd** at the prompt to see which directory you are in. You should be in your own area on the system. The reply message should look something like this: /user/home/userid/—that would be your directory on the system.

Microsoft Windows 95 includes a telnet client. To use the telnet client, click the MS-DOS prompt icon. At the DOS prompt, type telnet <host address>.

Now you have initiated a telnet session. The default directory when you telnet into the ISP system is always your user directory.

Figure 15.1 shows you what the screen looks like when you log on. If you are having trouble establishing a telnet session, call your ISP.

FIG. 15.1
Here's a new telnet connection.

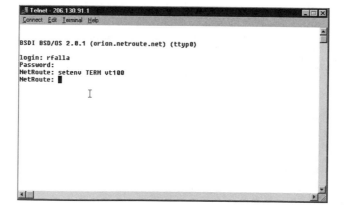

On your first telnet session you should take a few minutes to familiarize yourself with your surroundings. There are a few commands that will become useful during this and any future telnet session.

`ls`	List. Shows files and directories stored in the current directory that are not hidden.
`la`	List All. An alias for `ls -a`. Shows you all the files (including hidden files) and directories stored in the current directory (see Figure 15.2).
`mkdir`	Make Directory. Creates directories and subdirectories in the current directory.
`rm`	Remove. Delete files stored in the current directory.
`rmdir`	Remove Directory. Delete directories and subdirectories stored in the current directory.
`man <topic>`	UNIX manual. Displays the help files on the topic. `man mail` will provide the help files on the UNIX mail program.
`cd <directory>`	Change Directory. Change the current directory to another directory. To go up in the directory tree simply type `'cd ..'`.

TIP **If you want more information on the UNIX online manuals type man man.**

FIG. 15.2

la will list all the contents of the current directory, including hidden system files, which have a dot as the first character.

```
Telnet - 206.130.91.1                                          _ □ ✕
Connect  Edit  Terminal  Help
NetRoute: cd ..
NetRoute: la
.                        dos              old
..                       games            patches
X11                      home             private
X11R6                    include          sbin
adm                      install          share
bin                      lib              src
bootstraps               libdata          ucb
bootstraps.pre_2.0.1     libexec          var
contrib                  local
demo                     obj
NetRoute: ls
X11                      games            old
X11R6                    home             patches
adm                      include          private
bin                      install          sbin
bootstraps               lib              share
bootstraps.pre_2.0.1     libdata          src
contrib                  libexec          ucb
demo                     local            var
dos                      obj
NetRoute: cd ..█
```

Preparing the UNIX directory

The Web site files must be placed in a subdirectory of your home directory, specified by the ISP and usually called public_html. The public_html subdirectory is the default location the browser will look in, for all Web files, when it attempts to retrieve a Web page from your account. If there is no public_html subdirectory, the complete path for the Web site files must be supplied.

Also, the access permission level for the public_html subdirectory must be set to allow read-only access for everyone. Once the access permission for the public_html subdirectory is set, all subdirectories of public_html will share the same permissions as the public_html parent directory.

Not every UNIX is the same. The steps outlined in the following list are based on the BSDI 2.0.1 operating system. Some of the other UNIX systems will not inherit the permissions set for the directory. The best way to determine the requirements for any system is to ask your ISP.

Follow these steps to create the public_html subdirectory and set the appropriate access permissions:

1 Type **pwd** to make sure you are in your home directory.

2 Type **mkdir public_html**. This will create the public_html subdirectory in your home directory.

3 Type **cd public_html** to make it the current directory.

 TIP **Steps 3 and 4 can be combined into a single step by typing chmod 755 public_html or chmod 644 public_html** from the user directory.

4 Type **chmod 755** to set the access permissions of the directory to read and execute. All subdirectories of public_html will have the same access permissions unless you explicitly change them. If you would prefer to set the permission to read only, type **chmod 644** .

The directory is now ready for your Web files. You have created the directory to store the Web files, you created subdirectories as needed, and you even set the access permissions for all directories. The only thing left for your telnet session is for you to end it.

To end the telnet session, type **exit** or **logout** at the prompt. That is all there is to the telnet session—not so bad, eh?

Uploading the files

The next step to getting your Web site published so the world can begin to access it is to put the files in the proper directories. If you have already organized your files by type on your hard drive, you can move right into the next stage, transferring or uploading with an FTP client all the files needed by your Web site.

 NOTE **There are some ISPs who have accounts that do not have shell** access, and everything (including creating subdirectories and giving them the correct permissions) will be done via FTP.

Open your FTP client and follow these instructions to connect to your ISP. As with the telnet client, your home directory is the default directory you will be taken to with the FTP client.

 NOTE **The following is based on using the shareware FTP client** application WS_FTP. If you are using another FTP client application, the steps may be slightly different.

1 Create a new profile (see Figure 15.3) in the Profile Name area. (Or choose the preset profile for your home directory if one exists.)

2 Enter the host name **ftp.*yourhost*.net** (or com, org, whatever).

3 Select Automatic Detect in the Host Type area.

4 Enter your logon name in the User ID area.

5 Enter your password.

6 Check the Sa<u>v</u>e Password box and click the <u>S</u>ave button to save the new profile, so it's still there the next time you have to log on (for modifications to the Web site).

7 Leave the rest of the text areas blank and click the OK button. The FTP client will now connect to the host specified in the profile (your ISP).

8 Type the full path to and including your public_html directory in Remote Host under Default Directores.

FIG. 15.3

Setting up a new profile with WS_FTP.

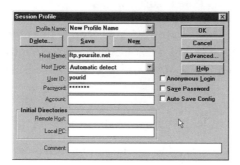

Once you are connected to the remote host, you will see a split window. On the left side is the local (your computer) directory tree; on the right you will see the directory tree of the remote host.

Both directory trees are broken up into three sections. The section nearest the top contains the path of the current directory. There is a separate path on both sides, the left representing your local system, the right representing the remote host.

The midsection contains the directory tree. The current directory is the highest on the tree and any subdirectories are placed under the current directory.

The bottom section contains the files that can be found in the current directory. The one on the left will show (by default) the files in the wsftp directory on your system. The right panel should show any files present in the current directory of the remote host.

Use the following instructions to upload your Web site files to your public_html directory and the pics subdirectory on your ISP's system.

1 In the local system panel (left side) select the directory your Web site files are located in. (Or you can click the ChgDir button and enter the exact path to the directory that contains the Web site files.)

2 In the remote host side, double-click the appropriate directory. In this case it is public_html. You will notice that the directory presently contains no files.

3 Using your mouse, highlight all the files that are to be transferred to the remote directory (see Figure 15.4).

 TIP Make sure the Binary option button is selected. Although you can use ASCII for transferring text files, it is much faster to just leave the setting to binary and transfer files of all types at the same time (bulk transfer).

4 Click the right-pointing arrow button to begin the transmission. A status box will appear, which indicates the progress of the transfer.

5 On the local system, go to any additional directories and transfer any relevant files to the appropriate remote directory.

FIG. 15.4

Select the files you wish to transfer and then click the button indicating which direction (remote-to-host or host-to-remote) you want them to go.

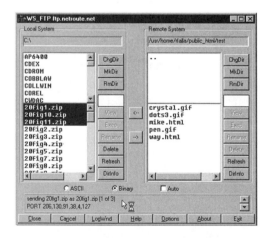

While still in the FTP client you can perform any file management tasks that are required. Depending on how you coded your files you may want to change the extensions of all your files to .html.

> **TIP** **Remember, There must be an index.html file for the Web site.**
> If there is not, the user must specify the exact name of your home page
> in the URL, **www.yourco.com/~yourid/pageone.html**. If there is an
> index.html, the user can simply put your Web server's domain and your user
> name such as **www.yourco.com/~yourid**.

You're finished! Using your favorite browser, test the URL for you Web site.
If it comes up properly you can begin testing all the links on your pages to
make sure your visitors will not end up clicking a dead-end link.

Now go out and announce your new site by using a search service like Yahoo.
Good luck!

Running your own server

If you are in the situation where you need to run your own server and you
have the resources to do it, then you need to choose the right server for your
operating system. You should also take your unique situation into consideration.

The right server

Selecting the right server for your corporate or organizational Web is extremely important. You do not want one that is too complicated or one that
doesn't perform to your requirements.

Take a few minutes to draw up a requirements outline. It should contain
information about capacity and speed expectations, whether or not you need
a secure server, script language requirements, and so on. You should visit the
Web sites of the various server manufacturers and read all the relevant Web
pages to determine if a server meets the minimum set of requirements you
have outlined.

Change the outline as often as is required until it describes your server
requirements in a clear and concise manner. As you read the product information pages, you may come across something that you hadn't thought of.
You should most definitely add those items to your requirements outline.

Once you have narrowed the candidates down to two or three possible servers, find out if you can download a trial version to test evaluate. Run each server through a vigorous evaluation procedure to see how well it performs in certain areas.

Your evaluation should include, in addition to anything you consider important for your circumstances, the following:

- Installation procedures—how easy or difficult are the installation procedures for the server?

- Technical support—what kind of technical support package is offered with the purchase of the server?

- HTML tools—does the server come with HTML authoring tools?

- Speed test—how well does the server handle at different speed benchmarks?

If you invest the time finding the right server, you will avoid many of the problems associated with getting the wrong server. A few days to a week of time spent investigating servers is worth many days or even weeks worth of headaches in the future.

 NOTE **For more information about server software refer to one of the** following Que books: *Running a Perfect Netscape Site, Special Edition Using Microsoft Internet Information Server 2,* and *Special Edition Using Netscape LiveWire.*

Putting your site online

When you are running your own Web server, the steps for publishing the Web site are slightly different. The biggest difference is you don't make a telnet or an FTP connection because the server is the local host. The following list will take you through the steps of publishing your Web site on your own UNIX server.

There are many other servers to choose from, depending on your operating system. If you are not using UNIX or Windows NT, you should purchase a book that is more specifically directed to the operating system you have chosen.

1 The first step is to create a root directory on your hard drive.

2 From the root directory create the directories user and home, which will allow you to add as many Web accounts as you want or need.

3 Create a Web account for your site in the user/home directory. Typically, your user ID is the account name.

4 Create the public_html directory in the Web account directory.

5 Assign the proper permissions.

6 Move the Web site files to the appropriate directories.

7 Change file names if required.

8 Test the links. Once again you are in the position where you must test the links on your site to ensure the visitor will have a nice unobstructed visit on your site. Test the links at least monthly. Find and fix broken links.

When you are running your own server you have a few additional options to consider.

- Should access to the site be restricted?

- Will it be a secure server site?

- What Web applications (if any) do I want to include?

Each of the three items in this bulleted list consists of many additional steps and procedures that must be followed. Don't be fooled by the brevity of the steps in publishing a Web site on your own server.

The list fails to mention the maintenance procedures that are required monthly on a Web server. It also says nothing of the many other (log report analysis, visitor count analysis, and so on) functions a server administrator must perform.

In the next section, you'll take a look at some of the Web servers that are presently available. This will give you a good starting point for finding and running the server that most meets your individual requirements.

Web Servers

Use the following section to help narrow your search for an appropriate Web server. Each Web server is presented with an introductory paragraph.

Microsoft Internet Information Server

Microsoft IIS is the Web server that comes bundled with the Windows NT operating system. IIS has been reviewed favorably by many Internet trade magazines. If Windows NT is your operating system then you should give this server serious consideration. It's free, anyway, with Windows NT version 4.

Company	Microsoft Internet Information Server
Web Address	**http://www.msn.com/** or **http://www.microsoft.com/**
Platform	Windows NT
Address	One Microsoft Way Redmond, WA 98052-6399
Telephone	(206)882-8080

IIS is a fairly complete Web server suite. There are no installation problems with this server, in part because it is automatically installed when you install Windows NT 4.0.

Although it performs superbly on the Windows NT platform, that is the only platform it is available on, at present. This platform limitation automatically eliminates many potential customers for Microsoft. Look to Microsoft to release a fully interoperable, multiplatform server in early 1997 with the release of the Active Platform.

The IIS comes bundled with an FTP server, WWW server, Gopher server, and WAIS server. In addition, IIS also includes an HTML editor to assist authoring of HTML documents, a slew of APIs, and SSL security support.

Another feature of the IIS package is the inclusion of the FrontPage HTML authoring application. FrontPage is an excellent authoring application for all Web developers—new to the Net—or veteran Web developers. Using FrontPage, you will have a Web site up and running in only a few short hours.

Luckman Web Commander

The people from Luckman are not new to the Internet. In fact, they have developed many other Internet-related applications, many of which are included in this package.

Company	Luckman Interactive
Web Address	**http://www.luckman.com**
Platform	Windows NT and Windows 95
Address	1055 W. 7th Street, Suite 2580 Los Angeles, CA 90017
Telephone	(213) 614-0966

Web Commander provides a complete Internet server solution package. From the time you remove the shrink-wrap to having the package fully installed on your system takes about an hour. There is helpful documentation included with the package to help you get everything running without a hitch.

The server software is only one component of the Web Commander package. Also included in the package are HTML authoring tools, secure-server applications, ODBC database support, WAIS Toolkit, Netscape Navigator, and Perl 5.

Where IIS is limited to operating only on Windows NT, Web Commander will work with both Windows NT and Windows 95, making it accessible to a wider group of information providers than IIS. In addition to working on both operating systems, Web Commander has a much better monitoring and logging program than IIS.

WebSite Professional

In keeping with their reputation for providing high-quality products, O'Reilly has produced the WebSite Professional.

Company	O'Reilly & Associates
Web Address	**http://www.ora.com**
Platform	Windows NT and Windows 95
Address	101 Morris Street Sebastopol, CA 95472
Telephone	(707) 829-0515
Fax	(707) 829-0104

Is security important to you? How about database connectivity? WebSite Professional provides excellent support for both, as well as a complete, GUI-based diagnostics application.

The documentation and manuals included with WebSite Professional are well written and easy to use, making installation and administration of your new server as easy as possible. There are no quick solutions to the problem of not understanding the technology. A few good books will go a long way toward improving your understanding.

Like IIS and Web Commander, WebSite Professional is also loaded with additional components. HTML authoring tools include HotDog, WSAPI, and Netscape Gold.

16

Search Engines and Advertising

● **In this chapter:**

● How are all those Web users going to find my site?

● Get yourself at the top of the list

● Target the search tools in this chapter

● Learn other methods for getting noticed

Current estimates show that the Web has more than 20 million pages. Even using the fastest connection and taking just seconds to glance at each page would take a reader the better part of a decade to see them all, by which time perhaps 10 times as many new pages would have appeared. Because of the scale of the Web, it is very unlikely that many people will find your page by pure chance. In fact, if your page has no links leading to it from other pages, it is very likely that no one will ever find it.

Because the reason to create a Web page in the first place is to publish information, you want to encourage other people to visit your page. The best way to bring people to your page is to make the job of finding it as easy as possible. That's what this chapter is all about. You'll learn how to list your site with the best search tools on the Internet. You'll also learn other methods you can use to get your site noticed.

Understanding what kind of advertising you need

The type of advertising that you do depends greatly on the nature of your page. If you are doing a page as a hobby, paying a thousand dollars to get a week's worth of exposure on one of the popular sites probably isn't worth the cost to you. On the other hand, if your site is the home page of a major multinational corporation, the attention that a professionally designed advertisement can bring more than justifies the expense.

 NOTE **Although I use the term advertising extensively in this chapter,** most of the methods listed here are free. A better term might be Web page promotion.

With this point in mind, you should take the first step toward advertising on the Web, which is to answer the following questions about your site:

- How much traffic do I want at my site?

- Does my site have a broad appeal, or is it for a more specialized audience?

- How much of a budget do I have to advertise my site?

- How much time can I devote to advertising my site?

- How important is it to the success of my business (or hobby or organization) that my site become well known?

If your page is just a hobby, where you share information with others who share your interests, you can mount a low-key advertising campaign. Most of the people who find your page will do so through links with other pages that cover the same topics. Think hard about the sites that you like to visit, and you'll probably find that most of your visitors like the same sites.

 NOTE **Even if you are starting a page just as a hobby, it doesn't need to** end there. Many of the most successful aspects of the Web began as part-time activities.

Nonprofit organizations can achieve tremendous exposure on the Web, far out of proportion to the amount of money invested. These organizations often have enough manpower to find a large number of free locations to advertise the site.

For a small business, the Web can be an excellent place to advertise. On the Web, unlike most other forms of advertising, even a small company can produce a presence that is equally impressive as is that of a huge conglomerate. Unlike the print world, the Web allows anyone access to full-color images and advertising regardless of budget. In the democratic world of the Web, all addresses are equally impressive, giving your company real estate that is just as valuable as that of your larger competitors.

If your company is a mail-order or service business that can support customers around the country, or even the world, investing a greater proportion of money and energy in Web advertising may well be worthwhile. If you work at one of these companies, you may want to consider using a commercial marketing service.

Listing with WWW search engines

Most people find what they're looking for on the Web by using one of the many available search tools. These systems are huge databases containing as many as 20 million Web pages, coupled with powerful indexing software that allows for quick searches. Many of the search engines are run on mainframe computers or large parallel processors that can handle hundreds of searches simultaneously. Other search engines run on arrays of Windows NT servers.

In the beginning of the Web, the first search servers were run by universities, but now most of these early efforts have been taken over by private companies. What benefit do these companies find in providing free searches on these expensive computers? Advertising! The index sites are some of the most frequently visited on the Web, and the maintainers of these sites can charge high rates to the companies that advertise on these pages. That doesn't mean that they charge you to list your site, though. Many of these companies have become so successful that they're now publicly traded on the stock exchange.

 In WebTrack's study of Web advertising, they discovered that five of the top 10 sites in terms of revenues from advertising were search tools.

In addition to the older sites, more than a hundred newer indexes are available. Some of them are restricted to a specific topic, and others are still very small, but all offer the opportunity to get your site noticed.

As you explore the Web, you soon discover that it possesses its own collection of fauna. The wildlife of the Web consists of autonomous programs that work their way across the millions of links that connect the sites, gathering information along the way.

These programs are known by such colorful names as robots, crawlers, walkers, spiders (a generic term), worms, and (in the case of one Australian program) wombats. What do these spiders do? Almost without exception, they arrive at a page, index it, and search it for any links to other pages. These new links are recorded and followed in turn. When all the links on a particular chain have been followed, the next path is restored from the database, and the process continues. Examples of these engines are Lycos and Webcrawler, which you'll learn more about later in this chapter. A large number of special-purpose spiders are also used to generate statistics regarding the Web. These programs do not generate databases that can be used for text searching, though.

 Most spiders index the title and content of each Web page they visit. In some cases—AltaVista and Infoseek—they also index the META tag if it's included on the page. (You learn about the META tag later in this chapter.)

The alternative to these spiders are the *structured systems*. Whereas spiders don't organize links hierarchically, structured systems store Web pages indexed against a series of categories and subcategories. You browse or search through the categories looking for entries. The hierarchical nature of these systems appeals to many people who are more comfortable using an index where they can see all the categories. For example, Yahoo! is a very popular index that almost looks more like an online service than a search tool.

The type of system on which you perform your searches is entirely up to your personal preferences. From the standpoint of advertising your site, you need to be aware of the differences. Some of the structured systems restrict you to a limited number of index entries. This limitation can mean that people who are looking for just the things that you offer may not find you because they are looking in the wrong place.

The major search engines

A complete listing of indexes would be out of date as soon as it was finished. New sites are added monthly, and even sites that are maintained by large corporations have disappeared. I have listed a few of the main sites in this section, but you should take the time to do some of your own searching when you decide to publish your pages.

In the big league, a handful of sites can claim to have indexed a sizable portion of the Web. These sites are the most popular systems, used by the majority of Web surfers. You need to register with these servers first to maximize your exposure. Table 16.1 lists the major search engines on which I recommend you list your Web site. The sections that follow describe each search tool in more detail.

Table 16.1   Major search engines

Name	URL
AltaVista	http://www.altavista.digital.com
Excite	http://www.excite.com
InfoSeek	http://www.infoseek.com
Lycos	http://www.lycos.com
Web Crawler	http://www.webcrawler.com
Yahoo!	http://www.yahoo.com

All of the sites in Table 16.1 are free to the user. They're sponsored by advertisers. Your listings are also free.

CAUTION **Some of the earliest robots were poorly written and could swamp** a server with hundreds of requests within seconds of each other. Fortunately, most recent robots are courteous enough not to overload their hosts. If your server does crash, check the logs for a single site that retrieved many documents within a short period of time. If such a site exists, try to contact the postmaster at the site that made the requests and let him or her know about the problems that you saw.

NOTE **In the September 1996 issue of PC World magazine, they gave** each of the search tools a grade: A+ to F, with A+ being the best. For your own amusement, here is how PC World graded the engines I've discussed in this chapter: Excite, A+; Yahoo!, A+; Lycos, A; Infoseek, A–; AltaVista, C–; WebCrawler, F.

AltaVista

AltaVista (see Figure 16.1) is a search engine that's owned and operated by Digital. It started indexing the Web in the summer of 1995 and went public with 16 million indexed pages in December of 1995. Now, AltaVista gets about 30 million hits per day.

AltaVista scours the Web looking for sites to index. When it finds a site, it indexes the site three levels deep. That is, it indexes the home page, any pages to which the homepage is linked, and any pages to which the second level pages are linked. When AltaVista indexes a page, it indexes the full text of the page. It stores the results in its database, on which a user's search is performed.

FIG. 16.1
Click Add URL to add
your site to AltaVista.

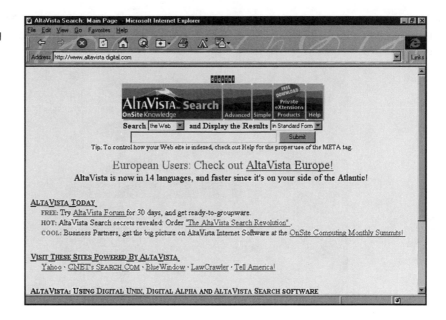

NOTE If your Web site changes, you don't need to relist it with AltaVista or most of the other search engines. AltaVista will visit your site periodically, reindexing the contents of the site that have changed. AltaVista is unique in that it notes how often your site changes, and will adjust the frequency of its visits to your site based upon the frequency of your changes.

To list your site with AltaVista, open AltaVista (**http://www.altavista. digital.com**) in your Web browser and click the Add URL link at the bottom of the page. Follow the instructions you see on the next page. To remove your site from AltaVista, follow the instructions you find at this Web site.

Excite

Excite (see Figure 16.2) was started in 1993. It currently indexes over 50 million Web pages, making it one of the largest databases on the Web. What makes Excite unique among the search engines is that it also contains over 60,000 reviews of individual Web sites. Thus, you can get a third-party perspective on the type and quality of information at a particular Web site before you visit the site.

FIG. 16.2
Click Add URL to add your site to Excite.

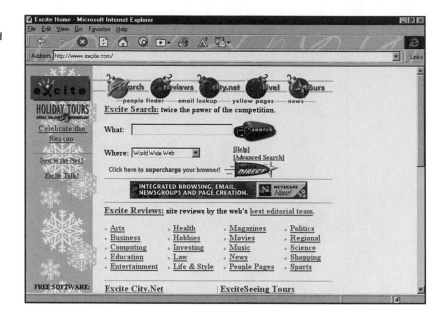

Excite does a full text index, just like AltaVista. What makes Excite's indexing unique, however, is that it also does a concept-based index. That is, if Excite finds the words Dog and Food on your Web site, those words will match a user's search if they use the terms Pet and Food. The user is more likely to find your site on Excite, because you don't have to be nearly as careful about picking just the right words.

Like AltaVista, Excite will index your site three levels deep: the homepage, its links, and the next level of links. Excite will reindex your site about every two weeks.

To list your site with Excite, open Excite in your Web browser (**http://www. excite.com**), and click Add URL link at the bottom of the page. Follow the instructions on the subsequent Web page. To remove your site from AltaVista, follow the instructions you find at this Web site.

 NOTE **If a spider wants to visit your site, there's really nothing you can** do to prevent it. Your site is on the Internet and the pages are available for the spider to access. On the other hand, if you want to keep spiders off of your Web site so that they don't affect its performance, most spiders will honor your request if you add a file called ROBOTS.TXT to the root directory of your Web server.

Creating this file is easy. Create a new text file in your root directory called ROBOTS.TXT. Add a line that begins with the field name **User-agent:**. This field must then contain the name of the robot that you want to restrain. You can have multiple User-agent fields, or if you want to exclude all agents not specifically mentioned in a User-agent field, you can use a field value of *****. The line following each User-agent field should begin with the field name **Disallow:**. This field should contain a URL path. Any URL that begins with the path specified in the Disallow field will be ignored by the robot named in the User-agent field.

Here are some examples you can use:

```
# Any text that begins with a pound-sign is treated as a
➡comment
User-agent: Webcrawler # Applies to the robot named
➡Webcrawler
Disallow: /webpages/data/ # Webcrawler will skip URLs in
➡this path

# This example is the universal "do not disturb" sign
User-agent: * # All robots
Disallow: / # Every URL begins with a / in the path
```

Infoseek

Infoseek started as a very meager search tool. It's all grown up now, however (see Figure 16.3). That is, it's a real contender for the best search tool on the Internet. It started in January of 1994 and has grown to the point that it indexes over 50 million Web pages.

Like the other tools, Infoseek does a full text index. It only indexes your site two levels deep, however. As well, Infoseek will only visit your site every three weeks, instead of every two weeks.

To list your site with Infoseek, open Infoseek (**http://www.infoseek.com**) in your Web browser. Then, click the Add Site link at the bottom of the page. Follow the instructions you see on the next page. To remove your site from AltaVista, follow the instructions you find at this Web site.

FIG. 16.3
Click Add Site to add
your site to Infoseek.

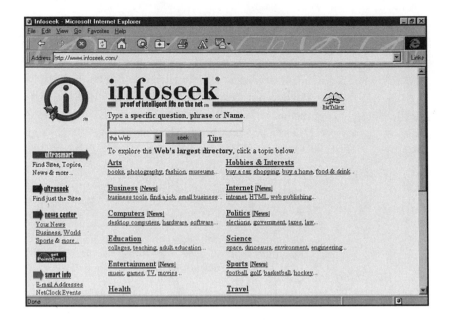

TIP   When submitting your Web site to a spider, only submit the top-
level page (homepage). The spider will traverse your site to find other pages
linked to the homepage.

Lycos

Lycos (see Figure 16.4) is one of the granddaddies of the Internet. It's been
around for a while, and has gone through some huge changes. It's user
interface is greatly improved. It's index is larger. And it's hierarchical database is better organized.

Lycos doesn't do a full text index like the other search tools. Instead, it
creates an abstract from your home page that describes the contents of your
site. Lycos will index your site three levels deep, and it'll revisit your site
about every two weeks.

To list your site with Lycos, open Lycos (**http://www.lycos.com**), and click
Add Your Site to Lycos at the bottom of the page. Follow the instructions you
see on the subsequent Web page.

FIG. 16.4
Click Add Your Site to Lycos to add your site to Lycos.

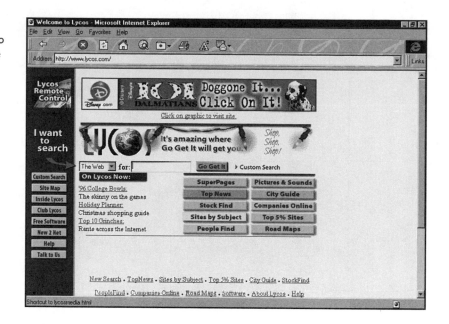

 NOTE **When you submit your Web site to one of the search engines,** don't expect immediate results. While the spider may index your site immediately, it can take from two to four weeks before your site actually shows up in the search database.

WebCrawler

WebCrawler (see Figure 16.5) started as an educational project in 1994. In 1995, America Online purchased it. Today, WebCrawler gets about three million hits per day.

WebCrawler does a full-text index. It only indexes your site one level deep, however, so the only information it's going to get is off of your home page. As well, WebCrawler will only visit about once a month. Because of these factors, WebCrawler has taken a beating in the press. PC Magazine recently gave WebCrawler a failing grade. You should not ignore WebCrawler, however, because it has a very large following given that it's owned by America Online.

FIG. 16.5
Click Add URL
to add your site
to WebCrawler.

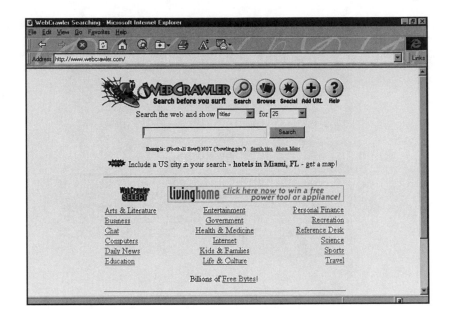

To list your site with WebCrawler, open WebCrawler (**http://www. webcrawler.com**) in your browser, and click Add URL at the top of the page. Follow the instructions you see on the next page.

Yahoo!

Yahoo! (started in 1994 as a hobby of its creators) is my favorite search tool. It's not a worm like the other tools. It categorizes Web sites that users submit into a hierarchical index. You find what you're looking for by either searching the hierarchy or traversing down each category until you find a Web site in which you're interested.

Yahoo! (see Figure 16.6) is one of the best-organized hierarchical indexes on the Internet. Beyond indexing Web sites, however, Yahoo! provides dozens of other services. For example, Yahoo! categorizes Web sites by their regional areas, such as my hometown of Frisco, TX. It also provides telephone books (white and yellow pages) in which you can look up a phone number and maps so that you can find a restaurant near you or get directions to your favorite computer store.

FIG. 16.6
You'll find Yahoo! on the Internet at **http:// www.yahoo.com**.

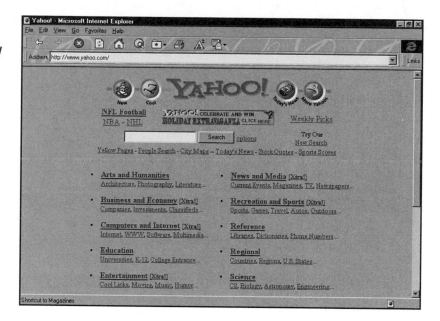

Adding your Web site to Yahoo! is a bit more complicated than adding your site to the other search tools. First, you have to locate the category in which you want to add your site. When you've located the appropriate category, click Add URL at the top of the Web page, and follow the instructions you see on the subsequent page.

Using submission services

You do not always have to do all the work yourself. Several good services submit your pages to the major search systems for you. Many of these services have a charge for this function, but a few services are available for free.

Submit It! is a nice forms-based system that allows you to enter all the relevant data for your page, after which it registers you with your choices of more than a dozen popular search tools (see Figure 16.7). This service is provided for free and can help you to hit most of the major search sites. You can find it at **http://www.submit-it.com**.

FIG. 16.7
Submit It! is a powerful tool for registering with multiple search engines quickly.

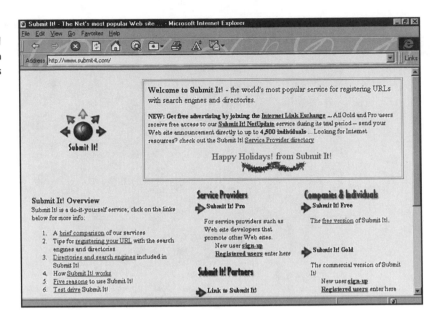

There are a number of other submission services available on the Web. Table 16.2 shows you a few to get you started.

Table 16.2 Submission services

Name	Free?	URL
AAA Internet Promotions	No	**http://www.websitepromote.com**
Ace Basic	No	**http://sffa/acebase.html**
Papparazi	Yes	**http://www.papparazi.com**

Just as with the search tools, any list of services on the Web is obsolete almost as fast as it is generated. Your best bet is to do a little checking on your own to see what else is out there. A good place to start looking is at the Web Announcements topic on Yahoo!.

The big advantage of a submission service is that it cuts down on the amount of work that you have to do. The disadvantage is that your submissions are made automatically, using the same categories and keywords for each database. This is probably sufficient if your page is personal or is intended for a specific audience.

If your page is the Web presence for your company or your organization, spending the time to learn about each of the databases yourself is probably better, so that you can ensure that your listing ends up under the right headings. After all, the time required to submit your page is nothing compared to the hard work that you've put into making it as good as it is.

Putting your site at the top of the list

Listing your Web site with a search engine is one thing. Making sure that it appears at the top of the list when a user does a search is a whole different matter. I've seen a lot of folks try their hardest to pick the right set of keywords, only to be disappointed when their site doesn't make it to the top of the list.

Good planning gets you on top

The best way to make sure your site appears at the top of the list is to do a bit of planning. Sit down with a piece of paper and a few of your colleagues and brainstorm on all the types of queries you think users will use to find your site. Try to anticipate them. Are you selling pet food? If so, people might use the following combination of queries to locate your site:

> pet and grooming and supplies
>
> dog and (food or supplies)
>
> dog and (flea or pest) and treatment
>
> pet and (leash or collar)
>
> dog and (toy or ball or bed)

The list can go on and on. Don't stop until you're absolutely out of ideas. You've covered every possible query you can think of. Then, make your Web site responsive to those queries:

1 Make a list of all the words in the queries you came up with.

2 Beside each word, write down the number of times that word appeared in your list of queries.

3 Sort the list, putting the words with the most number of occurrences at the top of the list.

4 Going down the list from top to bottom, make sure that each word appears in the homepage of your site at least one time. As well, you can use the META tag to list those keywords for the search engines that catalog the META tag.

Other tips for getting on top

Here are some additional ideas to make sure people find your site:

- *Use good keywords in your Web page.* As well, make sure that you use words that your prospective audience would choose to use, not what your technical staff would use. For example, your engineers may call it a super-duper widget, but your customers will probably call it a thingy.

- *Use the META tag to embed keywords into your homepage.* This doesn't work with all of the search engines, however, as only AltaVista and Infoseek use the META tag. The next section describes how to use the META tag.

- *Don't rely solely on graphics in your HTML file.* In particular, a homepage that contains nothing more than an imagemap is disastrous when it comes to listing with the search engines because you're given the searching engine nothing to index.

- *Keep your scripts, VBScript or JavaScript, away from the top portion of your Web page.* The search engines that create abstracts will display your scripts instead of a good abstract of your Web site.

- *Keep each Web page on your site focused on a particular topic.* That is, don't include information about pets on the same Web page that contains information about Windows NT Server. This will severely confuse concept-based search engines such as Excite. If each Web page is narrowly focused on a particular topic, you have a better chance of that page bubbling to the top of the list.

 **CAUTION** **Some folks will tell you that the way to get your site to the top of** the list is to fill it with the appropriate keywords, repeated over and over again. For example, if you want users to find your site when they search for the keywords **Windows 95**, then you might fill an HTML comment tag with those keywords over and over again. Don't do this. Many of the search engines are now catching on to this little trick and will knock your listing out of the index.

Categorize your site with the *META* tag

You can use the HTML META tag to tell the search engine a bit more about how to categorize your site. This doesn't work with all the search engines, however, as the concept- and abstract-based search engines don't necessarily use keywords to categorize a Web site.

The META tag is simple. It allows you to create pseudo-tags within your HTML file. Here's what it looks like:

```
<META NAME=name CONTENT=content>
```

You set the NAME attribute to the name of the tag you are creating and the CONTENT attribute to the content of that tag. This is only useful if something on the Internet, be it client, search tool, or whatever, is expecting to find a META tag by a certain name.

To help along some of the search engines that do look for the META tag, you can create two tags called KEYWORDS and DESCRIPTION. The KEYWORDS META tag provides a list of keywords, separated by commas, to the search engine. You can use this to specify keywords that aren't found within the text of your HTML file. The DESCRIPTION META tag contains a description of your Web site that the search engine will display to the user when the search engine displays your site in the list. Here's what both tags look like:

```
<META NAME="KEYWORDS" CONTENT="pet, dog, cat, food, toys,
➥grooming">
<META NAME="DESCRIPTION" CONTENT="My online pet store
➥provides all of your pet supplies."
```

TIP If your homepage uses an imagemap with little text, at least use a META tag for those search engines that parse the META tag.

Getting noticed by using other ways

On the Web, there are many other ways to get noticed. You're not limited to the search tools. The sections that follow describe a variety of these other ways. Some require a bit of work or expense on your part, whereas others are free.

Best of the Web listings

One of the more amazing things to come out of the Web has been the tremendous proliferation of "Best of the Web" sites. These systems generate listings under a variety of names, such as What's Cool, What's Hot, Top 5%, Best of the Web, Hot Picks, and so on (see Figure 16.8). In practice, of course, the selection of pages for these lists is completely arbitrary. For example, with the rapid growth of the Web, it is unlikely that anyone has ever even visited five percent of the sites currently available, let alone enough to make a reasonable judgment of which are the very best.

FIG. 16.8
Several organizations present "Best of the Web" awards.

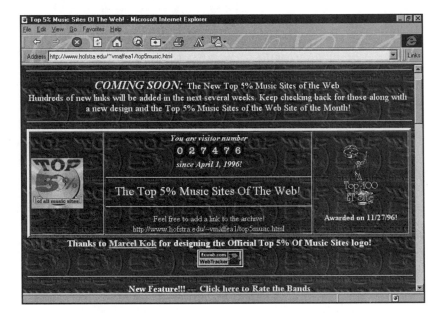

So how are these lists maintained? In most cases, you can submit the URL of your site to the administrator of the list, and he or she visits your site and reviews it. If your site meets whatever selection criteria the list is based on, you get added to the list.

Some of these lists provide you with a small graphic that you can display on your page to indicate that you have been awarded the honor, and virtually all the lists include links to your page after you have been accepted.

What is the real value of these lists? In the cosmic scheme of things, very little. But some of these lists are well known, and many people use them as launching points for random surfing. If you have a general interest site, getting it listed on a couple of these pages can really boost your traffic.

Some examples of these sites are:

- *Cool Site of the Day.* A strange and quirky site located at **http://cool.infi.net**.

- *Macmillan Winner's Circle.* A site that recognizes excellence in personal home pages at **http://www.mcp.com/general/workshop/winner**.

- *What's Cool.* If you can manage to get yourself onto Netscape's What's Cool page, you'll have to beat back the visitors with a stick. You can find this index of pages at **http://home.netscape.com/home/whats-cool.html**.

Links from other Web sites

Even more than the Web crawlers and structured systems, the primary method for traversing the Web is by using links found on other pages (see Figure 16.9). To expose your page to the maximum number of potential visitors, you should make an effort to get as many sites as possible to include links to your site.

FIG. 16.9
Many sites have long lists of links to other related sites.

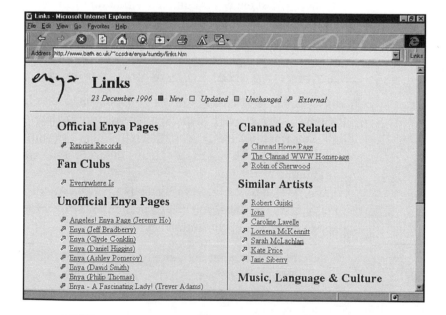

Most sites that cover a specific topic are more than pleased to include links to other sites that cover the same topic. By including as many links as possible, they make themselves more useful and, hence, more popular. To encourage people to link to your page, you need to identify sites that might be interested in linking to yours, and then contact the site administrator.

Finding sites from which to link

The best way to find sites to contact about linking to your site is to surf the Web. Find sites that are of interest to you, and you'll probably find the sites that are of interest to people who would visit your site. Where should you start surfing? The same places that your visitors would.

Start with the indexes and see what's out there. Try several of the more popular ones, and be sure to try both structured systems and Web crawlers. If one of indexes is particularly useful, you know that it is a good place to register your site. The ones that aren't useful can wait before you submit to them.

After you find some sites, visit them and see what they have to offer. You're looking for sites that have a theme that is similar to yours, without being identical. For example, if your page contains links to everything that a person might ever want to know about hog farming, pages that might make good links to your page include general farming pages, pages that cover animal husbandry, and pages for companies that do business with hog farmers, including both suppliers and consumers. Other pages that also cover aspects of hog farming but are not duplicates of yours would also be worth linking to.

Convincing sites to link to your site

The best way to get a link to your Web page is to simply contact the owner of the page that you'd like to be linked from and ask him or her to create the link. You can most easily accomplish this task by sending e-mail to the page author. In most cases, you should be able to find the address of the person who maintains the link on one of the pages at the site. Failing this, try sending e-mail to the address Webmaster at the site that interests you. Finally, if all else fails, you can examine the HTML source for the site's main page to see whether the author's address is included in a comment field.

Be sure to explain what your site is all about and to include the URL of the home page in your message. If the page that you want the other site to link to is not your home page, let the Webmaster know what the correct URL is. A brief (one-line) description of your page can save him or her some time when adding the link. Remember that the Webmaster is just as busy as you are and that anything that you can do to make his or her life easier will increase the chance that he or she links to your page.

Of course, you can expect that the person in charge of the other site will check out your page before adding a link. He or she will want to make sure that your page actually is what you say it is and that the quality is such that it will improve his or her site to be linked to yours.

Making your site worth a link

To make your site more worthwhile for others to link to, the first step is to ensure that it is free of HTML errors and that it loads correctly. Have your site examined by other people from outside your site to check that all the images are available and that all the tags display in the proper format. No one wants to be associated with a site that is filled with sloppy work.

Second, include useful, current, and interesting information and images. No one wants to spend time downloading a site just to find that it contains a mess of outdated or boring gibberish. Links to shareware programs can also make your page more popular.

 **CAUTION** **Before adding a link to download any program, be sure that the** program explicitly states that it is for freeware or shareware distribution, particularly if it is not stored on your server.

Finally, make it attractive. Ask yourself if the page makes you want to read it; then get the opinions of some people you can trust.

An important step toward making your site successful is to include a number of links to other sites that might be of interest to visitors to your site. The entire concept of the Web revolves around the interconnection of millions of sites. Don't make your page a dead end.

 TIP **Check occasionally that all the links on your page still lead** somewhere. Pages maintained by other people may disappear, often without notice.

If your site is a personal page, include connections to pages of your friends and colleagues. A hobby site should include as many links to other sites with similar interests as you can find. Check the links to make sure that they point to pages that you want to be associated to; then include them.

 NOTE **Although you can certainly add a link to a page without the prior** consent of the owner of the page, contacting the maintainer of the page to let him or her know of the new link is courteous. He or she may also have a preference as to which page you establish the link to.

Business and organization pages can include links to other sources of information related to your site. Including links to your competitors is not necessary, but having links that point to your suppliers and customers might be very effective. Encourage them to include reciprocal links back to your page. Remember that the most effective form of advertising is networking and that a link to your page is an implicit recommendation.

Specialized index pages

If your pages are focused on a specific topic, registering with any specialized index pages that cover your area of interest is well worth the time.

At present, you can find many sites for business-related topics. This fact isn't surprising, but what is amazing is the incredible variety of index pages available for other interests as well. A search of the Web turns up many specialized pages that contain dozens of links. The following are a few examples of these pages:

- *Art Planet.* A professionally run site that allows searches based on companies, keywords, or artists (see Figure 16.10). It is located at **http://www.artplanet.com/index.html**.

- *The Hamster Page*   This is the definitive hamster resource page, and you can find it at **http://www.tela.bc.ca/hamster**.

- *Special Needs Education Network*   A site that provides a number of links to resources for people with special needs and parents of children with special needs. You can find it at **http://schoolnet2.carleton.ca/ ~kwellar/snewww.html**.

- *Chess Space*   A comprehensive index to everything in the chess world. It is located at **http://www.redweb.com/chess**.

FIG. 16.10

You can use specialized search tools such as Art Planet to locate your page successfully.

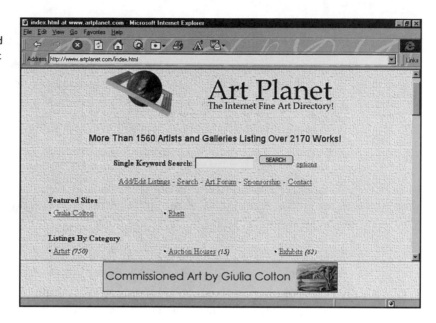

- *Points of Pediatric Interest*   More than 650 links dedicated to pediatric medicine and child care. You can find it at **http://www.med.jhu. edu/peds/neonatology/poi.html**.

- *Church Online*   A worldwide list of Christian churches. It is located at **http://www.churchonline.com/index.html**.

In the business world, pages exist for many different types of companies. You can see some of the tremendous variety in the following pages:

- *TruckNet*   A site specializing in just about everything that you might ever want to know about the trucking industry. It is located at **http:// www.truck.net**.

- *Petro-Links*   This site has links to oil companies, suppliers, petroleum industry magazines, and applicable government agencies. It is located at **http://www.findlinks.com/petrolinks.html**.

- *Fashion Net*   A service with hundreds of links to companies that are involved in the fashion and clothing industries. Not all these companies have Web sites, but many do. You can find Fashion Net at **http://www. fashion.net**.

- *Thomas Register* A site run by the company that publishes the famous Thomas Register of Manufacturers. If you work for a manufacturing company or if you supply manufacturing companies, you really should submit your site at **http://www.thomasregister.com**.

Using newsgroups effectively

A Web site is very difficult to find in the vast reaches of the Internet. Fortunately, you can use public bulletin boards to broadcast information to a number of people at the same time. These public areas are known as newsgroups, and they serve as public forums for communications and debate.

Much like everything else on the Internet, these groups have their own rules and customs. Very broadly, they fall into two categories: open and moderated groups. Open groups are pretty much what they sound like, in that anyone can post a message. Unfortunately, this freedom often leads to a very low signal-to-noise ratio. Moderated groups require that all postings are passed through a moderator (or group of moderators) who screens the messages and removes off-topic messages. This process greatly improves the proportion of postings that are relevant to the subject of the newsgroup.

Regardless of the type of newsgroup, proper use can greatly increase the traffic at your Web site. By the same token, however, improper use can cause ill feelings and will not attract the visitors that you are looking for.

The announcement groups

The first newsgroups to use when spreading the word about your new Web site are the announcement groups. These groups are dedicated to the purpose of broadcasting messages dealing with new sites and services (see Figure 16.11). Most of these groups are moderated and do an excellent job of keeping messages on topic.

comp.infosystems.www.announce lists virtually every site that is submitted to it. The rules of this group are standard for many of the announcement groups. Postings should be relevant to the purpose of the group and should not have a commercial purpose other than the announcement of a Web site that provides further information about a commercial product or service. The message announcing the site should have the URL of the page clearly listed in the message, preferably on a separate line. The message should also include a clear but brief description of the nature of the site. Finally, the subject of the message should be clear and precise. It is recommended that the subject begin with a word or two that clearly defines your site. See the example shown in Figure 16.12.

FIG. 16.11
comp.infosystems. www.announce is the number one site for posting new sites.

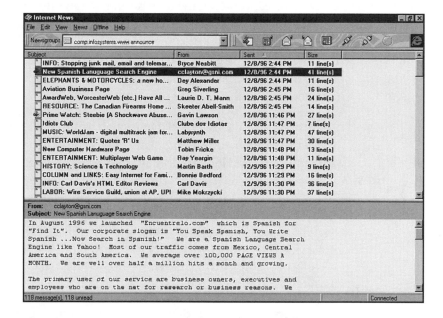

FIG. 16.12
This announcement is clear and concise, and it lets potential visitors know what they can expect.

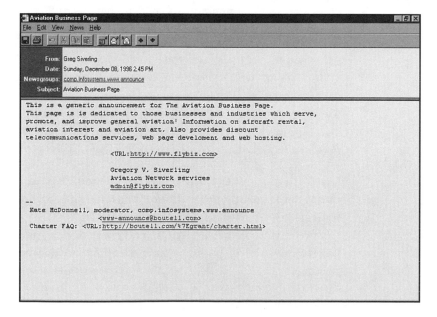

Other good groups to announce in are **comp.internet.net-happenings** and **misc.entrepreneurs** (for business sites).

Other newsgroups

After you have posted on the announcement newsgroups, you should take some time to find any other groups that may involve topics covered in your Web site. Far more than 20,000 newsgroups are operating right now, although your Internet provider may cache only a fraction of this number. With this kind of diversity present, finding the groups that most closely match your interests is normally not difficult.

After you narrow down the field to a small handful of groups, the next step is to read the various messages that are posted. Try to identify people who are regular posters, and look for threads that have a long life. This practice of reading messages on a group without posting is known as lurking. You lurk in a group to become more familiar with it before you post.

One of the features of many groups is the occasional posting of what is called a FAQ. This message is a list of Frequently Asked Questions, and reading it carefully can help you avoid asking any questions that might have been answered repeatedly in the past.

The primary benefit to lurking is that when you are ready to post messages, you can do so in a manner that is perceived as highly competent and professional.

After you do start posting, you should make a special effort to ensure that your posts are well written and on topic. Remember that you are not just carrying on a friendly conversation, but rather you are advertising your page. Avoid mentioning your Web site in the body of your posting, but include your signature at the end of the message. If your postings are worth reading, people will make an effort to visit your pages, too.

One form of message posting is not recommended: Sending large numbers of messages to post on many different newsgroups, regardless of the group's topic, is known as *spamming* (see Figure 16.13). This kind of posting is a tremendous waste of bandwidth, and many people, particularly those who pay for their access based on time spent logged in, do not appreciate your postings.

FIG. 16.13

The message about saving on long-distance charges is off-topic for this group and is an example of spamming.

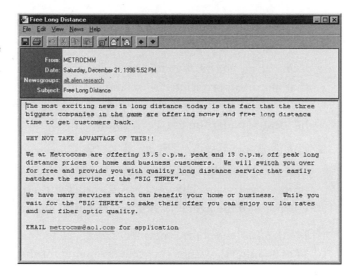

An unfortunate side effect of spamming is that it tends to attract retaliation from residents of the Internet. This retaliation can begin at the annoyance level and rapidly escalate. To avoid any unpleasantness, you should follow the rules and act in a responsible manner.

NOTE **The primary offense caused by spamming is the waste of huge** amounts of storage space on computers around the world. To help curb the problem, many newsgroups have programs that can excise spamming messages automatically from the group, often before most people even see the message. One side effect of spamming is that you may become black-listed, which can expose you to remarkable levels of harassment from cybervigilantes.

Using a publicity consultant

As you may have noticed, developing an effective Web advertising campaign can be a lot of work. For someone working on a page for a hobby, all this work might not matter much, but for a busy professional who is trying to build up business through the Web, the time required may be more than he or she can afford. One solution to this problem is to use a publicity consultant. This person is an agent who handles the details necessary for getting your site noticed.

Some of the functions that a publicity consultant should perform are as follow:

- *Submitting your site to all the major search engines* and to any others that may be appropriate. This submission should be followed up to make certain that the database actually added your site and that it can be located under the correct headings.

- *Locating appropriate newsgroups.* Some agents also identify threads that are relevant to your site, and then post messages that subtly promote your site. This task is rather delicate, so you should ask to see examples of the agent's work before hiring him or her for this job.

- *Identifying pages for reciprocal links.* An agent should also take care of contacting the other sites and arranging for the links.

- *Locating and purchasing advertising space* on commercial Web pages. An agent with many contacts and clients may be able to arrange lower rates than you could by yourself.

- *Developing and editing your Web site.* Most agencies also do Web site development work. This can be useful if you are too busy to develop your own site or if you have limited creative abilities. Even if you are a skilled artist or writer, having a professional critique your work and make suggestions may be productive.

 TIP **Before you enter into a contract with anyone, you should ask for** references from previous clients. Contact the references and ask if the agent was aggressive in promoting their sites and prompt in communicating with the clients. Also take the time to look at the client sites themselves. Are they professional in appearance? Well-designed pages indicate that the client's recommendation should carry a solid weight.

The cost of consultant services can range from a few hundred dollars to tens of thousands, depending on the scope of the work. When you do contract with one of these consultants, consider the possibility of basing his or her fee on the amount of traffic that is received at your site. This approach requires that the agent put his or her money on the line and increases the incentive to provide good service. Be aware that this tactic may increase the cost of services to you because the consultant is now sharing some of the risk.

Advertise your site in print

In this chapter, you've examined a number of ways that you can advertise your site on the Internet. This certainly does not mean that you can't increase your exposure through other methods. Indeed, if you don't use these other techniques, you may miss out on many opportunities.

The simplest of all of these methods is to include your site's URL in the signature on all your e-mail. Including your URL costs nothing and has the advantage of appearing before an audience that is (or at least should be) receptive to your message already.

You should also add your Web site URL to your business cards and stationery. In effect, your Web site is your office in cyberspace, and you should include its address alongside your physical office. Before you do so, however, remember to walk through your site carefully to check for a professional and finished appearance. You wouldn't invite potential clients into a half-finished office covered with graffiti, and you shouldn't show them your work in progress on the Web, either.

Finally, include your URL on any ads that you might place in magazines, newspapers, or trade journals. For many people, the discovery of a Web site in an advertisement is an illicit thrill. It's a way of letting people with access to the Web feel that they're an exclusive group and that you're catering especially to them. Take advantage of the cachet that comes with being on the Web whenever you can.

Creating a Personal Web Site

In this chapter:

- **Create a great site with simple HTML**

- **Keep your site organized and each page simple**

- **Make sure your personal Web site is solid**

When the chapters in this book were being assigned to individual authors, I hoarded this one for myself. The plumber's sink is always the one that leaks, they say, and the same thing holds true when you write books about the Web—for months my personal Web site has been a shining example of how *not* to do a Web site. I just haven't had the time to update it. I've been too busy writing.

But now all that is going to change—I've cleverly arranged to get paid for redoing my personal Web site by writing this chapter, and as I go through the steps of redesigning and planning my site, gathering together all the artwork and text files, and actually writing the HTML code for my new site, you can come along and hopefully get some good ideas for creating your own personal Web site.

This chapter will focus on using basic and intermediate HTML to create a useful, entertaining, and well-organized Web site. We won't get into CGI scripting, Java applets, or other advanced topics. The intention here is to learn to use a couple of basic "hand tools" to create a functional, fun, personal Web site. In fact, the only tools we'll use for creating this site are two excellent shareware programs: the HTML tag editor **HTML Writer** and the graphics editing program **Paint Shop Pro**.

Planning and designing any HTML document involves the same up-front steps, no matter what the content or complexity. While documents that include Java and other advanced features are harder to build, the goal is the same—to create informative documents that are compelling, useful, and easy to use. This chapter will get you grounded in the basics so you can move on to creating your own killer, high-tech HTML documents, with all the bells and whistles.

Getting started

My Web site is a mess (see Figure 17.1). My links are outdated, my graphics are all jammed onto one page, and the bibliography I'd carefully assembled was lost in a server crash months ago. Since I earn my living telling other people how to create good Web sites, the situation is especially embarrassing. It's well past time to redo my personal site, and make it the showplace it ought to be!

FIG. 17.1
Though enhanced by a photo of a strikingly good-looking man, my Web site is long overdue for a complete refurbishing. I even admit it on my home page!

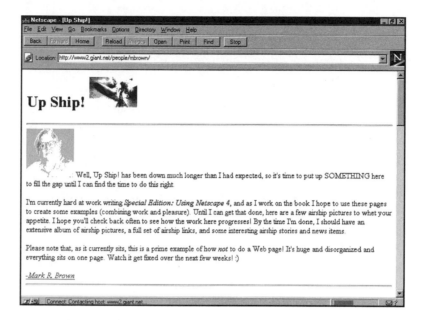

In fact, there's enough wrong with my Web site that I think it's best to just start over. So we'll begin at the beginning.

Choosing a focused topic

Surprisingly enough, the first step in setting up a personal Web site is often the most difficult—choosing a topic for each page.

Notice first of all that I said *a* topic, not a *bunch* of topics. The World Wide Web is a unique medium in that just about anyone can put up a site and sit back and see who visits. The problem is, that's just what happens. Most Web sites—especially personal Web sites—aren't very well thought out. Many people put up a site that includes everything they're interested in: their family, hobbies, line of work, and so on. Let's face it, the odds are against you that anybody surfing into your site will be interested in all the things that interest you.

The first thing you need to do is pick a topic. If you really, really want to cover more than one topic, set up two separate Web pages, or even more. Nobody's stopping you. You can even create a tasteful "Table of Contents" page that directs people to your various topics if you really want to. But keep things carefully separated, or you'll lose your audience by making a bad first impression.

And, let's face it, on the Web all you have is a first impression. With hundreds of thousands—soon, millions—of sites on the Web, nobody's going to stick around your site long if you don't grab them quickly. They'll surf off to a more appealing site.

Once you have your topic, it's important to narrow it down even more. If your interest is rock'n'roll, it might be best to concentrate on a single group. There are literally thousands of generic rock-n-roll sites out there, and you've got to attract a more elite clientele if you're going to make a name for yourself. If the group you choose to focus on is the Beatles, you'll have to create an extremely good site. If it's the Shirelles, you may stand a chance of becoming a Web legend—at least among Shirelles fans.

For me, my passion is airships, which means I already have a nicely focused topic. It's not as generic as "airplanes" or even "fighter planes." In fact, when I first set up my site two years ago, an eternity in Web years, it was the first site on the Web devoted to the topic. Now a search of Yahoo! (see Figure 17.2) shows a short list of sites with similar topics, but I'm convinced I can still compete.

FIG. 17.2

When choosing a topic for your Web site, check out Web indexes like Yahoo! **(http://www.yahoo.com)** to see who your competition is, and find out what they've already done.

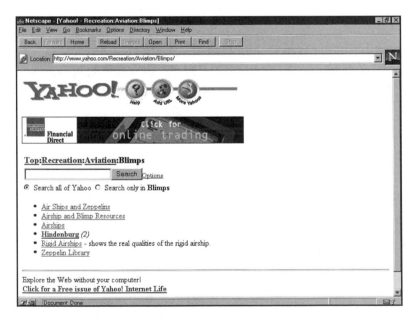

If you're creating a personal Web site for personal gratification or artistic outline more than as a resource for other users, you don't need to worry as much about keeping your pages focused. Just have fun and experiment to your heart's content.

Selecting content

After selecting a focused topic, the next step is to choose the types of content you'll provide on your site.

Depending on your subject matter, you may want to include video clips, audio files, graphics, lists of hyperlinks, text files, or database information.

It's best to go with what you have access to that is unique. If the same material has already appeared on other sites, there's no reason to include it on yours. With the hyperlinked nature of the Web, if someone has something online that you'd like to refer to, all you have to do is add a link to it. Why reinvent the wheel?

In the case of my airship site, I've have an extensive library of airship photos I've scanned in, digitized from videos, or downloaded from public domain sources, so I definitely want to include a library of airship images. I've also archived some interesting text articles over the years, so I'll include them. And I have collected a much more extensive list of airship-related links than Yahoo!, so I'll put those online, too.

 All of the material I'll be putting online is in the public domain. If I'm not sure of the copyright status of an item, it won't go online. Though there's a lot of "borrowing" on the Web, there's no need to violate copyright laws when you're putting up your Web site. Make sure you have permission from the copyright holder if you plan to use any copyrighted material on your Web site.

Later on I want to add a bibliography of airship-related books, so I'll make sure there's a place for that on my site, too.

Organizing the site

Form follows function. Now that I know what I'm going to put online, it's time to organize it. I have four categories of information I'm planning to use:

- Photos
- Links
- Text
- Bibliography

I think having a home page with a link to a directory page for each category would work fine. I'd like to keep a navigational directory handy for those who are roaming around my site, so I think I'll use frames in my design. I'd also like a title graphic so people remember where they are on the Web.

If I were designing a more complex site, I'd sit down and map out the organization of my site. But since this is a fairly simple site, with only four information "areas," I don't think that's really necessary.

Creating the bones

Before I can hang any flesh on my skeleton design, I have to create the bones that make up that skeleton. That means getting out an HTML editor and starting to create the code for my home page.

I'm most familiar with HTML Writer, so let's boot that up and get started. Figure 17.3 shows the HTML code that creates my basic home page.

There are four main HTML files that define my site, two to create the framesets that create the screen layout, and two that contain the content for the title and navigation bar frames. Here's the HTML file for the outermost frameset:

```
<html>
<head>
<title>Up Ship!</title>
</head>
<frameset rows ="20%,*">
  <frame src="title.htm" name="title">
  <frame src ="frameset.htm" name="frameset">
</frameset>
</html>
```

FIG. 17.3
HTML Writer displays
the basic HTML code
that will serve as the
framework for my new
Web site.

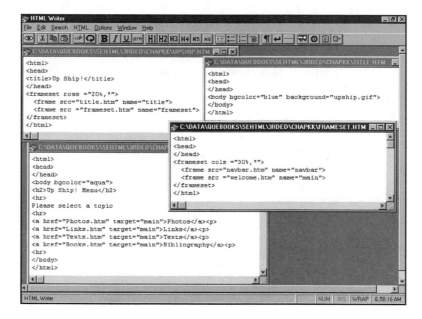

UpShip.htm

This file sets the title of my site as "Up Ship!", which is the command that was shouted to the ground crew to launch an airship. This has been the title of my site for over two years, and I see no reason to change it now.

The FRAMESET definition in "UpShip.htm" produces two frames arranged as two rows. The top frame holds the file "title.htm", which will contain just the GIF graphic titlebar of my site (see Listing 17.1).

Listing 17.1

title.htm

```
<html>
<head>
</head>
<body bgcolor="blue" background="upship.gif">
</body>
</html>
```

title.htm

The bottom frame calls a second frameset definition file called "frameset.htm". Listing 17.2 shows you what it looks like.

Listing 17.2

framset.htm

```
<html>
<head>
</head>
<frameset cols ="30%,*">
  <frame src="navbar.htm" name="navbar">
  <frame src ="welcome.htm" name="main">
</frameset>
</html>
```

frameset.htm

This file creates a frameset which breaks the bottom frame into two frames that form two columns. The end result of the FRAMESET tags in both files is that we have a single frame running across the entire top of the screen which will hold title graphics, and two frames in the bottom portion of the screen, one for the navigation bar and one for the main content frame.

The navigation bar frame is defined in the file "navbar.htm" (see Listing 17.3).

Listing 17.3

navbar.htm

```
<html>
<head>
</head>
```

```
<body bgcolor="aqua">
<h2>Up Ship! Menu</h2>
<hr>
Please select a topic
<hr>
<a href="Photos.htm" target="main">Photos</a><p>
<a href="Links.htm" target="main">Links</a><p>
<a href="Texts.htm" target="main">Texts</a><p>
<a href="Books.htm" target="main">Bibliography</a><p>
<hr>
</body>
</html>
```

navbar.htm

This file contains a heading that identifies the menu, and a list of targeted hyperlinks that can change the content in the main frame. For the time being, I've created a batch of dummy files, like the one following, so that when we test the page we won't get a bunch of errors telling us that files can't be found. We'll fill in content later, but here's what each looks like so far:

```
<html>
<head>
</head>
<body>
Photos
</body>
</html>
```

photos.htm

One exception is the file "welcome.htm", which is just my current home page, stuck in for the time being as filler.

Figure 17.4 shows what all this preliminary code nets us when displayed in Netscape Navigator.

FIG. 17.4

My first pass at a new home page. Now, we start tweaking!

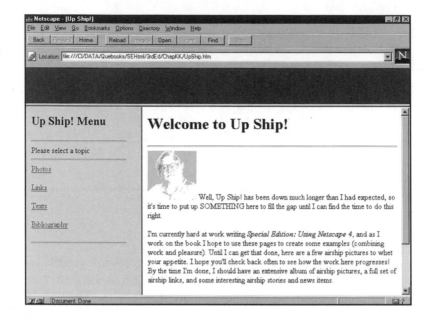

Making adjustments

Well, it's a start. The blue background in the title frame looks like a mistake, and I forgot to create the title graphic "upship.gif". I don't think I really want it as a BACKGROUND graphic, either, since it will tile differently at different browser window sizes. I just didn't think that one through. We'll make it an inline image instead. And, of course, we've got to create it in the first place. That means firing up Paint Shop Pro.

Paint Shop Pro (at version 4.0 as this is written) is one of the best all-around image manipulation tools around. The fact that it is shareware doesn't hurt anything, either. I'm going to use it to turn a couple of airship images I have into a title graphic (see Figure 17.5).

I've decided to take one image of the Graf Zeppelin and one of the Hindenburg in flames and combine them, adding some text at the same time.

I can accomplish all of this in Paint Shop Pro, right down to "smearing" the images to give the graphic some continuity. Saving it as a GIF file called "UpShip.gif" gives us the image we need to complete the Up Ship! home page.

FIG. 17.5

Paint Shop Pro at work resizing images and combining them into a new work of art.

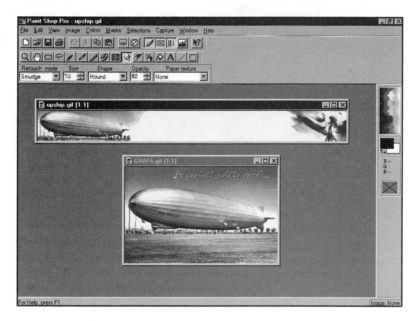

A look at the navigation bar shows that I forgot to include a link to the Welcome page. Even though it comes up by default when a visitor enters the Up Ship! site, I've given them no way to go back to that page if they want to. So I'll add a link for "Welcome" to the "navbar.htm" file. The text lines on the navigation bar seem too far apart, as well, so I think I'll change the <P> tags into <BR> tags. That'll push the lines closer together. I'm still not sure about the "aqua" background color for the navbar, either, but I'm pretty sure I want it a different color than the other frames, so I'll leave that for now.

Figure 17.6 shows Up Ship! after these changes.

I think I can live with the look and feel of this set of frames for the time being. Now it's time to start to work on content.

FIG. 17.6
After a few relatively
minor changes, my
home page is starting
to look like I intended.

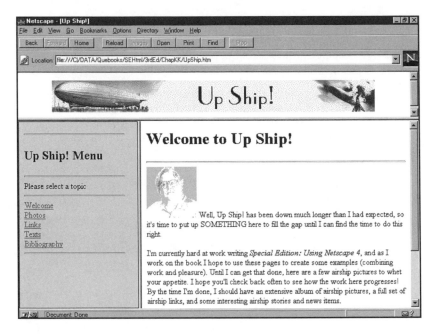

Bringing the content together

"Begin at the beginning," said Humpty Dumpty to Alice, "and go on until you reach the end." That's pretty good advice for content creation, too, which means I should probably work on the Welcome page first.

I really like that picture of the handsome guy, and the <H1> level heading that says "Welcome to Up Ship!" is okay, though it looks a bit redundant to have two huge "Up Ship!" signs so close together. I think I'll change that to just "Welcome." And, of course, it's time to update the text. No need for apologies now that the site is being updated! And I think I'll move that e-mail address over to the navbar, where it will be available all the time. This means a subtle change to "navbar.htm" as well as rewriting the text in "welcome.htm."

I also happened to notice that ugly scrollbar in the title frame, so I went into the "upship.htm" file and set SCROLLING="NO" for the FRAME definition for that frame.

Figure 17.7 shows what the Welcome screen looks like after making these changes.

FIG. 17.7
With a friendly new welcome screen and a few other minor changes, Up Ship! is starting to look ship-shape!

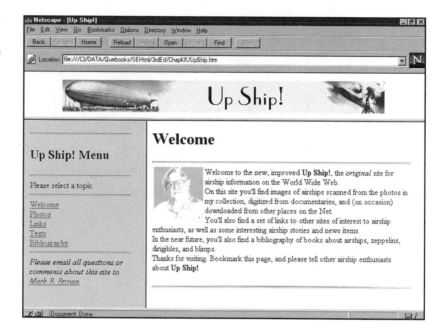

Creating the photo album

Now comes the toughest part of the site: creating an album of airship photos. I have a *lot* of digitized airship photos. For the time being, I'm going to pick 10 to put online, then I'll add to the collection as time permits.

My graphics are already the right size, but I need to create a set of thumbnails to use as a graphic menu. After all, I don't want to just shove kilobyte after kilobyte of photos down my viewers' throats! I want to let them choose which ones they want to see. So it's time to fire up Paint Shop Pro again. This time, I'll use the Resize command on the Image menu to create the thumbnails I need (see Figure 17.8).

The thumbnails I created are all a uniform 60 pixels in height, and use only 16 shades of gray. They should load quickly and make a good looking page.

Speaking of which, it's time to create one.

FIG. 17.8
Creating thumbnails is an essential part of building an online image album, and Paint Shop Pro does the job extremely well.

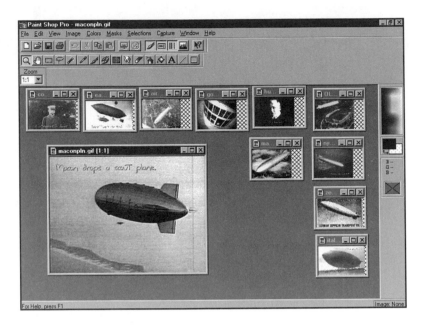

After much thought, it seems to make sense to divide the main frame into two frames for displaying images. I'll create a frame on the right to hold the thumbnails, and will keep enough of the main frame intact to display individual images. By grouping the thumbnails with their captions to create a scrolling list, I should be able to create a compact, easy-to-use, and interesting-looking display.

It's time to load up HTML Writer and go to work on creating the frameset and two frames that will make up the image viewer.

photos.htm

The first, "photos.htm", shown in Listing 17.4, creates the two frames I need. The first will initially contain a beginning image called "image.gif". (I've chosen to have this image unavailable from the scrolling menu—it's a photo of the burning Hindenburg, and I'd like it to be a sort of unselectable memorial.)

Listing 17.4

```
photos.htm

<html>
<head>
</head>
<frameset cols="3*,*">
  <frame src="image.gif" name="image" scrolling="no">
  <frame src="thumbs.htm">
</frameset>
</html>
```

The second frame calls the file "thumbs.htm", described in the next section.

thumbs.htm

Listing 17.5, thumbs.htm, creates the scrolling image menu. Each link combines the thumbnail image of a larger graphic with a targeted link that loads the full-size version into the named frame "image."

Listing 17.5

```
thumbs.htm

<html>
<head>
</head>
<body>
<hr>
<h2>Airship Image Directory</h2>
<hr>
<a href="Pic01.gif" target="image"><img src="Thumb01.gif"></a>
<br>
Santos-Dumont over Paris?<br>
<hr>
<a href="Pic02.gif" target="image"><img src="Thumb02.gif"></a>
<br>
Count Ferdinand von Zeppelin<br>
<hr>
<a href="Pic03.gif" target="image"><img src="Thumb03.gif"></a>
<br>
Airship photographed from biplane<br>
<hr>
<a href="Pic04.gif" target="image"><img src="Thumb04.gif"></a>
<br>
```

continues

Listing 17.5

Continued

```
Hugo Eckener<br>
<hr>
<a href="Pic05.gif" target="image"><img src="Thumb05.gif"></a>
<br>
Nobile's airship Italia<br>
<hr>
<a href="Pic06.gif" target="image"><img src="Thumb06.gif"></a>
<br>
Zeppelin travel poster<br>
<hr>
<a href="Pic07.gif" target="image"><img src="Thumb07.gif"></a>
<br>
Hindenburg over the Olympics<br>
<hr>
<a href="Pic08.gif" target="image"><img src="Thumb08.gif"></a>
<br>
Hindenburg over New York City<br>
<hr>
<a href="Pic09.gif" target="image"><img src="Thumb09.gif"></a>
<br>
Graf Zeppelin's gondola<br>
<hr>
<a href="Pic10.gif" target="image"><img src="Thumb10.gif"></a>
<br>
U.S. Navy airship Macon<br>
<hr>
</body>
</html>
```

That's all we need, besides the individual GIF image files themselves. Figure 17.9 shows the result.

You know, it looks like there's enough room under those images to add a nice scrolling text file someday. We'll have to add another frame, but that should be no problem. The problem is finding time to write the text files to associate with each image. We'll leave that for future expansion.

FIG. 17.9
Our image menu splits
the main window into
two frames, one for a
scrolling thumbnail
menu, and one to
display the full-size
image.

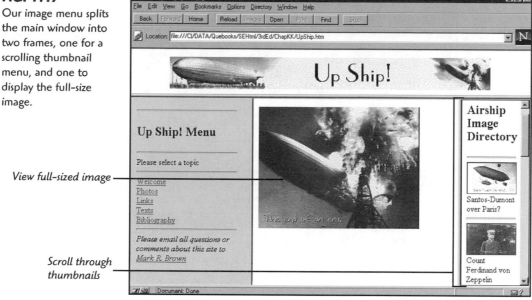

View full-sized image

*Scroll through
thumbnails*

NOTE **You may have noticed that I'm giving little thought to anybody** who uses a nongraphical browser, or those who are still operating at 640×480, rather than 800×600 resolution. Because this site is image-intensive, and because so many people are operating at the higher resolution these days, and because this is just a fun site anyway, I've decided it probably doesn't make any difference.

But, if I were concerned about folks with nongraphical browsers, I'd provide text alternatives for each image. At the very least, consider adding a disclaimer to your Web site stating that it's graphically intensive.

If you think otherwise, e-mail me from the link on my Web site, and let me know your opinion.

Some useful links

What would the Web be without links? Over time, I've compiled a list of good airship links, and my next step is to add at least part of that list of links to my site. For this, all I need is my trusty HTML editor.

I've always been of the opinion that links without comments are somewhat less than useful, so I'll add a bit of personal commentary to my links. Figure 17.10 shows what I ended up with.

FIG. 17.10

I chose to put my links into a bulleted list, with some commentary.

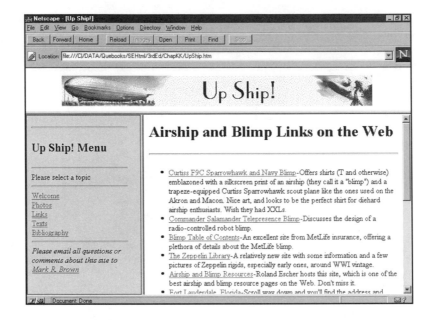

Listing 17.6 shows the HTML that created my list:

Listing 17.6

List of links

```
<html>
<head>
</head>
<body>
<h1>Airship and Blimp Links on the Web</h1>
<hr>
<ul>
<li><A HREF="http://www.white-hawk.com/image-pages/rw-2.html"
target="_top">Curtiss F9C Sparrowhawk and Navy Blimp
</A>-Offers shirts (T and otherwise) emblazoned with
a silkscreen print of an airship (they call...
</ul>
<h3>Return soon! More links to come!</h3>
</body>
</html>
```

links.htm

The entire page consists of nothing but an unordered (bulleted) list of links.
Each link uses the TARGET="_top" attribute to wipe the screen clean and fill it
with whatever is at the linked site. Otherwise, the linked site would just
appear in the main frame, and that can get mighty crowded mighty fast. The
page concludes with an admonition to return soon, because I have a lot more
airship links bookmarked that I'd like to add later.

Adding some articles

Now it's time to add some of the text articles I have waiting on my hard drive.
This should be easy—in fact, text loads so quickly that I think I'll just shove it
into the main frame all in one file, with a "Table of Contents" of internal links
at the head end. After a bit of manipulation and formatting in HTML Writer,
the end result is shown in Figure 17.11.

FIG. 17.11
Though just a loose
amalgam of more-
or-less random articles,
there's enough
interesting information
in this text file to hold
an airship fan hostage
for more than a few
minutes.

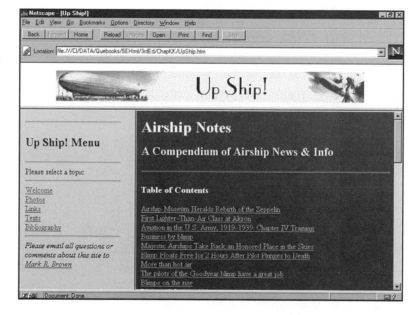

Here's a short sample of the HTML that creates this content:

```
<html>
<head>
</head>
<body bgcolor="blue" text="white" link="yellow" vlink="aqua">
<h1>Airship Notes</h1>
<h2>A Compendium of Airship News & Info</h2>
<hr>
<h3>Table of Contents</h3>
<a href="#museum">Airship Museum Heralds Rebirth of the
Zeppelin</a><br>
...
<a name="museum"><h3>Airship Museum Heralds Rebirth of the
Zeppelin</H3></a>
<hr>
Germany at last has a museum honoring the Zeppelin,
one of the defining images of the 1920s and 30s, and a
glimpse of a new airship that aims to...
```

texts.htm

The "Table of Contents" section of "Texts.htm" consists of a set of anchor tag links that HREF to the headings of each article, which are themselves named using the <A> tag NAME attribute. It's all pretty straightforward. Each article has its own name; each link in the Table of Contents links to that name.

Under construction

It's inevitable that every Web site have an "Under Construction" icon somewhere. Mine comes in the Bibliography. I had a killer bibliography of airship books that I lost in a server crash. What about my backup, you say? I *thought* I had one. But I couldn't find it anywhere, so maybe I was hallucinating. It took me several days of research to put it together the first time, so I hope my viewers will forgive me if I put off recreating it until another time. But I've been told it was my most useful resource, so I'll definitely add it to my site as soon as I can. In the meantime, I'll create an apologetic "books.htm" file that tells the whole sad story of why there isn't currently a bibliography on Up Ship!, and add an "Under Construction" icon to the Bibliography header. Figure 17.12 shows the state of my site after this addition.

 NOTE **Under construction icons can be annoying. Use them sparingly and** only when they truly indicate a Web page that is coming soon. Consider just not putting a Web page online until it's available, unless you want people to know that it'll be available soon.

FIG. 17.12
Though I hated to do it, I just didn't have time to create the bibliography I want to add to my site. I hope I can soon.

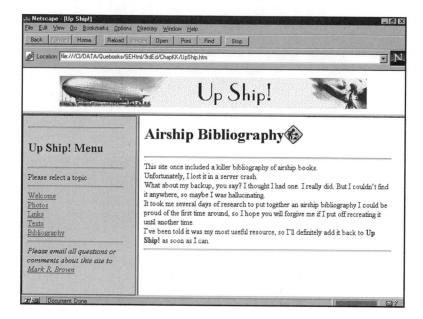

Putting it on the Web

Now that I'm relatively happy with my new site, it's time to put it all online. Like most people putting up a personal Web site, I rely on my local ISP (Internet Service Provider) to host my site for me. My $19.95 flat access fee includes a UNIX account with 10M for my pages, so I have plenty of room.

I use FTP to transfer my files to my ISP, so it's time to fire up my FTP program of choice, WS_FTP32 (see Figure 17.13). A few quick clicks and my site is updated.

FIG. 17.13
With a program like WS_FTP32, uploading your files to your ISP only takes a couple of minutes.

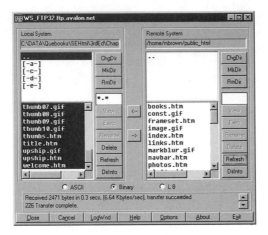

Your personal Web site

Well, that's about it for my personal Web site. But what about yours? While you're certainly welcome to borrow anything you want from my site, I'll reiterate: "Form follows function."

Your site is bound to be different than mine, or anybody else's, because the information you want to present on your site is unique.

Strive to give your Web site its own personality, its own flavor, its own look and feel. And, I'll see you on the Web!

Part V: Appendixes

HTML Editors: HomeSite, HotDog Professional, Web Media Publisher Pro, and BBEdit Lite

In this chapter:

- **The HTML editor HomeSite came into being because of one document author's level of disappointment with existing HTML editors**

- **Sausage Software's HotDog HTML editor is still a favorite among Web publishers**

- **Web Media Publisher Pro is a straight forward, easy-to-use HTML editor**

- **BBEdit Lite is practically a "must-have," according to Mac Webmasters**

S ince HTML files are just text files, all you really need to write one is a plain-text editor like Notepad or a word processing program that will save in plain text format. But if you use this approach to authoring HTML files, you'll soon discover the tedium involved in typing (and retyping) the same tags over and over again. Then, as you sit in the middle of a complex table layout, you might find yourself asking: "Isn't there any way the computer can help me with any of this?" Thanks to several software developers in the world, the answer is "Yes."

Many individuals and corporations have taken it upon themselves to create HTML tag editor programs—software tools that free you from much of the drudgery that can be involved in preparing a document for the Web. Through use of toolbars and drop-down menus, these programs give you point-and-click access to virtually all of the HTML tags in use today. Whenever you want to place a tag, you just click the appropriate button to place it—no more typing it out by hand. Tags that take lots of attributes are composed in extensive dialog boxes that collect your requirements and then write the tag out for you. Complicated forms, tables or framed layouts are handled by wizards that walk you through each step of the creation process. In short, these programs automate much of what made HTML authoring such an uninspiring task in the past and empower you to focus more of your attention on the design quality of your documents.

This chapter introduces you to three of the more popular HTML editors available today. They are:

- HomeSite
- WebEdit
- HotDog Professional
- BBEdit Lite

Each of these is available on the CD-ROM included with this book. To get the most out of this chapter, be sure to install the program and follow along as you read.

 NOTE **Using an HTML editor doesn't necessarily free you from having to** know HTML. Indeed, the most effective users of these programs are the ones who have a good command of standard HTML before they use them. Because of their knowledge, they can see what attributes a dialog box might be prompting for or they can better understand how to use one of the wizards. Make sure you have some comfort level with HTML before you start—it will help you learn the programs faster and will maximize your effectiveness while using them.

HomeSite

HomeSite is a product of Bradbury Software LLC that has become something of a sensation among Web authors. Indeed, the program was written by an author who was disappointed with the other HTML editing software on the market. The rest of us are the benefactors of that disappointment, however—HomeSite is an outstanding program that is well worth the $39.95 U.S. for a single user license.

The HomeSite interface

The intelligent design of the HomeSite user interface is a big part of the reason the program is so popular. The clean, tab-oriented HomeSite window puts just about every type of tag you could ever need within easy reach (see Figure A.1). And any tags that aren't right at hand can easily be set up in one of HomeSite's customizable toolbars or drop-down lists.

FIG. A.1
The HomeSite
interface puts
commonly used tags,
your computer's file
system, an edit window
and a preview window
right at your fingertips.

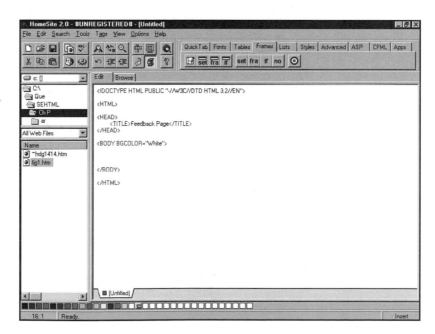

The bulk of the interface is the Edit window. It is here that you will compose your document and see the HTML markup you place displayed. Note that there is a Browse tab behind the Edit window. Clicking this tab lets you preview the document as it would look in a browser.

CAUTION **For the Browse feature to work most effectively, you need to have** Internet Explorer selected as your default browser.

The toolbar you see at the upper left (which is made up of two rows of buttons) is the Main Toolbar. It plays host to commonly seen toolbar buttons like New, Open, Save, Save All, Cut, Copy, Paste, and Undo. Additionally, you can find buttons there for some of HomeSite's other nifty features, like Spell Check and Projects (collections of related documents).

To the right of the Main Toolbar, you'll find the HTML Speedbar—a set of toolbars stored on a sequence of tabs. Buttons on each tab are logically grouped according to function. HomeSite provides tabs for run-of-the-mill authoring work like marking up text, composing forms, setting up framed documents and tables, and creating lists. It also has toolbars for more advanced tasks like Cold Fusion Markup Language (CFML), client-side imagemapping, placing embedded objects and ActiveX controls, and building scrolling marquees. You can also add up to five custom tabs to the speedbar to suit your own authoring preferences.

Down the left hand side of the screen, you'll see what is essentially a miniature version of the Windows Explorer. This is the Document List, and it makes browsing to a desired file a snap. Once you browse to a target directory, you can choose to open as many of the files as you want. Each open file gets its own tab along the bottom of the Edit Window.

Along the very bottom of the window are the Status Bar and the Color Bar. Helpful messages pop up in the Status Bar as you work with HomeSite and the Color Bar gives you quick access to the 16 colors in the standard Windows palette. These are the same colors that can now be referenced with English-language names in an HTML document.

 TIP **All of HomeSite's toolbars can be revealed or hidden from the** View menu.

Getting started

You need to put something in the Edit window to start using HomeSite, and there are two easy ways to do that. You can choose File, New to reveal the dialog box you see in Figure A.2. If you want a clean slate, choose the Blank Document template. Otherwise, you can choose from any of the other templates you see—including ones that you've made up yourself.

 TIP **Once you have a blank document, choose Tools, Quick Start**
to have HomeSite collect information about global document settings from you. Once you enter all of your parameters, HomeSite will place the HTML tags that set up the document according to your specifications.

FIG. A.2
HomeSite comes with three standard templates for popular kinds of Web pages.

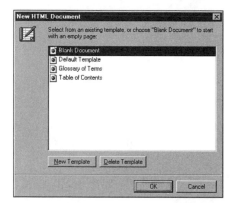

Your other choice is to select one of the "open" options under the File menu. The regular Open option lets you browse to an HTML document, text file, or style sheet file. You can choose the Open from the Web option to download a document from a server for editing as long as you have a working connection to the Internet. Finally, the Reopen option presents you with a drop-down list of the last 10 files you had open.

 TIP **If you have the Document List open, you can use that to browse**
to any documents you want to open.

Formatting text

HomeSite works like most other HTML tag editors when it comes to formatting text. To apply a style, you simply highlight the text to be formatted and click the button corresponding to the style you want. Bold, italics, and underlining are available on the QuickTab tab of the HTML Speedbar. The Fonts tab is home to buttons for the six heading style, strong, emphasis, preformatted text, and the <FONT> tag and all of its attributes. You can configure your own styles under the Styles tab. When setting up a style, you have an extensive number of characteristics that you can set (see Figure A.3).

FIG. A.3
HomeSite allows you to control virtually all aspects of a font's appearance.

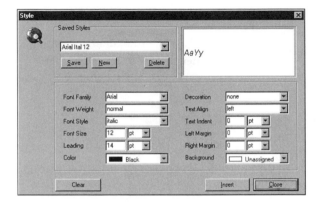

Buttons for block formatting tags are found back on the QuickTab tab. These include paragraph breaks, line breaks, nonbreaking space, centered text, and right-justified text.

Placing images

HomeSite is very supportive when it comes to placing potentially complex tags like the <IMG> tag. By choosing Tools, Quick Image or by clicking the QuickImage button on the QuickTab tab of the HTML Speedbar, you get the dialog box you see in Figure A.4. In addition to the one mandatory attribute (SRC), you get to specify virtually all of the extended attributes of the <IMG> tag as well. The options at the bottom of the dialog box are for the Microsoft Internet Explorer extension to the <IMG> tag that lets you use it to place an AVI movie in a document. The scrollable preview window in the dialog box is a nice touch since it lets you do a quick check to be sure you chose the right image.

 TIP For quick access to a tag and all of its attributes, you can right-click on the tag in the Edit window.

FIG. A.4
Composing an intricate
<IMG> tag is simple
when HomeSite is
doing all of the work.

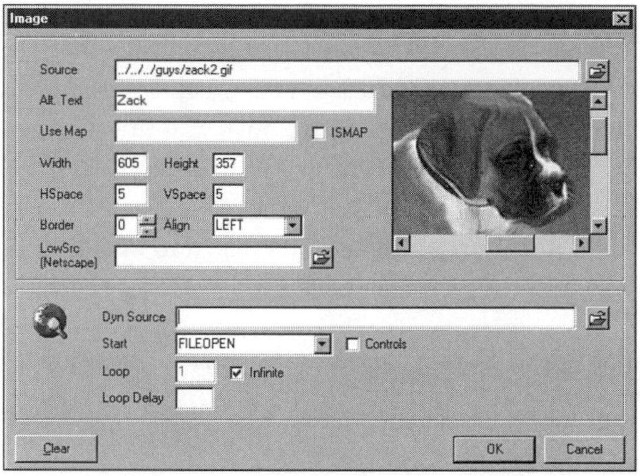

Setting up links

Establishing hyperlinks is even easier than placing an image. Once you highlight the text you want to serve as the hypertext anchor or the <IMG> tag that places the image you want to be the anchor, you can click the QuickAnchor button on the QuickTab tab of the HTML Speedbar or choose Tools, Quick Anchor to reveal the dialog box you see in Figure A.5.

FIG. A.5
You can choose one
of your Netscape
bookmarks or your
Internet Explorer
favorites for the HREF
attribute when setting
up a hyperlink.

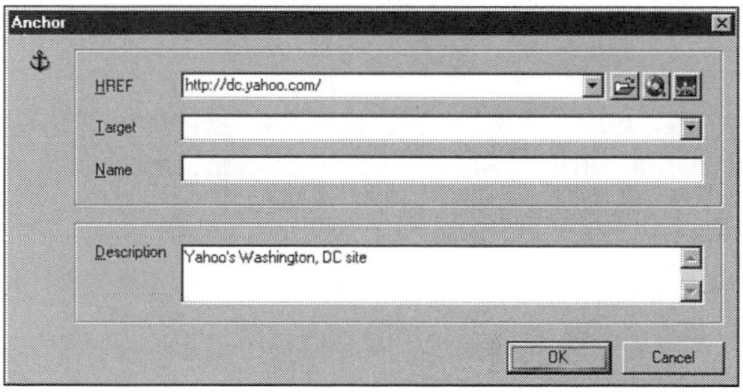

More often than not, you'll be just filling in the HREF attribute, setting it equal to the URL of the document you're linking to. If you're using frames, you may need to also specify a Target frame so that your linked document loads in the proper place. Linking within a document will require you to set up named anchors within the document by using the Name field. The Description field will automatically be populated with the anchor text or the <IMG> tag you highlighted.

Setting up tables

The HomeSite Table Wizard lets you set up the structure of a table in an interactive dialog box (see Figure A.6). The first thing you'll want to do is set the number of rows and columns to the desired values. On the Table Properties tab, you can also specify your caption, background color, table width, border width, cell padding, cell spacing, and global horizontal and vertical alignment properties.

FIG. A.6

The Table Wizard lets you give all the content and specs for your table, then it writes in the HTML tags necessary to create the table.

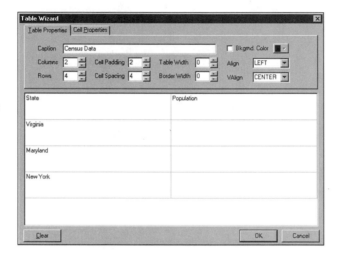

Next, you can enter the content you want to appear in each cell of the table. Remember that table cells can contain text, images, form fields, nonbreaking space (to produce an empty cell), and even other tables!

Finally, if needed, you can tweak the attributes of individual cells from the Cell Properties tab. These include height, width, background color, horizontal and vertical alignment, text wrapping, and the number of rows and columns the cell should span.

 NOTE **There is no support for aligning your caption or setting a cell to be** a table header in the Table Wizard. You'll have to add these instructions by using buttons on the Tables tab of the HTML Speedbar or by hand.

One other option for creating a table is to use the QuickTable button on the Tables tab of the HTML Speedbar. Clicking this button displays a drop-down box with a grid. You can trace out the size of the table you want on the grid, and HomeSite will set up the tags to create the table. It's up to you to go into the Edit window and enter content in the cells.

Creating framed layouts

The HomeSite Frame Wizard is probably your best bet for composing a framed layout. You invoke the Wizard by clicking the Frame Wizard button on the Frames tab of the HTML Speedbar or by choosing Tools, Frame Wizard. The Wizard will first ask whether you want the browser window initially divided into rows or columns. From there, you can indicate how you want each row or column subdivided. Once HomeSite has this information, it presents you with a dialog box like the one you see in Figure A.7. It is in the last dialog box where you specify what's going on inside each frame—where it should draw content from, the frame's name, margin sizes, whether or not the user can resize the frame, and whether or not there should be scrollbars. Once you set all of these attributes, clicking OK instructs HomeSite to place the necessary frame tags into your document.

FIG. A.7
HomeSite walks you through the complex process of setting up a framed layout.

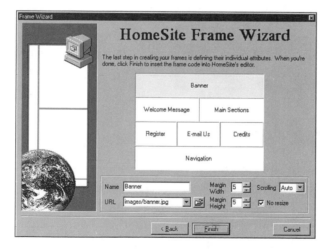

If you don't want to use the Wizard, you can avail yourself of the buttons on the Frames tab of the HTML Speedbar. There are buttons for the <FRAMESET>, <FRAME>, and <IFRAME> (with and without dialog boxes to support the attributes) tags and also a button you can use to set the base target for all of your hyperlinks.

Other useful HomeSite features

By now, you can probably tell that HomeSite is a pretty complete HTML editor that will support you with most major authoring tasks. But it also comes with a few other nice features that are worth noting. These include:

- **Date and time insertion**—HomeSite will insert the current system date and time in any one of four different formats. Choosing Tags, Insert Datetime reveals a listing of the four choices.

- **Tag List**—If you want constant access to a full list of HTML tags and attributes, you can select View, Tag Selection to call up the HomeSite Tag List (see Figure A.8). With the Tag List open, all you need to do to place a tag or attribute is scroll to its position in the list and click it.

FIG. A.8
You can place any tag or attribute by using the HomeSite Tag List.

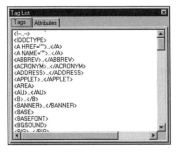

HotDog Professional

Sausage Software has struck again—this time with version 3.0 of their popular HTML editor HotDog. This particular HotDog comes in two flavors: a 32-bit, professional version for Windows 95 and a 16-bit, standard version for Windows 3.1. Both versions of the software are included on the CD-ROM, but this section of the chapter will discuss the 32-bit version of HotDog. Most functionality is common to both programs.

The HotDog interface

When you start HotDog for the first time (and get past the nag dialog box reminding you to register the software), you'll see the screen shown in Figure A.9. The interface may seem a little overwhelming at first, so it is helpful to take a moment to understand each part.

FIG. A.9

The busy HotDog interface puts a lot of the program's features within easy reach. But which button does what?

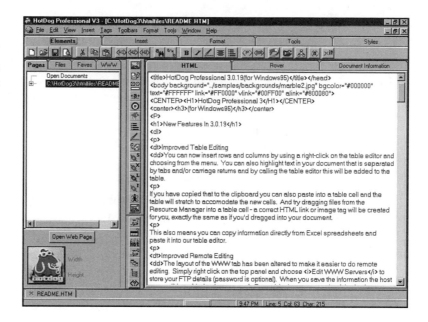

The set of five tabs you see across the top of the screen is the Main Toolbar. Each tab on the Main Toolbar contains logically grouped buttons that perform related functions. The Element tab plays hosts to file operation buttons, buttons for placing common HTML formatting tags (physical styles, heading styles, horizontal lines, lists, and so on). Buttons on the Insert tab let you place things like images, hyperlinks, ActiveX controls, and embedded items into your document. The Format tab repeats some of the buttons on the Element tab plus it adds a few others related to how HTML tags appear on screen. Finally, you can define buttons on the Style tab for specifying text attributes.

The large area below the Main Toolbar and to the right is where you will compose your documents. You'll note that the window is divided into three tabs: HTML for creating the actual markup; ROVER (Real-time Output ViewER), which will give you a decent approximation of what your document will look like in a browser; and Document Information, where you can set up much of your document head section, and where you can get a sense of how long it will take your document to download with different connection speeds.

The interface element down the left side of the screen is HotDog Resource Manager. The Resource Manager has four tabs—Pages to show what pages you have opened currently; Files for easy browsing to files on your hard drive; Faves to let you specify favorite blocks of text, tags, or links; and WWW to download a page from a Web server out on the Internet. You can select anything from the Resource Manager, and move it into your document by double-clicking it or by dragging and dropping it into the HotDog document window.

Sandwiched between the Resource Manager and the document window, you'll find two toolbars. The Insert toolbar replicates much of what you'll find under the Insert tab of the Main Toolbar. Below that is the Customize-O-Tron toolbar. Clicking a Customize-O-Tron button invokes one of the many ways you can customize HotDog. If you don't want these toolbars hanging around, you can hide them by unselecting them under the View menu.

NOTE There are other features that you can reveal or hide by using the View menu. In addition to the Insert and Customize-O-Tron toolbars, you can also reveal the Color and Background Builder, a list of all of the HTML tags HotDog knows, the HotDog File Manager, and the Special Characters list.

Getting started

HotDog gives you a bunch of different ways to get started with a new document. Choosing File, New reveals the dialog box you see in Figure A.10. From here, you can select from one of six document templates, the HotDog Page Builder (for building a personal home page), or a Normal document. If you go with a template or the Page Builder, HotDog will open up a new page and add content to it as you provide information over a series of dialog boxes. Starting a Normal document instructs HotDog to set up the structure tags for a blank page.

FIG. A.10
HotDog has preprogrammed templates for many common types of pages.

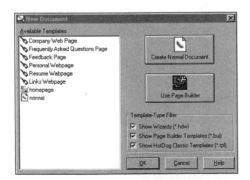

If you want to open an existing document, you can choose File, Open and browse to the desired file. Or, even better, if you have the Resource Manager open, you can click the File tab and browse to the file from there. Double-clicking the file loads it into HotDog.

NOTE   **Webmasters for large sites may have grouped their pages into a** HotDog project by using the Project Manager. To open a project, choose File, Open Project.

Formatting text

Marking up your text in HotDog is much the same as it is in the other programs discussed in the chapter. You simply highlight the text and choose the desired style to apply—from either a button bar or a menu option. The key in HotDog is knowing where to get quick access to the available formatting options.

The Main Toolbar is a good place to start. Bold and italic formatting, as well as the first three heading levels, can be found on the Elements tab. Block formatting instructions like centering, paragraph breaks, line breaks, and list structures live on the Elements tab, too.

You might think the Format tab would be chock full of formatting buttons, but you'd only be about half-right. In actuality, only the first five buttons are really helpful. In addition to buttons for bold, italics, and centering, you also get a button for making the first letter of a word larger and one for opening a dialog box where you can change many different font attributes (see Figure A.11).

FIG. A.11
The Format Text dialog box lets you change typeface, base type size, or color, and it gives you access to all of the physical styles.

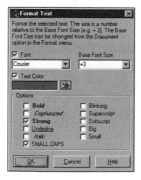

Another way HotDog supports you in formatting text is by options under the Tags menu. Choosing an option under this menu launches a floating dialog box from which you can choose from a host of related tags. Options that would be helpful during text formatting include Content, Headings, Font, and Lists.

TIP **Inserting a text file into your document? Just place the cursor** where you want the document to go, browse to the file in the Resource Manager, and drag-and-drop it to the editing area.

Placing images

If you're placing a run-of-the-mill <IMG> tag with just the basic attributes, there are two ways you can go about it. The easiest way is to browse to the desired image file in the Resource Manager, click it, drag it to the editing window, and drop it there. HotDog automatically writes the <IMG> tag for you complete with SRC, HEIGHT, WIDTH, and ALT attributes. You can even see a preview of the image at the bottom of the Resource Manager.

The other way to place a simple <IMG> tag is to choose Insert, Image. This presents you with a dialog box that allows you to browse to the desired image file and to enter a text-based alternative to the image. You can also make the image into a hyperlink anchor by specifying what document you would like it to link to.

A more complex <IMG> tag will require you to choose Insert, Image (Advanced). This gets you to a dialog box where you can set other image attributes like height, width, border size, how much space to leave around the image, a low-resolution alternative, and how the image should be aligned (see Figure A.12)

TIP **Clicking the image preview in the Image Properties dialog box** opens a second dialog box, where you can alter GIF and JPEG properties like transparency and compression.

Setting up links

HotDog's drag-and-drop functionality extends to setting up hyperlinks as well. If you need to link to an HTML document that's on your hard drive, simply browse to the file in the Resource Manager and drag-and-drop it to the editing area. HotDog will set up the appropriate <A> tag for you. Just be sure to change the text anchor as HotDog uses the file name for this and very often that is not sufficiently descriptive to tell users where they'll go if they click the link.

FIG. A.12
If you want more than just your basic <IMG> tag, you need to use HotDog's advanced image insert feature.

You can take a more traditional approach to placing a link by choosing Insert, Simple URL. When you do, you'll get a dialog box that prompts you for the URL to link to, the text to serve as the hyperlink anchor, and the name of any frame you would like to target with the link.

Setting up tables

HotDog has a facility that can help you compose a table. To call it up, choose Insert, Table, and you'll see the dialog box shown in Figure A.13. From there, you can set up the table's caption and other global attributes like width, cell padding, cell spacing, and the number of rows and columns. The grid adjusts itself to the number of rows and columns you specify, leaving you able to place content in the cells.

CAUTION You can load an existing table into this dialog box by highlighting its HTML code and choosing Insert, Table. If you do this, however, you will lose any attributes you may have set up. The dialog box only handles the tags.

FIG. A.13

You can set up a basic table, with no special formatting in the cells, from a single HotDog dialog box.

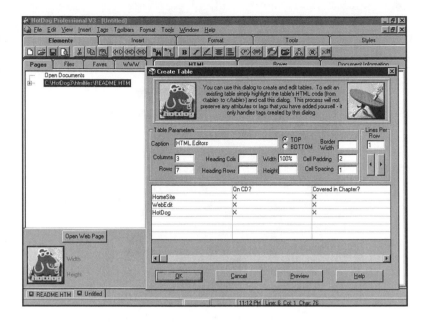

Once you have the basic table set up, you'll probably want to enhance it by adding some attributes to <TR>, <TH>, or <TD> tags. A quick way to get access to these attributes is to choose Tags, Attributes to get a floating dialog box containing a clickable list of attributes. Not all of them are table-related, but it's a fairly simple matter to sort through the list for the attributes you want.

Creating forms

HotDog has very nice support for placing a control element on a form. Choose Insert, Form Element to reveal the dialog box you see in Figure A.14. The first thing you should do is click the button corresponding to the type of form control you want to place. When you do, the bottom of the dialog box will change to allow you to enter the attribute information appropriate to the type of control you chose.

One thing that's missing from the dialog box is something that allows you to place the <FORM> tag itself. One way you can do this is to type it in yourself. Or, you can select the Forms attribute under the Tags menu to reveal a dialog box of form-related tags and attributes. You can select the <FORM> tag, as well as the ACTION and METHOD attributes, from here.

FIG. A.14
HotDog's Define Form Elements dialog box takes the headache out of composing tags to place form control elements.

Creating framed layouts

You probably didn't know this, but HotDog does frames by using a plug-in called a *snaglet*. Once you're aware of this designation, it becomes pretty easy to invoke HotDog's support for creating documents in frames—you just choose Insert, Snaglets, Frames. When you do, you'll see the first of two dialog boxes that will help you develop your framed page. This first box asks you if you want the screen split into rows or columns first and how many rows or columns it should use. From there, you move on to the second dialog box where you can give each frame a unique name and URL. You can also further subdivide a selected frame by clicking the Add button or remove a selected frame by clicking Remove (see Figure A.15). When you're done, click the Done button to instruct HotDog to place the frame tags that create the layout you designed.

FIG. A.15
Frames, along with client-side imagemaps, animation, and text effects, are considered "snaglets" in HotDog vernacular.

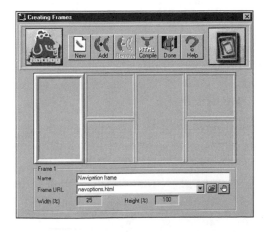

NOTE **The HotDog frames dialog boxes do not let you set attributes like** NORESIZE, SCROLLING, MARGINWIDTH, and MARGINHEIGHT.

Other useful HotDog features

As with the other HTML editors covered in this chapter, there is room to show how to accomplish HotDog tasks that will comprise 90 or more percent of your Web authoring activities. But in so doing, it's easy to overlook some of the special features a program has. This is especially true with HotDog which has plenty of neat extras like:

- **Customization of the Interface**—Every release of HotDog has been touted for how much the user can customize the interface, and the current version is no exception. You can configure eight different tabs of program options (Tools, Options), all toolbars (Tools, Customize Toolbars), all shortcut keys (Tools, Shortcut Keys), and even what sound effects the program uses (Tools, Mixing Desk).

- **HTML Syntax Checker**—HotDog will check the validity of your HTML without the support of an external program (choose Tools, Check HTML Syntax).

- **Text Effects Generator**—If you select Insert, Snaglets, Text Effects, you get to configure one of six different text effects that are supported through Java applets. All you need to do is fill in the dialog box and HotDog will write out the applet-related tags for you.

- **Animated GIF Maker**—You can use HotDog's Animated GIF Maker to select the individual images that comprise the animation and then write the whole thing out to an animated GIF file. To invoke this feature, choose Insert, Snaglet, Animator.

- **Dynamic Images**—HotDog's Dynamic Image maker lets you label an image with text, converting it instantly into a usable button (choose Insert, Dynamic Image).

- **Bandwidth Buster**—The Bandwidth Buster can help you assess what documents will have unacceptably high download times. Then, where possible, it will give you options for shrinking the bandwidth requirement, perhaps by compressing the document's images to a higher ratio. To make use of this feature, select Tools, Bandwidth Buster.

Web Media Publisher Pro

Web Media Publisher Pro is a straightforward, no-nonsense HTML editor produced by Steve Jackson. It is easy to use and highly customizable—in fact, two entire toolbar tabs are completely set up by the user! Add to that the built-in browser preview and support for most HTML tags (both standard and extensions) and you have a very useful authoring tool in your arsenal.

The Web Media Publisher Pro interface

When you use Web Media Publisher Pro, your work environment will look like the one you see in Figure A.16. The major component of the interface is the set of tabs you see near the top. The first tab is the Toolbar tab. The Toolbar is full of buttons that cover you in the most common of authoring situations. You can apply styles (physical, logical, and heading styles), set up lists, place images, create a form, or even place an embedded object with buttons on the Toolbar tab.

FIG. A.16

Most of Web Media Publisher Pro's authoring support comes from the tabs of toolbars near the top of the screen.

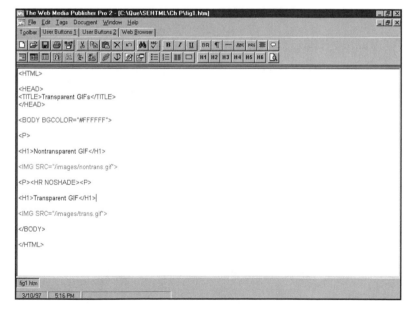

The next two tabs—User Buttons 1 and 2—are all yours. You can customize them to place any tag or tags you'd like. This is particularly useful if there is a certain combination of tags you use frequently. By storing them on a User Button tab, you can apply the tags more quickly than if you typed them out by hand or used Web Media Publisher Pro support for the tags individually.

To customize a button, just follow these easy steps:

1 Right click your mouse on the button you wish to customize.

2 You will then see a dialog box like the one shown in Figure A.17. Give the button a name and then specify the beginning and ending tags the button should apply.

FIG. A.17
Configuring your own toolbar buttons is a breeze with Web Media Publisher Pro.

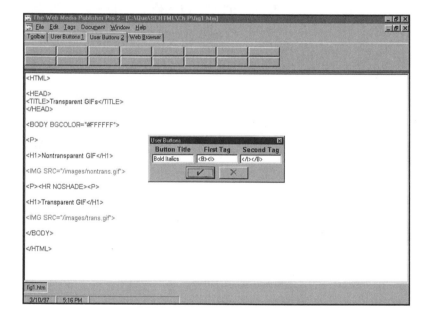

3 Click the checkmark button in the dialog box. The customized button will now appear with the name you gave it. When you click this button, the tag or tags you specified will be applied to any highlighted text.

The last tab is the Web Browser tab. It allows you to preview your document without launching a separate application. Rather, Web Media Publisher Pro uses the Internet Explorer executables already on your system to support its own browser preview feature.

Getting started

To get started with Web Media Publisher Pro, you have two basic options. The first is to start a new document by either clicking the New Document button on the Toolbar tab or by choosing File, New. Either option will give you a blank file where you can begin your work. Once you have the blank file, you can fill it in quickly by using a template. You can find templates under the Document menu—either the Default Template to place the standard document structure tags or a User Template that you've defined yourself.

Your other option is to open an existing file. To accomplish this, click the Open File button on the Toolbar tab or choose File, Open. Either approach will let you browse your hard drive for the file you wish to open.

Formatting text

Text formatting with Web Media Publisher Pro is very similar to using a word processing program. You simply highlight the text you want to format and then apply the desired style or effect. More often than not, you'll apply an effect from the Toolbar tab, but don't forget about Web Media Publisher Pro's handy menu options. Options under the Tags menu will reveal pop-up lists of tags that you can place simply by selecting them.

Block-level formatting is handled most easily from the Toolbar tab since the major formatting tags can be found there. These include paragraph breaks, line breaks, horizontal lines, lists, and centered alignment.

Placing images

Web Media Publisher Pro gives you good support when placing an image in your document. Clicking the Image button on the Toolbar tab reveals the dialog box you see in Figure A.18. From there, you can browse to the image file you want to place in addition to a lower-resolution version of the image. Other fields let you specify image width and height, how much white space to leave around the image, whether or not you want a border, whether or not the image is being used for a client-side or server-side imagemap, and a text alternative to the image.

TIP   **If you're making the image a hyperlink anchor, you can assign the** URL the image links to in the same dialog box. This saves you from having to set up the link in a separate step.

FIG. A.18

The standard attributes of the <IMG> tag can all be set from Web Media Publisher Pro's Image dialog box.

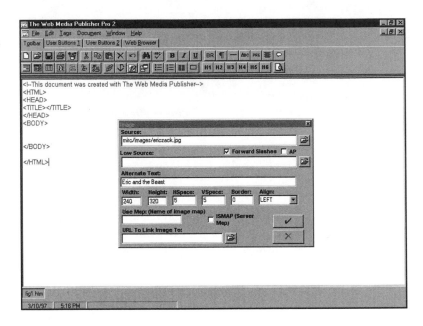

Setting up links

Transforming text into hypertext is also simple with Web Media Publisher Pro. To start, highlight the text you want to make clickable and then click the Link button on the Toolbar tab. This calls up a dialog box where you can specify the URL the hypertext should be linked to. You can select the protocol from a drop-down list of standard protocols. Then you need to give the server name, directory path and file name. If you're linking to a named anchor within that file, you can enter the anchor's name in this dialog box as well.

If you're setting up a hyperlinked image, you would follow virtually the same steps, except you would highlight the <IMG> tag that places the image rather than highlighting text. This places the <A> and </A> tags on either side of the <IMG> tag, thereby making it hyperlinked.

NOTE **If you're using a framed layout, you can target a link from this** dialog box as well. Just enter the target frame's name into the Target field.

Setting up tables

Placing a table with Web Media Publisher Pro is much easier than typing out all of the individual table-related tags by hand. Instead, you can click the Table button on the Toolbar tab to reveal the dialog box you see in Figure A.19. Your first step in the dialog box is to set up the basic structure of the table. As you change the number of rows and columns, you'll see the window inside the dialog box change to reflect the new values you're entering. At this point, you can also caption your table and set up global table attributes like cell padding, cell spacing, border size, and the width of the entire table.

FIG. A.19
Web Media Publisher Pro collects the information it needs to construct a table in this dialog box and then writes the HTML tags for you.

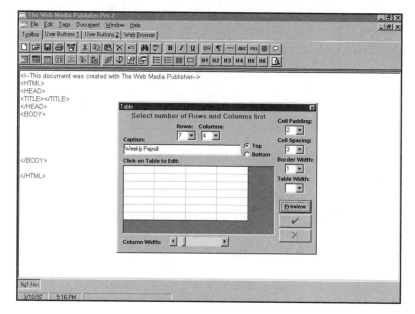

Next, you need to place content in each of the cells. To do this, click a cell to call up a subordinate dialog box that you can use to enter content and to specify alignment and background color within the cell.

 TIP **The Preview feature in the Table dialog box is a neat feature as it** lets you check your work as you build the table. This way you can make any necessary changes before the HTML tags are written into your file.

Creating forms

If you're composing an HTML form, you'll definitely want Web Media Publisher Pro's Forms dialog box close at hand (see Figure A.20). The box displays all of the possible form controls in buttons down the left-hand side and, as you choose different form controls, the appropriate attributes show up on the right-hand side of the box. This makes it almost impossible to forget an attribute in a form-related tag—they're all right there for you!

FIG. A.20

If all of the variations of the <INPUT> tag get you down, you'll love Web Media Publisher Pro's support for form-related tags.

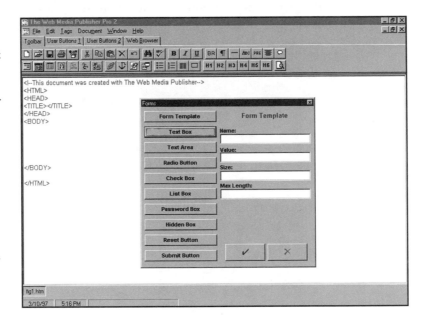

One of the buttons in the Forms dialog box works a little differently though. Notice the Form Template button at the top. Clicking this button prompts Web Media Publisher Pro to ask you for the URL of the script that will process the form. Once it knows that, the program will write out the <FORM> and </FORM> tags complete with the correct ACTION attribute.

Creating framed layouts

Web Media Publisher Pro can help you out with simple framed layouts, too. Clicking the Frames button calls up a dialog box, where you can set up a layout with multiple horizontal or vertical frames. With your frames set up, you can click each one to reveal a dialog box that lets you specify the URL of the document to be presented in the frame, as well as other attributes like margins, scrollbars, and whether or not the user can resize the frame.

CAUTION   **If you're doing nested framesets, Web Media Publisher Pro may** not be able to help you very much because it allows for horizontal or vertical frames *only*.

Other useful Web Media Publisher Pro features

Web Media Publisher Pro comes bundled with a few other neat features that make it an even more worthwhile package. These include:

- **Spell Checker**   Spell checking your documents is always a worthy quality assurance effort. Web Media Publisher Pro will spell check your document whenever you click the Spell Check button or when you choose Edit, Spell Check.

- **Webpage Wizard**   If you need to put together a personal Web page quickly, just choose Document, Webpage Wizard. This fires up the wizard—a series of dialog boxes that gather information for the page and, when you're done, writes out the HTML to produce the page.

- **Projects**   Web sites are rarely made up of single files. A Web Media Publisher Pro project is a collection of related files that you store, open, and edit together. This makes it much easier to be consistent in your editing across multiple files.

BBEdit Lite for Mac

While the Mac world offers a variety of commericial and shareware HTML editing solutions, most Mac Webmasters seem to agree that a copy of BBEdit or BBEdit Lite (**http://www.barebones.com/freeware.html**) is a must-have for professional-level design. Created as a programmer's text editor, BBEdit offers features like linefeed translations (for working with cross-platform text files), auto-indenting, and high-powered searching.

For our purposes, however, the most important and impressive aspect of BBEdit is its ability to use "Extensions" to add to its functionality. For instance, using the add-on BBEdit HTML Tools, written by Lindsey Davies, turn your copy of BBEdit into an impressive HTML editor.

NOTE **Open the HTML Tools folder and you'll see another folder called** "for BBEdit Extensions Folder." Select all of the files in this folder and drag them to the BBEdit Extensions Folder located inside BBEdit Lite's main folder. Just like Mac OS Extensions, these little snippets of code extend BBEdit's capabilities into the realm of HTML editing.

The BBEdit interface

Figure A.21 shows a menu item, called Extensions, within an open HTML document. Extensions holds all of the various HTML commands that HTML Tools support, including commands for adding basic HTML formatting, document, image, and list tags. Commands in this menu can even be added by using a simple scripting mechanism.

FIG. A.21

BBEdit's simple interface actually allows amazing flexibility through hot keys and scriptable extensions.

Extensions	
Set Keys...	
◇ Anchor...	⌥⌘A
◇ Document...	⌥⌘D
◇ Form Elements...	⌥⌘F
◇ Heading...	⌥⌘H
◇ Image...	⌥⌘I
◇ Line Breaks...	⌥⌘B
◇ Lists...	⌥⌘L
◇ Preview...	⌥⌘P
◇ Style...	⌥⌘S
◇ Translate...	⌥⌘T
◇ User's Markup...	⌥⌘M
◇ Utilities...	⌥⌘U
Concatenate Files...	
Convert to ASCII...	
Copy Lines Containing...	
Cut Lines Containing...	
Educate Quotes	
Make Prototypes...	
Prefix/Suffix Lines...	
Send PostScript™...	

Other nonHTML specific commands exist on the BBEdit interface as well, including drop-down menus for changing the way the window wraps text or displays quotation marks, for choosing the computing platform for which files are formatted (DOS, Mac, UNIX), and for pasting the contents of other text files into the document (see Figure A.22).

FIG. A.22
The buttons in BBEdit's editing window may look like icons, but they act like drop-down menus for quick access to common options.

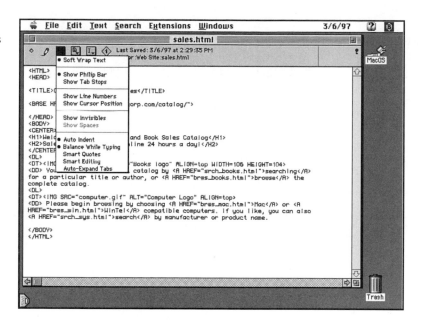

TIP   **The Mac OS, UNIX, and DOS use different newline conventions** when saving ASCII text, which can make those files difficult to read when saved in the wrong format. If you plan to allow DOS or UNIX users to edit your HTML documents, you might want to save them by using one of those conventions—you'll always be able to load it in BBEdit, regardless of the format.

Getting started

By default, BBEdit opens a new document window after it's launched from the Finder. If you're interested in starting a new HTML document, you can begin immediately with the Untitled document window.

Choose Extensions, Document to enter values for the Head section of your HTML document (see Figure A.23). The Document dialog box allows you to determine what document tags you want added to your page (SGML, HTML, HEAD, and BODY) by using check boxes at the top of the dialog box. You can then enter a Title, Base URL, and Next ID, and LINK attributes for META tags. Enter the elements that interest you and click the Insert button to add them to your document.

FIG. A.23
Using this dialog box you create the basic framework for your HTML document.

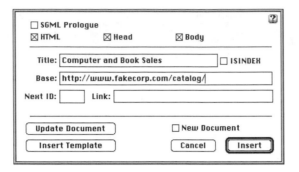

If you want to open an existing file, you can use the File, Open command to browse for the file by using the standard Open file dialog box. BBEdit also gives you the opportunity to search for a file by using the File, Open Selection command. The File, Open Recent allows you to reopen files you've been editing recently.

TIP   **Highlighting a file name (for instance, in an URL) and choosing** File, Open Selection from BBEdit's menu bar will open that file (if it's on your hard drive) for editing. You can then switch between windows by using the Windows menu or the assigned keyboard shortcuts.

Once your file is opened, you can simply begin typing text for your page—or you can paste it in from other documents. The best way to work in BBEdit is to first type all of your page's text, then go back with the mouse and highlight elements for formatting.

Formatting text

BBEdit is a text editor, not a WYSIWYG HTML editor, so you'll see the actual HTML tags when you edit your documents, not a preview of your Web page. You'll probably find this is a powerful way to work, since you already understand HTML.

Once you've entered text on the screen, formatting is a snap. Simply highlight the text on the screen and choose the Extensions, Style command from the menu bar. In the resulting dialog box you have your choice of physical and logical styles (see Figure A.24). Choose a style (for instance, Bold) by clicking on the style name and clicking the Apply button.

You should see the text flanked with <B> and </B> tags, or with the appropriate HTML tags for any of the text styles you choose.

TIP **If some of the options in the dialog box are "grayed-out," click** the check box next to HTML-2 in the bottom left-hand corner of the dialog box.

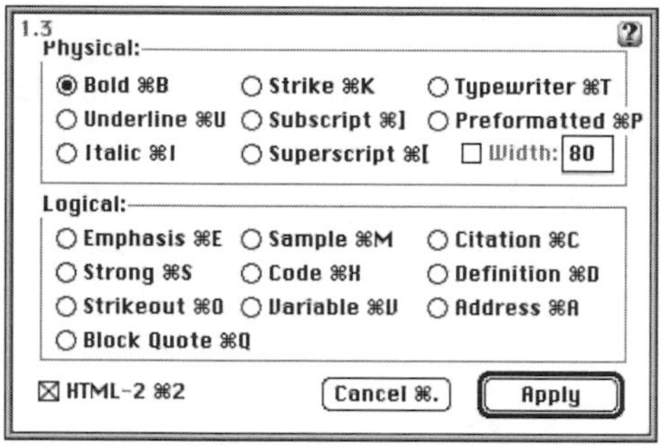

FIG. A.24
Hold down the
Command key to
see the keyboard
shortcuts for styles
in this dialog box.

Creating HTML lists is just as easy. Begin by typing in your list, hitting Return after each item. Next, highlight the list with the mouse and choose Extensions, Lists from the menu bar. The resulting dialog box gives you the choice of creating a variety of HTML lists. You can also choose to indent the items in the list to make the HTML document more readable.

Inserting images

To place an image in your document, start by placing the cursor at the point in your document where you want the <IMG> tag to appear. Next, select Extensions, Image from the menu bar. A dialog box appears, allowing you to enter an URL for the image (or filename for a relative link) and ALT text for nongraphical browsers. You can also choose the alignment for the image, enter size attributes (in pixels), and choose whether or not the image is an imagemap (see Figure A.25).

Click the Insert button and the appropriate <IMG> tag and attributes appear in your document.

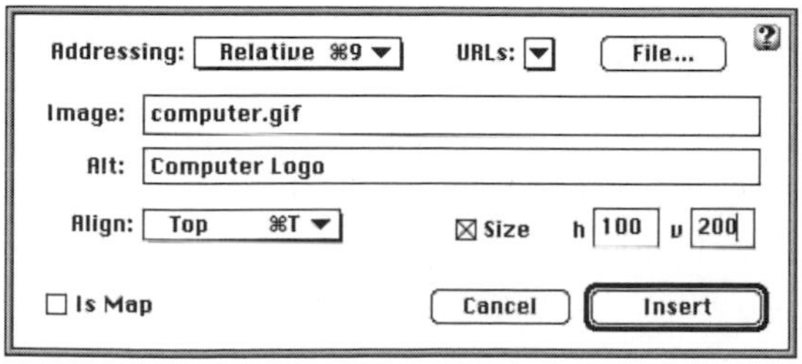

FIG. A.25
You can change the
style of addressing via
the Addressing menu
even after you've
entered an URL for
your image.

There are two other ways to enter Image URLs—using the URL pull-down menu and the File button. The URL menu relies on the existence of a Hotlist, which you can import from the bookmark files of a number of different Web browsers. To use the File button, you'll need to set your Preferences for BBEdit HTML Tools.

NOTE **To set Preferences for HTML Tools, choose Extensions, Utilities** from the BBEdit menu bar. Then click the Preferences button in the resulting dialog box. As with any HTML Tools dialog box, you can click the "?" icon to turn on Balloon Help and read about a particular entry or option.

Setting up links

Adding a link to your document is very similar to adding images with HTML Tools. Begin by highlighting the text you want to use as a hypertext link, then choose Extensions, Anchor from the menu bar. In the dialog box, you enter the URL or the file that you'd like to link to (see Figure A.26).

FIG. A.26
Enter the URL or file name in the HREF text box to create a link. You can also use the drop-down menu to change between relative and absolute addressing.

1.3				
Scheme: ▼	Hotlist: ▼	URLs: ▼	File... ⌘O	?
HREF:	search.html			
Name:				
Addressing:	Relative ⌘9 ▼			
			Cancel ⌘.	Insert

And, of course, there are other ways to create anchors by using the Anchor dialog box. Among them are a pull-down menu for your Hotlist sites and a pull-down menu that keeps recently entered URLs. You can also click the File button to search for a local file. Using the Scheme pull-down menu automatically enters the appropriate prefix for accessing a particular protocol with your URL (for instance, **ftp:// for file transfer protocol links**).

Creating forms

The HTML Tools are actually rather intelligent about HTML forms. The first time you select Extensions, Form Elements from the tool bar, you'll be asked for information required to create the FORM container tags—information like the URL to your processing script (for the ACTION attribute) and the METHOD you prefer to use. (METHOD is set to GET by default, so if you want to use the POST method, you need to click the radio button next to POST.) Enter those values and click Insert.

 TIP **If you don't want your form to automatically appear with hori-**
zontal lines dividing it from the rest of the page, uncheck the Rules checkbox.

The clever part in HTML Tools' handling of forms is the fact that the Form Elements dialog box won't ask you again for ACTION or METHOD information as long as the cursor is between the two FORM tags. Just select Extensions, Form Elements every time you want to add another element. If you do put your cursor elsewhere in the document, you'll be creating a second pair of FORM tags.

And adding an element is pretty straightforward. Begin at the top of the dialog box by choosing the type of form element you want—Input, Select, or TextArea (see Figure A.27). Depending on which of those you choose, the rest of the dialog box will change to reflect your options for that element. For instance, with TextArea selected you can enter a Label to appear on the page, a Name (for storing the values in the textarea), and how many rows and columns will appear on screen.

FIG. A.27
"Label" isn't an HTML attribute—it's HTML Tools' way of allowing you to enter optional text that will describe this form element on your page.

Element:	○ Input	○ Select	◉ TextArea	?
Label:	Comments:			
Name:	comment_text		Rows: 5	
			Cols: 80	

[Cancel] [Insert]

If you want to enter more form elements, choose Extensions, Form Elements again from the menu bar and continue the process.

Creating your own extensions

To be honest, the combination of HTML Tools and BBEdit Lite isn't the most powerful in the world of HTML editors—but that has something to do with the freeware nature of BBEdit. The full version of the BBEdit software is considerably more powerful, and more powerful extensions have been written for it.

That said, it's still possible to configure HTML Tools to do nearly anything you can conceive of in HTML—once you get used to its method for creating your own HTML commands.

From the Extensions menu, choose User's Markup. In the resulting dialog box, you'll see that you have an interesting little toolbox at your fingertips for creating additional extensions for Web design (see Figure A.28).

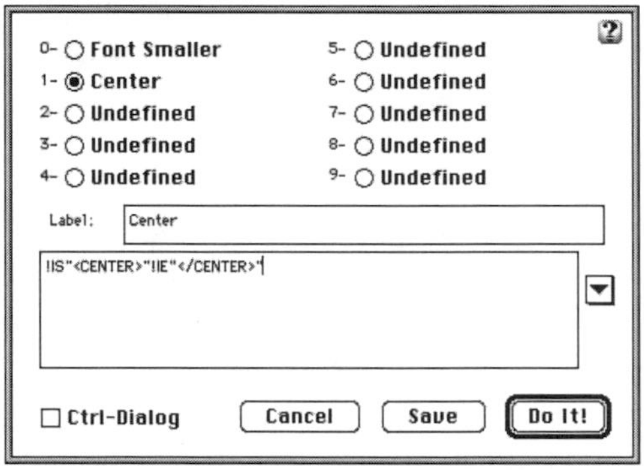

FIG. A.28

This dialog box features advanced tools for creating up to 10 unique commands yourself.

Things may seem a bit complicated in this dialog box, but it's fairly easy to get started. To create your own HTML command, choose one of the "Undefined" markup routines at the top of the dialog box. Once it's active, you can give it a name in the Label textbox.

Then, it's time to define what this routine is going to do. You'll find many different types of commands available from the pull-down menu to the right of the textarea—commands that do anything from copying a particular selection to inserting the current date. Experiment with them to find what's useful.

You'll probably use the Insert menu item most often for creating new HTML tags. For instance, choose Insert, Start of Selection and you'll see a little code appear with quotes in the textarea. Enter <CENTER> between the quotes. Now, if you selected a word (or series of words) in your document, then accessed the "Center" routine, you'd force the tag <CENTER> to appear before the selected word in your document.

The Insert, End of Selection menu item, then, can be used in the same way to complete the routine by appending </CENTER> to the end of the selection.

CAUTION   **If you leave the Ctrl-Dialog checkbox selected, then exit the** dialog box back to your document, you'll find that the "default" (last selected) routine will automatically run when you next select the Extensions, User's Markup command. If you want to get back to the dialog box for more editing (or to select a different routine) hold down the CTRL key while choosing the User's Markup menu item.

What's on the CD?

● **In this chapter:**

● **Browsers for the taking**

● **Choose among HTML editors**

● **Over 80 plug-ins included**

● **Software for building and maintaining a Web site**

● **Also, utilities and helper applications to pick from**

Τ
he CD-ROM included with this book is packed full of valuable programs and utilities. This appendix gives you a brief
overview of the contents of the CD. For a more detailed look at any of these
parts, load the CD-ROM and browse the contents by using your favorite Web
browser.

Web browsers

We have included Microsoft's latest browser, Internet Explorer, on the CD
along with:

Internet Explorer 3.0 (Internet Mail, Internet News, Active Movie,
Net Meeting, HTML Layout Control)

SlipKnot

HTML editors and utilities

Save yourself the trouble of creating HTML pages with Notepad by choosing
among the following HTML editors and special-purpose utilities:

BBEdit Lite	Map This!
Color Manipulation Device	WebForms
EasyHelp/Web	Webmania
HomeSite	Web Media Publisher Pro
HotDog Professional	

Web plug-ins

Plug-ins are great,but finding and downloading these can be a hassle and is
definitely time consuming. We've provided over 80 plug-ins covering the
following topics:

Audio

Remote Access

Graphics

VideoVRML

Miscellaneous

VRML

Productivity

Web servers

The CD contains software necessary to build and maintain a regular Web site or an intranet.

Apache

NCSA HTTPd

Internet Information Server

Web Quest

Web utilities, helper applications

Here you will find graphics and compression utilities:

ARJ

MHONArc

BinHex

Swish

Excite

StuffIt

GetStats

UUCode

Hyper Mail

WinCode

LISTSERV & trade

WinZip

LSMTP & trade

WWWWais

Mail Serv

Index

Check out Que® Books on the World Wide Web
http://www.quecorp.com

As the biggest software release in computer history, Windows 95 continues to redefine the computer industry. Click here for the latest info on our Windows 95 books

Make computing quick and easy with these products designed exclusively for new and casual users

Examine the latest releases in word processing, spreadsheets, operating systems, and suites

The Internet, The World Wide Web, CompuServe®, America Online®, Prodigy®—it's a world of ever-changing information. Don't get left behind!

Find out about new additions to our site, new bestsellers and hot topics

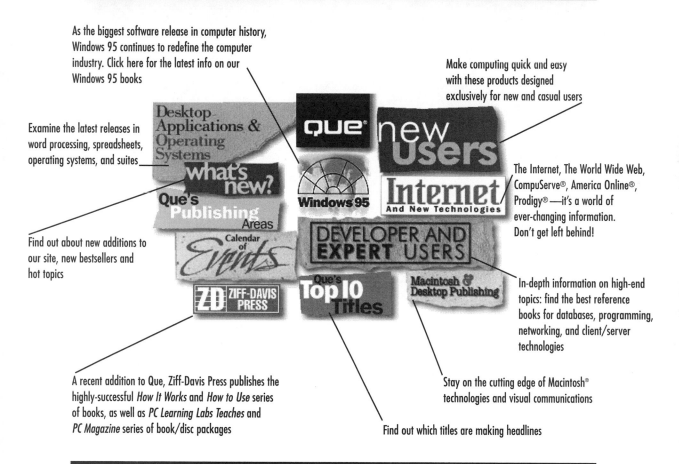

In-depth information on high-end topics: find the best reference books for databases, programming, networking, and client/server technologies

A recent addition to Que, Ziff-Davis Press publishes the highly-successful *How It Works* and *How to Use* series of books, as well as *PC Learning Labs Teaches* and *PC Magazine* series of book/disc packages

Stay on the cutting edge of Macintosh® technologies and visual communications

Find out which titles are making headlines

With 6 separate publishing groups, Que develops products for many specific market segments and areas of computer technology. Explore our Web Site and you'll find information on best-selling titles, newly published titles, upcoming products, authors, and much more.

- Stay informed on the latest industry trends and products available
- Visit our online bookstore for the latest information and editions
- Download software from Que's library of the best shareware and freeware

Complete and Return this Card
for a *FREE* Computer Book Catalog

Thank you for purchasing this book! You have purchased a superior computer book written expressly for your needs. To continue to provide the kind of up-to-date, pertinent coverage you've come to expect from us, we need to hear from you. Please take a minute to complete and return this self-addressed, postage-paid form. In return, we'll send you a free catalog of all our computer books on topics ranging from word processing to programming and the internet.

Mr. ☐ Mrs. ☐ Ms. ☐ Dr. ☐

Name (first) ☐☐☐☐☐☐☐☐☐☐☐☐ (M.I.) ☐ (last) ☐☐☐☐☐☐☐☐☐☐☐☐☐☐☐☐

Address ☐☐☐☐☐☐☐☐☐☐☐☐☐☐☐☐☐☐☐☐☐☐☐☐☐☐☐☐☐☐☐☐

City ☐☐☐☐☐☐☐☐☐☐☐☐ State ☐☐ Zip ☐☐☐☐☐ ☐☐☐☐

Phone ☐☐☐ ☐☐☐ ☐☐☐☐ Fax ☐☐☐ ☐☐☐ ☐☐☐☐

Company Name ☐☐☐☐☐☐☐☐☐☐☐☐☐☐☐☐☐☐☐☐☐☐☐☐☐☐

E-mail address ☐☐☐☐☐☐☐☐☐☐☐☐☐☐☐☐☐☐☐☐☐☐☐☐☐☐

1. Please check at least (3) influencing factors for purchasing this book.

Front or back cover information on book .... ☐
Special approach to the content .... ☐
Completeness of content .... ☐
Author's reputation .... ☐
Publisher's reputation .... ☐
Book cover design or layout .... ☐
Index or table of contents of book .... ☐
Price of book .... ☐
Special effects, graphics, illustrations .... ☐
Other (Please specify): _____ ☐

2. How did you first learn about this book?

Saw in Macmillan Computer Publishing catalog .... ☐
Recommended by store personnel .... ☐
Saw the book on bookshelf at store .... ☐
Recommended by a friend .... ☐
Received advertisement in the mail .... ☐
Saw an advertisement in: _____ ☐
Read book review in: _____ ☐
Other (Please specify): _____ ☐

3. How many computer books have you purchased in the last six months?

This book only .... ☐
2 books .... ☐
3 to 5 books .... ☐
More than 5 .... ☐

4. Where did you purchase this book?

Bookstore .... ☐
Computer Store .... ☐
Consumer Electronics Store .... ☐
Department Store .... ☐
Office Club .... ☐
Warehouse Club .... ☐
Mail Order .... ☐
Direct from Publisher .... ☐
Internet Site .... ☐
Other (Please specify): _____ ☐

5. How long have you been using a computer?

☐ Less than 6 months   ☐ 6 months to a year
☐ 1 to 3 years   ☐ More than 3 years

6. What is your level of experience with personal computers and with the subject of this book?

	With PCs	With subject of book
New	☐	☐
Casual	☐	☐
Accomplished	☐	☐
Expert	☐	☐

Source Code ISBN: 0-7897-1249-0

7. Which of the following best describes your job title?

Administrative Assistant .... ☐
Coordinator .... ☐
Manager/Supervisor .... ☐
Director .... ☐
Vice President .... ☐
President/CEO/COO .... ☐
Lawyer/Doctor/Medical Professional .... ☐
Teacher/Educator/Trainer .... ☐
Engineer/Technician .... ☐
Consultant .... ☐
Not employed/Student/Retired .... ☐
Other (Please specify): _____ ☐

8. Which of the following best describes the area of the company your job title falls under?

Accounting .... ☐
Engineering .... ☐
Manufacturing .... ☐
Operations .... ☐
Marketing .... ☐
Sales .... ☐
Other (Please specify): _____ ☐

9. What is your age?

Under 20 .... ☐
20-29 .... ☐
30-39 .... ☐
40-49 .... ☐
50-59 .... ☐
60-over .... ☐

10. Are you:

Male .... ☐
Female .... ☐

11. Which computer publications do you read regularly? (Please list)

_____
_____
_____
_____
_____
_____
_____
_____
_____
_____

Fold here and scotch-tape to mail.

Comments: _____
_____
_____

NETCOM Interactive
Website Hosting Services

http://www.netcomi.com
1.888.638.2664 (toll free)

Complete Access

NETCOM owns and operates one of the largest and most robust networks in the industry today. The international network of SMDS, ATM, T3 and T1 highspeed lines connect hundreds of thousands of worldwide businesses and individuals to the Internet with reliable service and readily available access.

■ Complete Support

At NETCOM, we can assist you with designing inter-marketing strategies. We specialize in setting up complete websites that include domain registration and routing, configuration of your server (or virtual server), CGI scripting, image mapping, interactive forms, databases, secure transactions and usage statistics. We support the emerging technologies for your business to utilize.

Complete Control

The exclusive NETCOM Business Center is a full service, on-line support center, open 24 hours every day. Our clients have a number of hosting options to select features such as: e-mail boxes, daily site back-up, CGI and FTP access, security keys, traffic logs, stats, disk space and monthly transfer rates. We allow you to customize your site so you have complete control.

Visit our website or give us a call @ 1.888.638.2664
Mention this reference code QNI00297 and receive a 20% discount.

NETCOM Interactive
1607 LBJ Freeway
Dallas, TX 75234
972.481.5700

NETCOM

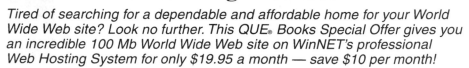

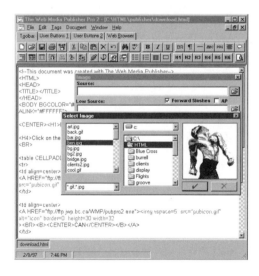

Need Premium Web Tools? Get BBEdit 4.0.

BBEdit 4.0 combines drag and drop HTML tools with maximum performance and usability.

Bare Bones Software, Inc. is pleased to offer a special deal to Que readers. Use this coupon to order BBEdit 4.0 for $79 (a $40 savings).

BBEdit is an award-winning Macintosh product used for the development of both HTML and traditional code. Both the freeware and demo versions of BBEdit are on the companion CD for this book. Try them out!

BBEdit is extremely popular with HTML authors and programmers. Market-leading integrated HTML editing and site management tools have made it the weapon of choice for Web authors and designers all over the world. Its power and ease of use make it suitable for both novices and professionals.

Visit Bare Bones Software at: **http://www.barebones.com** to obtain further information or place an order online.

Complete and fax or mail this form to Bare Bones Software, Inc.:

Name:

Company:

Address:

Phone: Fax:

E-Mail:

VISA / MC / AMEX #:   Exp. Date:

Cardholder Signature:

Order Information:

BBEdit 4.0Que Books Special Offer:	**$79.00**
	+
Sales Tax (**Massachusetts Residents**):	$ 3.95
	+
Shipping (US Priority or US Airmail):	$ 5.00
	=
Order Total:	

Bare Bones Software, Inc.
Post Office Box 1048
Bedford, MA 01730-1048
USA
voice: 617.778.3100
fax: 617.778.3111
sales@barebones.com

Bare Bones
Software, Inc.

Allaire HomeSite 2.5

The award winning Web design tool that is capturing the attention of Web developers worldwide.

Page Editing

- **HTML and Script Color-Coding.** Troubleshoot your code at a glance with automatic color-coding.
- **Built in HTML 3.2 Preview.** HomeSite links to Microsoft Internet Explorer® 3.01.
- **Tabbed Multiple Document Interface.** Move seamlessly between documents.
- **Drag-n-drop and Right Mouse Click.** Be productive with just a few clicks.
- **Integrated Spell Checker.** Correct your content without changing your code.
- **Global Search and Replace.** Update entire projects, folders, and files simultaneously.
- **Image and Thumbnail Viewers.** Browse image libraries directly in your editor.
- **Customizable Toolbars and Menus.** Configure the editor to your preferences.
- **Online Help.** Access documentation for HTML, CFML, and other popular scripting languages.

Project Management

- **Project Management.** Define multiple projects for easy site construction and maintenance.
- **Link Verification.** Keep track of all your dependant documents and connections
- **Document Size.** Analyze Internet download times to check site efficiency.
- **Validation Support.** Use the CSE 3310 HTML Validator for integ-rated HTML verification.
- **Dynamic Page Preview.** Real time preview of pages that include server-side scripts.
- **Common Templates.** Save time and energy by re-using templates across projects.
- **Remote File Open and Upload.** Maintain pages at off-site servers.

Code Wizards

- **Frame Wizards.** Build frame-based Webs quickly and easily.
- **Table Wizards.** Rapidly develop multiple tables.
- **JavaScript Wizards.** Use the JavaScript dialog box to create client-side scripts quickly.

Application Development

- **Cold Fusion and Active Server Toolbars.** Add scripts and tags from these popular Web application development tools.
- **JavaScript Object Viewer.** Easily create and edit client-side JavaScript.
- **Color-Coded Client and Server Scripts.** Visually distinguish client and server scripts.
- **Reuse Code.** Create up to 60 different custom toolbar items for easy code reuse.

Cutting Edge

- **Custom Style Sheets**
- **Key Server-Side Tags (CFML)**
- **Full HTML 3.2 Support**
- **Netscape and Microsoft HTML Extensions**
- **Embedded Multimedia and Plug-in Support**
- **ActiveX and Java Controls**

THE SKEPTICS WERE RIGHT: THE WEB WILL FOLD!

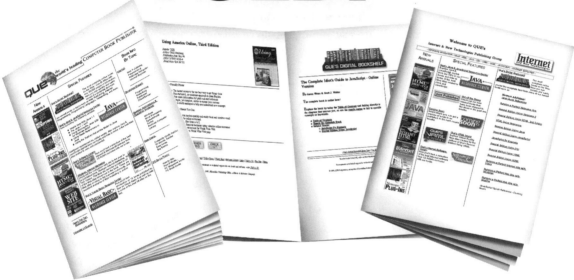

Fold the Web and take it with you. WebPrinter instantly turns Internet, CD-ROM and Windows files into portable, double-sided booklets. With just two clicks, your favorite articles, reference materials, product literature and even photos are transformed into convenient booklets.

WebPrinter is simple to use and works with any laser or inkjet printer. It intercepts standard-sized pages and reduces, rotates and realigns them to print as booklets. WebPrinter even walks you through double-sided printing.

Fold the Web For Free!

Included on this book's CD ROM is a free version of WebPrinter that lets you print any four booklets of your choice. Use it to turn the content of CD ROMs or pages on the Que Web site into handy booklets. The free version is limited to one 4-pack installation per computer.

WebPrinter, the best way yet to print the 'Net.

FORE FRONT™

The ForeFront Group, Inc.
1330 Post Oak Boulevard, Suite 1300
Houston, Texas 77056   http://www.ffg.com

Call us at 1-800-653-4933

Before using any of this software on this disc, you need to install the software you plan to use. See Appendix B, "What's on the CD?" for directions. If you have problems with **HTML 3.2 Starter Kit**, please contact Macmillan Technical Support at (800) 545-5914 ext. 3833. We can be reached by e-mail at **support@mcp.com** or by CompuServe at **GO QUEBOOKS**.

Read this before opening software

By opening this package, you are agreeing to be bound by the following:

This software is copyrighted and all rights are reserved by the publisher and its licensers. You are licensed to use this software on a single computer. You may copy the software for backup or archival purposes only. Making copies of the software for any other purpose is a violation of United States copyright laws. THIS SOFTWARE IS SOLD AS IS, WITHOUT WARRANTY OF ANY KIND, EITHER EXPRESSED OR IMPLIED, INCLUDING BUT NOT LIMITED TO THE IMPLIED WARRANTIES OF MERCHANTABILITY AND FITNESS FOR A PARTICULAR PURPOSE. Neither the publisher nor its dealers and distributors nor its licensers assume any liability for any alleged or actual damages arising from the use of this software. (Some states do not allow exclusion of implied warranties, so the exclusion may not apply to you.)

The entire contents of this disc and the compilation of the software are copyrighted and protected by United States copyright laws. The individual programs on the disc are copyrighted by the authors or owners of each program. Each program has its own use permissions and limitations. To use each program, you must follow the individual requirements and restrictions detailed for each. Do not use a program if you do not agree to follow its licensing agreement.